18/XII/86

ARABS AND AFRICANS

Arabs and Africans

Co-operation for development

ANTHONY SYLVESTER

with a Preface by Dr Chedly Ayari
President of the Arab Bank for
Economic Development in Africa

THE BODLEY HEAD
LONDON SYDNEY
TORONTO

A Sadok, mon ami

British Library Cataloguing
in Publication Data
Sylvester, Anthony
Arabs and Africans
1. Economic assistance, Arab-Africa
I. Title
337.1'17'4927   HC502
ISBN 0-370-30332-6

© Anthony Sylvester 1981
Printed in Great Britain for
The Bodley Head Ltd
9 Bow Street London WC2E 7AL
by Thomson Litho Ltd, East Kilbride
set in monophoto Ehrhardt
First published 1981

CONTENTS

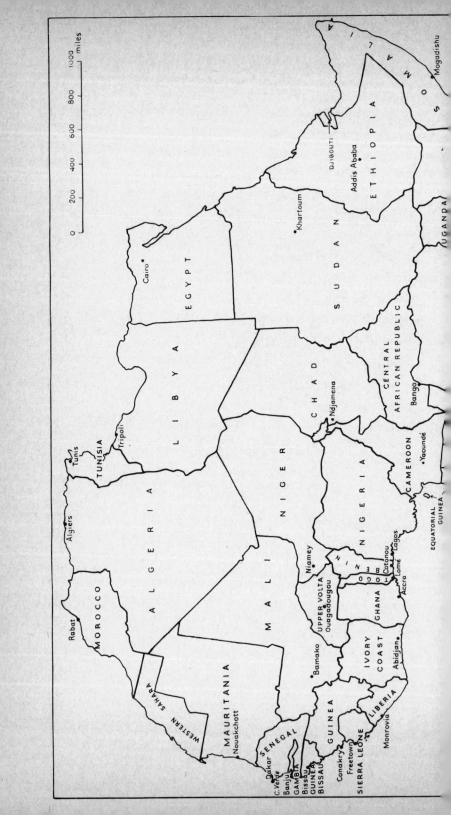

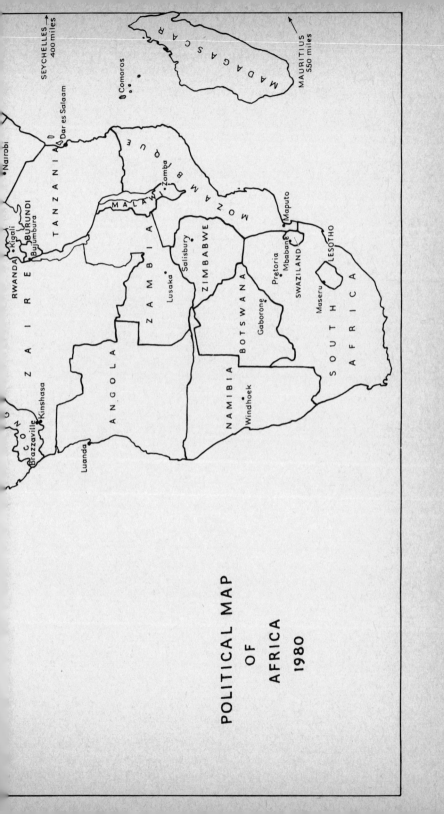

POLITICAL MAP
OF
AFRICA
1980

PREFACE

When I was recently in Senegal several people in that West African country asked me whether I, a Tunisian, regarded myself as Arab or African. I said I had never put the question to myself, but I thought I was both.

On the same theme I remember President Léopold Sédar Senghor talking to me some time ago about the very pronounced African characteristics that could be found among the Gulf Arabs. Displaying his usual penetrating powers of observation, he spoke to me particularly of the traces of African arts, music and rhythm that he had detected among these Arab people which, he said, were even more noticeable than in the Arabs in North Africa.

President Senghor has understood better than most not only how the Arab–Berber and Negro–African civilisations differ but how they complement each other, when human rather than materialist values, social and cultural achievements rather than the accumulation of riches, are considered.

The two civilisations have discovered the ability to work together, providing an instance of what is now called 'horizontal' co-operation, that is co-operation between the underprivileged peoples of the Third World themselves. And in the light of this discovery the peoples concerned have given their partnership a Charter, institutions and funds so that the solidarity of the disinherited countries may be turned into concrete action in the area of development. This is how Arab–African co-operation was conceived by the Arab and African Heads of State gathering together for the first time, in the spring of 1977.

This was an act of solidarity, certainly, but also a joint defence in the face of the iniquitous system of international exchanges imposed on the South by the North.

By employing this device with increasing intensity through the decades of failed development in which the Third World was treated as peripheral and of marginal significance, the wealthy countries of the North tried to prevent the economic, social and cultural emancipation of what we are now used to calling the South.

Dramatic data on deaths, famine, malnutrition, illiteracy and the cultural and social degradation of one-third of mankind have never in the course of these past three decades diverted the privileged industrial countries from their attempts to escape the historical, political and economic—in one word human—responsibilities for these thousand million condemned men and women who have grown tired of lectures, conferences and humanitarian aid.

But then again, what is at stake today? Survival, no less: the survival of the peoples of this earth, as Willy Brandt has reminded us in a report which aroused so many hopes but which the wealthy nations have chosen to shelve together with so many other similar pleas.

Survival, as Brandt has put it; or to repeat a recent catchphrase of the Organisation of Economic Co-operation and Development, 'basic or minimum needs'; or *human development*, to recall the central theme of the World Development Reports of the World Bank, or, again, one could speak of the 'costs of man', as explained more than 30 years ago by the great teacher François Perroux. This, in a nutshell, is what the matter is about as far as the thousand million human beings are concerned who have placed so much faith in the past three decades of development, believing that one day they would, as Peterson has said, become 'partners in development', instead of being left without hope.

The shattering of these hopes constitutes a major defeat for the international community, and anticipating a future that is only too predictable we call it the failure of the century. Yet this century has so much from which to redeem itself in the eyes of history, in the eyes of humanity: two murderous world wars and the pillage, suffering and injustices inflicted by the colonial domination of the North on the hundreds of millions of people in the South. Only if a more equitable system of international exchanges is instituted between the privileged and the under-privileged; only if survival is guaranteed as a first step to those who now live below the line of absolute poverty, to be followed by true development; only if a new, and juster and fairer, economic, social and cultural international order is created will the terrible blemishes attached to this century be cleansed.

Now, we know that it is in Africa more than anywhere else that the question of survival for hundreds of millions of human beings assumes its most penetrating and dramatic meaning. It is in this continent that the past and present unjust international exchanges and political, economic and cultural domination have produced their most harmful and degrading consequences.

There is no need to clog this preface with figures. Anthony Sylvester, the author of this book, quotes them in abundance. Yet listen to what such prominent African statesmen as Léopold S. Senghor, Sekou Touré, Kenneth Kaunda and Julius Nyerere, or for that matter Edem Kodjo, the Secretary-General of the Organisation of African Unity, have been saying in African and international assemblies about their Africa, our Africa, of yesterday and of tomorrow! And you will then understand why neither drought nor disease, famine nor malnutrition, nor illiteracy, in short all its past and present miseries, could daunt the hopes and aspirations of an Africa that is aware of its culture, its natural and human resources, its unique place in the history of mankind and its future role in the concert of nations.

It is to these hopes and aspirations that Arab–African co-operation has sought to give a response. Without claiming to be comprehensive in its scope, let alone a model of co-operation between peoples, or in any way an exemplary undertaking free of failure or error, Arab–African co-operation is nonetheless profoundly significant and marks an *event* in the history of the Third World and international relations.

Denounced by some as a stratagem by which the Arab countries have been seeking to purchase African support for their political causes, particularly in the matter of Palestine, or for their economic interests, particularly in regard to the confrontation between the OPEC and industrial countries, it has yet been hailed by Africans and Arabs as well as others as proof of an active solidarity between the two communities living in the Third World—the Arab and the African.

However that may be there is little doubt that Arab–African co-operation is here to stay, having gained the recognition and respect of the international community thanks to the quality and

achievement of the Arab bilateral and multilateral institutions—
BADEA being one of them—designed to make true the ideals of
mutual co-operation.

Mr Sylvester's book can be regarded as another testimony to
this co-operation, one of special value given the quality and
wealth of information it contains, and the expertise and
commitment of the author—a tireless researcher and traveller.
Statesmen, economists and students of international relations and
others in Africa, in the Arab region and elsewhere will find it
well worth reading.

Mr Sylvester has endeavoured to draw his information from
original sources, by meeting a large number of influential people
concerned with Arab–African co-operation, on the Arab as well
as on the African side, and this has enabled him to put the matter
in a proper perspective based on the facts as they are.

It is true however that the inadequacies of this co-operation
have been the subject of much negative comment in the past so
that one can understand why Mr Sylvester wanted to distance
himself from this chorus of disparaging voices, wishing instead to
bring out the more positive, and hitherto little noticed, aspects of
the matter.

It has already been said often enough that Arab–African co-
operation needs a fresh initiative, additional resources and a new
perspective. This is our opinion too. Such new development
should be the theme of discussions at the next, the second,
Arab–African Summit conference which we hope will be held as
soon as possible.

But while we wait for this new Summit we can look on the
experience of the past seven years, if one goes back to the Arab
Summit in Algiers in 1973 when Arab–African co-operation
could be said to have started, or simply of the past three years, if
one goes back to the first Arab–African Summit held in Cairo in
1977, as demonstrating that Arab–African co-operation has been
neither a tactical move, nor a matter of compensation, nor, least
of all, an Arab attempt to buy African consciences.

We said the same thing five years ago at the very birth of
BADEA. We repeat it today with a conviction that is all the
stronger seeing the road that has been travelled and the tangible
achievements of this co-operation.

Yet in spite of all this Arab–African co-operation remains

unilateral and one-dimensional. It is so in so far as it has been confined to simple financial transfers from the Arabs to Africa, notwithstanding the fact that the Cairo Charter, adopted by the first Arab–African Summit of March 1977, laid down an eleven-point programme of joint economic activities.

There are still many missing links in this co-operation, in the areas of commerce, private investment, information and culture, to name only a few sectors, all of which are of great potential help in improving and amplifying the co-operation and making the Arab–African partnership both more varied and more integrated.

With the financial resources so unevenly distributed between the Arab and African regions it is scarcely surprising that Arab–African financial co-operation should at present mainly take the form of Arab capital transfers in the direction of Africa. But, joint assessment of Arab and African resources of all kinds will eventually have to be undertaken to make a true common project for Arab–African co-operation. If Anthony Sylvester's book helps to stimulate and enliven, as we believe it will, the much needed debate on Arab–African co-operation, the author's principal aim will have been achieved.

CHEDLY AYARI

AUTHOR'S NOTE

This book represents a research effort extending over more than five years, in the course of which I travelled extensively in Africa and the Middle East, interviewing many people involved in Afro–Arab co-operation.

This co-operation, although at present largely confined to the flow of Arab funds for development in non-Arab Africa, has assumed important dimensions, especially remarkable as it constitutes a growing partnership for development between two communities in the Third World itself. It is therefore a pioneering venture of considerable future potential, not only for the Arabs and Africans, but for the entire world. I believe this momentous initiative deserves study and appreciation and I hope I have made a small contribution to the debate on this topic.

I will not hide the fact that in writing this book I was moved as much by sentiment as by intellectual curiosity, as I regard the aspirations of what are still largely underprivileged and poorly understood peoples very much as my own. This applies to both Arabs and Africans, many of whom are my personal friends. This work must therefore be regarded above all as an effort in communication: to present to the world the views and feelings of people I like and admire. Nonetheless, I have taken fully into account the negative aspects of the situation as well as views critical of, or hostile to, Afro–Arabism. It is common knowledge that such views are very prevalent in the West, motivated as they are by sectional interests and political bias or are simply due to ignorance.

My book should not be seen as an apologia for whatever the Arabs or Africans have been doing, right or wrong. But it is fair to say that I have looked particularly for the positive and constructive side of the emergent partnership. It is also my conviction that a fruitful co-operation between the Arabs and Africans is in the highest interest of the country of my adoption, Britain, as indeed it is of value to all people with a fair mind and concern for world development and improvement.

14

I have placed Afro–Arab co-operation in a broader context, attempting to throw light on the general problem of financial surpluses accruing to oil-exporting countries and the economic situation in Africa, especially its non-Arab region, the two topics making up separate chapters.

I had embarked on the study of Afro–Arab co-operation entirely on my own initiative, as a sequel to my interest in the Sudan where the settlement of a long conflict between the Arab North and the African South much impressed me. I owe a great deal to a large number of writers whose works and articles on the subject I read and whose ideas inspired me. I must particularly mention the book *Arab Aid: Who Gets It, For What, and How* by John Law, published by Chase World Information Corporation.

As my research progressed I was considerably assisted by several institutions and their personnel, including the Arab Bank for Economic Development in Africa (BADEA), the Kuwait Fund for Arab Economic Development (KFAED), United Nations Development Programme (UNDP) and Economic Commission for Africa (ECA) of the United Nations.

I am grateful to all these and many other people for their help and co-operation, but the responsibility for the views expressed in this book is wholly mine.

Oxshott, Surrey,
December 1980.

INTRODUCTION

To talk about Afro–Arab, or as some prefer to say, Arab–African co-operation and partnership, is to talk above all of a community of interest of peoples who had till very recently been, and to some extent still are, colonised or otherwise treated as second-class citizens in their own countries because of their race.

It seems to me only yesterday, although it was in fact nearly 20 years ago, that few Frenchmen seemed to think that Algeria could ever be anything but 'française'. More recently, Dr Henry Kissinger, former US Secretary of State, a man of extraordinary intelligence and grasp of world affairs, had thought his Government ought to endorse the Portuguese empire in Africa as a bulwark of American interests in that region—only very shortly before this colonial set-up suddenly and totally collapsed in 1974. Still more recently, many usually well-informed and influential people in Britain thought white supremacy in Rhodesia would and ought to endure. Whatever the motives of these advocates of outdated and unjust political systems they were above all proved wrong and misguided. They misunderstood and underestimated the irresistible urge, and because of that the power, of the people living in bondage to be free and accepted as equal human beings.

That this urge for human emancipation has taken the form of nationalism, that is for the creation of independent and sovereign States, is perhaps regrettable: many independent nations are ruled by tyrannical and iniquitous regimes. But there can be nothing more unjust and painful than to be doomed from one's very birth to live a disinherited life because of one's race.

It was the struggle against racism and colonialism which first brought the Arabs and Africans closer together again after their ties of culture, commerce and other contacts had been largely broken by European imperialism. It is still the struggle against racism which provides one of the concrete bases for their political co-operation, as the Arabs fight for the rights of their people in

Palestine and much of southern Africa remains to be freed.

This Afro–Arab political co-operation must be seen as a facet of the world-wide movement of non-alignment, a platform for the independent nations of the Third World to assert their claims and interests, a way to safeguard their recently won independence from machinations and designs of the great powers. The fact that some of the members of this movement are in effect closely allied with one great power, the USSR, may appear to be contradictory in terms of the non-alignment principle. It is nonetheless true that the vast and growing majority of independent nations in the Third World adhering to most varied and disparate ideologies continue to regard it as being in their interest to belong to the non-alignment movement and work with it. In spite of everything the movement has had some notable successes to its credit, not least in the area of resistance to racism, and is now able to exert considerable pressure on world affairs, notably through the United Nations Organisation.

While struggle on the political front has brought successes, especially in Africa, there has been far less achievement on the economic front where the underprivileged nations are fighting for a New International Economic Order which would be more just and at the same time more economically productive and beneficial to all concerned than the present system.

The report published in 1980 by the Brandt Commission, which included among its members several prominent statesmen and experts from the West as well as from the developing nations, presented the problem eloquently, as can be seen from the following passage:

'The North, including eastern Europe, has a quarter of the world's population and four-fifths of its income; the South, including China, has three billion people—three-quarters of the world's population, but living on one-fifth of the world's income. In the North, the average person can expect to live more than 70 years; he or she will rarely be hungry, and will be educated at least up to the secondary level. In the countries of the South the great majority of people have a life expectancy of closer to 50 years; in the poorest countries one out of every four children dies before the age of five; one-fifth or more of all the people in the South suffer from hunger and malnutrition; 50 per cent have no chance to become literate...

'Behind these differences lies the fundamental inequality of economic strength. Over 90 per cent of the world's manufacturing industry is in the North. Most patents and new technology are the property of multinational corporations of the North, which conduct a large share of world investment and world trade in raw materials and manufactures. Because of this economic power northern countries dominate the international economic system—its rules and regulations, and its international institutions of trade, money and finance.'

One interesting point made by the Brandt Commission is that it would be in the interest of the developed nations themselves to do more to help the Third World onto its feet as this would enable the poor nations to purchase more goods and services from the industrial world and thus help its growth and employment. A great deal of discussion has followed this historic report, but the dialogue between the North and the South has so far produced precious little.

In this world-wide movement and debate for a change in the international economic system an important event took place in 1973 when the oil-exporting nations suddenly succeeded in imposing a more realistic price for their commodity on the world markets. It was the first time that a group of the Third World countries, in this case operating through their own organisation, the Organisation of Petroleum Exporting Countries (OPEC), seven out of 13 of its members being Arab, could assert their economic interests in this way. This gave heart to all those in the developing world who too have been waiting for their claims to be similarly met.

The question now was what the Arabs, and other petroleum exporters, were going to do with the very substantial revenues coming their way.

It is important in this context to point out first of all that the oil-rich Arabs have categorically affirmed their loyalty to the cause of the underprivileged. In spite of the change in their financial circumstances these Arabs have continued to regard themselves as part of the Third World and its problems. In international assemblies, in which they now gained considerable influence, they supported the idea of a New International Economic Order.

Then, they have allocated very considerable resources for

direct help to developing nations as well as to finance international institutions designed for development.

Yet they will be the first to admit that on both these counts success has been limited as so far much of the money spent by the Arabs in many parts of the world has gone to benefit the industrial nations rather than the developing because it is the advanced countries which control the tools of development.

The financial resources which the Arab oil-exporting countries have deployed for economic and social development have, however, been huge. Understandably, the Arabs have made particularly large allocations for development plans in their own countries which had been largely poor and undeveloped before the petroleum revolution.

But very considerable resources have been employed to help the outside world as well. This effort has been especially remarkable when measured against the total wealth, the Gross Domestic Product, of the donor country concerned. According to OECD statistics, in 1977 Kuwait disbursed over 10 per cent of its GDP for concessional aid to other developing countries and Saudia Arabia 4·3 per cent. In 1979 the percentage for Kuwait was 5·14 and for Saudi Arabia 3·15. In that year the USA disbursed only 0·19 per cent of its GNP for development aid, some of this going to Israel and southern Europe which are not usually regarded as part of the Third World.

It is true, as has often been pointed out by the detractors of the Arab aid effort, that a larger proportion of this total effort has gone to benefit other Arab countries. But it is normal that one should first help one's own family particularly if this includes some of the world's poorest and least developed countries or populations with extremely low incomes, such as Egypt, Sudan, Mauritania, the two Yemens and Somalia. But very substantial financial assistance has also been extended to non-Arab developing countries, including Sub-Saharan Africa. It is estimated that total direct Arab commitment for the benefit of non-Arab Africa amounted between 1973 and 1979 to nearly $4·4 billion, of which more than $3 billion was on concessional terms, i.e. including a grant element of at least 25 per cent.

The International Monetary Fund, not known for any bias in favour of developing countries, wrote in its Annual Report 1980: 'The net flow of funds from oil-exporting countries directly to other developing countries, mostly in the form of official foreign aid and provided on concessional terms, is estimated to have amounted to about $8 billion in 1979 ... It is expected that such disbursements will increase in 1980. Activities of both bilateral and multilateral aid institutions sponsored by the oil-exporting countries are expanding, and announced or anticipated Government contributions to these should facilitate this expansion.'

But, say some, what the Arabs are doing is merely 'robbing Peter to pay Paul' as the increased prices of petroleum have brought to them more money from the developing countries than they spend for aid to the Third World. The Arabs reply to this that most of the money they receive for their oil comes from the industrial countries and not from the developing, particularly not from the poorest among them as these only import modest amounts of petroleum. That among the countries now suffering from higher petroleum prices are also the non-oil developing countries is unfortunate, the Arabs say, but it cannot be helped because it is for technical reasons impossible to have different prices of petroleum for different countries. Besides, most of the oil trade is not in the hands of the Arabs but of the big transnational petroleum companies.

Again, some argue that the large increases in the prices of oil in 1973/74 and again in 1979/80 have played havoc with the international economic system, causing inflation, recession and unemployment, which in turn had extremely serious effects on the developing countries. No, say the Arabs, it is not the higher prices for petroleum that have caused inflation. This was under way in the industrial countries well before the first jump of petroleum prices and continued unabated even when prices of oil were actually declining or stagnating in the seventies. The world recession, the Arabs argue, is due principally to the misguided policies of western governments, who have allowed inflation to spiral and cause recession and unemployment.

The Arabs also emphatically refute the idea that their aid to developing countries is a form of compensation for higher oil prices. There is no relationship between the amount of oil any country imports and the assistance it receives from the Arabs. Some heavy importers of oil, like Brazil, get no Arab aid while certain countries which are net exporters of oil, such as Tunisia, obtain substantial development help.

Petroleum, the oil-exporting countries argue, is like any other commodity subject to the interplay of supply and demand. The price is high because the demand is so high, especially in industrial countries. People should use less oil, in fact by raising their prices the oil-exporting countries are doing the world a service. Higher prices will encourage conservation of energy and utilisation of alternative sources of power. If the Arabs were concerned with their self-interest only they would keep much more of their oil in the ground as this would keep its value while petrodollar surpluses are being steadily eroded by inflation and also, in the seventies at any rate, by the decline in the relative exchange value of the dollar. The Organisation of Arab Oil Exporting Countries (OAPEC) has estimated that the nominal revenues of its members of $86,462 million in 1977 represented a real value of only $33,254 million in terms of what the money had been worth in 1970, for Saudi Arabia alone the difference being between $42,384 million and $16,301·5 million.

The Arab aid effort, the Arabs say, is creditable by any standards. It must be looked at on its own, unrelated to the higher prices for oil which the developing countries are now paying, although these prices have enabled the Arabs to provide such aid as they do. The Arabs disclaim any responsibility for world poverty, which, they argue, is largely the result of western policies, going back to colonial times. It is the industrial countries which must bear the responsibility for helping the poor of the world.

The Arabs particularly resent exhortations addressed to them by the West that they should give more aid, pointing to the puny percentages of the GDP allocated by most western countries for such aid. Arab aid is to be seen not as an obligation, but as a gesture of solidarity with the Third World. The Arabs admit that now, with the situation rapidly deteriorating in developing countries, particularly in Africa, for whatever reason this might be, there may be need for more aid, including Arab. They appear ready to discuss new ways of helping the world, either by the creation of new institutions to channel the flows of development capital, or by raising the capital of the existing agencies. They are generally eager to discuss world economic problems and have endorsed the Brandt Commission's call for a World Economic Summit Conference. What they are not ready to do is to discuss the problems of oil supplies and prices in relation to world poverty as a separate item on the agenda and without reference to other global problems, including a better deal for the developing countries and their trading as envisaged by the New International Economic Order.

All these matters of Arab aid, petroleum prices, endeavours to bring about a New International Economic Order, and the political affinities and interests of countries sharing the problems of development, assume a special significance in relation to Afro–Arab co-operation. The movement, promoted by the respective organisations of the two communities, the Arab League and the OAU, began to take the shape of concrete measures in the same year of 1973 when petroleum prices and revenues of oil-exporting countries rose sharply.

In the course of that year many more African countries embraced the Arab cause and broke their diplomatic relations with Israel. This made a profound impression on the Arab community as an act of solidarity, and the Arabs for their part decided to reciprocate, giving their proof of solidarity, by beginning to channel very substantial funds for aid to Black Africa.

Both sides have emphatically denied that the two moves of solidarity were a kind of quid pro quo. Nevertheless each side has been measuring the benefit of the new co-operation at least partly by the character and extent of what the other side was doing to help in those two matters of great importance to them; the support for the cause of Arab Palestine and economic and financial co-operation with Black Africa, respectively.

At a meeting of the Arab Heads of State in Algiers in November 1973 one of the decisions favouring Afro–Arab co-operation was to create a special institution for development aid exclusively to non-Arab African countries. The institution, the Arab Bank for Economic Development in Africa, known also by its acronym, BADEA (Banque Arabe pour le Développement Economique en Afrique), began operations in Khartoum in 1975 and has by the end of 1980 achieved remarkable results not only as a source of development capital on concessional terms from which nearly all African countries eligible for its aid have now received at least some assistance, but also as an agency to promote African interests in the Arab world generally.

BADEA has co-operated closely with other Arab Funds, such as the Kuwait Fund for Arab Economic Development which now became available also for aid to non-Arab Africa.

The Afro–Arab movement saw a high point in March 1977 when the Heads of States of the two communities met for the first time and decided on a comprehensive and institutionalised long-term co-operation programme, covering both political and economic matters. Although the institutions created then have not been able to develop their activity as planned, because of the dispute that arose in regard to the representation of Egypt, which the Arab League had suspended from its membership, the conclusions of the first Summit stand and have been repeatedly affirmed and endorsed by both sides.

There have then been ups as well as downs in this Afro–Arab partnership. This is not difficult to understand. The Arabs on their own and for that matter the Black Africans on their own have not been noted for unity. Internal differences and disputes inside each community have inevitably affected relations between the two.

There has been a certain frustration on the Arab side at the way their main political problem, that of Palestine, has dragged on without a solution—something that will be clear from the account of my conversation with the Secretary-General of the Arab League, Chedli Klibi, in Tunis at the end of the book. In Africa, economic problems have overshadowed other pre-occupations as famine and growing destitution grip the continent. Arab aid, however substantial, is far from sufficient in the face of these difficulties the causes for which are multiple and complex. They are both internal, as the first Economic Summit Conference of the OAU held in April 1980 in Lagos, the conclusions of which are summarised in the book, made clear; and external. Among the latter, the unfavourable terms of trade with the industrial countries and high cost of imports and services derived from them are particularly significant.

Yet when non-oil developing Africa has seen its oil bills increase in current dollars by 15 times over the decade, 1970–1980, and many of the Sub-Saharan countries are facing enormous problems of adjustment to the new cost of fuel, one will understand why many Africans today see their co-operation with the Arabs dominated by these issues.

Those whose interest is to drive wedges between the two communities and destroy the emergent partnership have seized eagerly on the opportunity presented for their propaganda by these problems.

On the other hand one witnesses the serious and substantial commitment of the oil-rich Arab countries for help to Africa continuing. On the African side too a sober analysis of the situation inexorably leads to the conclusion that Afro–Arab co-operation ought to continue and indeed expand, precisely because of the grave economic problems of the continent.

As will be seen from these pages, the Afro–Arab movement as a practical political programme is an innovation of very recent date. The awareness of its long-term value and significance may still not be shared by some on either side. But it is growing and becoming more pronounced as the benefits of co-operation are seen and measured against the alternatives.

I

Petrofunds for Development

By and large the world received with surprise and shock the sudden sharp increases in the prices of petroleum in 1973/74. In the West it was almost regarded as an act of war, as more than a threefold jump in the average price for a barrel of crude coincided with the October War in which America decisively supported Israel. It also coincided with the embargo on exports of oil decreed by the Organisation of Arab Petroleum Exporting Countries* in respect of the USA and the Netherlands. The Arabs were now confronting the West with a new and powerful weapon. OPEC suddenly emerged from the obscurity in which it had lived since its foundation in 1960. It soon became unpopular in many parts of the world.

It was the first time that a group of developing countries had been able to assert their commercial interests successfully. Moreover, the oil exporting countries made plain their intention to use their new power not only to promote their own interests but to help the entire Third World with which they ostensibly remained identified, and to assist in bringing about changes that would make the international economic order juster and fairer.

OPEC has successfully weathered many storms and resisted attacks and criticism from outside as well as pressures and dissensions from within. By 1979 it was seen by many oil-importing countries as a responsible and rather beneficial organisation. Owing to sudden shortages of oil at a time of high demand, prices of the fuel sold outside the organisation, in spot markets, considerably exceeded those decreed by OPEC. The moderating stance of Saudi Arabia, which accounts for about one-third of the total production by OPEC of some 30 million barrels a day, was particularly noticed. The suave and articulate

*The organisation, largely outside the scope of this book, includes Bahrain, Egypt and Syria in addition to the seven Arab members of OPEC—Algeria, Iraq, Kuwait, Libya, Qatar, Saudi Arabia and United Arab Emirates.

Sheikh Yamani, Saudi Arabia's Minister of Petroleum, came to personify this mood.

It was clear that Saudi Arabia at any rate was a friend of the West, anxious to safeguard the supplies of oil to industrial countries at reasonable prices and in sufficient quantities, although it would have been more profitable for her to reduce production and keep the depletable resource in the ground. This was particularly noticeable at times of crisis, as in 1980 when the Gulf War caused the suspension of supplies from Iraq and Iran.

There was another danger now. It became fashionable in certain quarters in the West to take the friendship and co-operation of Saudi Arabia and other leading Arab oil exporters for granted, in spite of Iran where the Government of the Shah became wholly alienated from the feelings of the broad masses of the Iranian population precisely because of his blatant pro-western policies and disregard for religion and traditions. When the Shah's rule collapsed like a pack of cards America and the West lost heavily by having backed the wrong horse.

The regimes in Saudi Arabia, Kuwait and the United Arab Emirates are sustained by traditions which the Shah sought to undermine. Yet everybody ought to know that any Arab regime friendly to the West is under pressure from its own people: what is the West doing for the Arabs? It is wrong to believe that oil-rich Arabs, because they want to keep their money or because they are afraid of Russia and communism, can be indefinitely blackmailed into support and endorsement of the West.

Despite the pressures from their own people, and Arab people generally, which the conservative Arab regimes must heed, and even granted that these rulers and Governments see their future tied to the fortunes of the free world, they still have much room for manoeuvre. They can be more or less friendly, more or less co-operative as far as the West is concerned. They can also discriminate between one industrial country and another, to suit their ideas and interests. In simple terms, what the Arabs have managed to do with their oil weapon is to enforce the principle that there must be give and take in their relations with the outside world, particularly with the economically advanced countries, a partnership in inter-dependence rather than the kind of domination on the part of the industrial West which had marked these relations in the past.

Many influential people in the western world find this new situation hard to accept, however. Powerful influences in the media and elsewhere have been at work to upset the emerging partnership, to discredit the Arab countries and belittle their importance. Much of this effort has been thoroughly misguided and damaging to the West's long-term interests.

The image of the self-indulgent and greedy Arab oil shcikh, indifferent to the plight of the world, has been studiously cultivated. Yet all the oil exporting countries had done in 1973/74 was to correct, most belatedly, a historical injustice. For many years price of oil had been too low. Oil was 25 per cent cheaper in 1970 in relation to the prices of other goods than in 1955. This had led to profligate waste of a uniquely important and non-renewable resource. The higher price for oil is a blessing in disguise when one considers the need to conserve energy. But it is the inordinate demand for the fuel that causes the escalation of fuel costs, particularly in America. One American uses as much commercial energy as two Germans, or three Japanese, or six Yugoslavs, or 15 Chinese or 438 Malians.[1]

It is a common fallacy to blame the higher oil prices for world inflation and for the accompanying recession and unemployment. These problems had all been well under way in the industrial countries before 1973/74 and were due to wrongly conceived policies in the countries concerned or the inability of Governments to assert the national weal against sectional interests of particular groups, such as powerful trade unions.

The best proof of this is that some western countries have been able to cope much better than others in the face of rising costs of fuel. In West Germany or Japan there has been little inflation. The West German Government for example took measures to ensure that higher prices of imported oil were not simply accommodated into the price structure in such a way that all the prices were now moving upwards. If people now had to spend more on fuel they had less money to spend on other things and inflation could be kept within reasonable limits where monetary discipline prevailed. Elsewhere oil price rises were regarded by businessmen and trade unions as a signal that the cost of their goods and services could now go up proportionately and more. As a recent study of the General Agreement on Tariffs and Trade (GATT) makes clear, the inflationary spiral is generated by the expectation that prices and costs will go on rising. Once the Government takes the necessary measures to impose monetary stability inflation will be curbed. Moreover, recession and unemployment will be cured as well because these are, according to GATT economic experts, a direct result of inflation and bad co-ordination with the economy, aggravated by the uncertainties caused by inordinate increases of costs and prices.

GATT has described the view that higher petroleum prices in 1978 and 1979 caused a resurgence of inflation in the industrial countries as 'dangerously wrong':

'At the outset it is important to stress that the petroleum price increase which occurred in several steps between December 1978 and June 1979 did not *cause* the present resurgence of inflation in the industrial countries, nor the recession now beginning in the United States. In both the United States and Western Europe, inflation rates were already rising by the middle of 1978 when the impression that a petroleum glut existed was widespread. Already in the second half of 1978, with the economic expansion in the United States well into its fourth year, and monetary and fiscal policy developments increasingly focused on the need to reverse the upward trend in inflation, a sharp slowing down, if not recession, was widely anticipated. Thus the evidence forecloses the dangerously wrong view that the petroleum price increase was a major causative factor behind the resurgence of inflation and the expected rise in unemployment.'[2]

It has also been suggested that the effect of higher prices of oil and surpluses accumulated by oil exporting countries had a deflationary effect on the world economy in general and the economies of advanced western countries in particular. What happened, of course, was that major shifts were now taking place in the balances of payment of the oil-exporting and oil-importing countries respectively. Surpluses on one side were matched by deficits on the other.

When more purchasing power had to be used for buying fuel there was less available for other goods, hence the deflationary effect of the oil price increases. But in assessing this particular aspect of the new situation it is also necessary to take account of the recycling of petrofunds that has been taking place all these years. This has been very successfully handled thanks to the world banking system, high demand for goods in the oil exporting countries and, again, the exemplary sense of international responsibility on the part of the major Arab petroleum exporters.

Since the recycling of petrofunds is an important aspect of this book's theme it is necessary to give a broad outline of these developments.

No oil-rich Arab country had experienced any large-scale development prior to the petroleum bonanza. Their populations were largely poor, even destitute, and lacking the skills which modernisation would call for. Oil money provided a chance to lift these people out of the backwardness and poverty, and every single oil-rich Arab country was determined to seize this opportunity. Money cannot do everything, however. Given the lack of development in the past, all manner of constraints continued to bedevil the planners. As the Saudi Minister of Planning, Sheikh Hoshman Nazer, has said pointedly, 'it would be an illusion to believe that any problem could be solved by throwing a bundle of banknotes at it.'[3]

Much of the progress is based on past mistakes as there are no ready-made models to follow anywhere in the world. But with lessons learned the next development plan will no doubt be more effective and more efficiently implemented.

The Arab development programmes have a great deal in common as the conditions under which they started and the needs they were designed to meet were similar in many respects. Everywhere there was need for improved infrastructure, and many roads and other transport communications have been built. Most of the countries concerned endeavoured to develop their petroleum industries, to refine the product at home, and some began the construction of petrochemical plant. Everywhere there were huge outlays on education and training, partly to lessen dependence on foreign labour and technicians. Efforts have been made to develop import substitution industries which may later become exporters. Increasing attention is being paid to farming and rural development, often under very difficult climatic and soil conditions. Also typical of the region has been the predominant role played by the State in economic and social development and the importance of the public sector. What follows is a brief description of development in four oil-rich countries that can serve as examples of progress in the entire area.

Saudi Arabia, the most important of the oil exporting countries, had begun development from a very low level, with no other natural resources except petroleum and a population as remote from modern life as almost any in the world. Yet in a relatively short space of time, with purposeful and planned economic development, assisted by outside expertise, mostly American, the country has been transformed, although this has not affected the traditional social fabric and way of life. Helped by an expatriate workforce numbering well in excess of one million, Saudi Arabia, with a native population of about eight million, has now laid the required infrastructure and established the pre-conditions for a full-scale modern development. The third five-year plan starting in 1980 can consequently be devoted more directly to the creation of productive industries and private enterprise activities. The original estimate of the cost for this programme was put at nearly $250 billion, but it now looks more likely to cost in excess of $300 billion. The previous plan, 1975–1980, started with an estimate of nearly $150 billion but in the end $60 billion more was in fact spent. In 1980 Saudi Arabia is expecting to have a revenue from oil in the region of $80 billion.[4]

Saudi Arabia is now capable of producing most of the building materials, including cement, required for the gigantic construction programme that is in progress up and down the country, and many other industries have been set up, especially petroleum refining and production of fertilisers and other petrochemicals. The gas gathering and processing programme, to utilise a resource that has previously been flared, is being completed in 1980 and soon billions of cubic feet of gas a day will be produced and treated in association with petroleum. Huge hydrocarbon- and mineral-based manufacturing industries will be located at Jubayl and Yanby where most of the required infrastructure had already been put in place by 1980. Large-scale petrochemical, fertiliser, aluminium, steel and other industries will operate in the two new industrial centres.

Among the achievements of the preceding, second five-year plan, was the expansion and improvement of port facilities which eased the supply of goods that had been considerably delayed before and thus also helped bring down the inflation rate to manageable proportions. In one year alone, 1978/79, well over 1,000 miles of asphalted roads were constructed, something that usually takes a decade or more to complete in a developing country.[5]

Agriculture is making progress in spite of almost impossible climatic conditions, and a large irrigation network is being completed at Jezan where a dam was recently built. Production of cereals, such as wheat, of potatoes, vegetables and fruit has increased, although Saudi Arabia remains a major importer of all types of food. Fish catches too have improved although, again, most of the fish consumed in Saudi Arabia is imported.

Over the past 11 years eight desalination plants have been constructed and work started on a major new desalination complex at Jubayl to supply with fresh water the Eastern Province as well as Riyadh, the capital. Water is the key to much of the development in arid and desert-like Arabia, but massive investments in desalination and related technologies often lead to more effective and less costly processes being invented and developed, to help other, less privileged regions of the world.

In the field of social progress an expanded house building programme in Saudi Arabia has all but eliminated the housing shortages which previously made life very difficult for native people as well as expatriates. By generous subsidies the Saudi Government managed to bring down the cost of living by 2 per cent between 1977/78 and 1978/79. It must have been the only Government in the world which was able to do that in those years. In the same two-year period the number of doctors working in the country rose by nearly 500 to reach more than 3,300, or an increase of 17·4 per cent. There has been a spectacular expansion of schooling and vocational training. In 1977/78 there were a total of just over 1·2 million students in Saudi Arabia, over 420,000 of them female. Of these over 32,000 male and over 9,100 female students were in higher education establishments.

Kuwait, whose reserves of oil are second only to those of Saudi Arabia, has nonetheless been busily diversifying its economy, preparing itself no doubt for the time when petroleum dries up. While 60 per cent of the Gross Domestic Product in 1980 originated from crude petroleum and natural gas production the rest derived from other economic activities, most of them newly established. Apart from petroleum refining and industries directly based on hydrocarbons, such as the production of fertilisers, the small Gulf country of only about 1·2 million inhabitants, more than half of them not native to the country, has begun the construction of a wide range of manufacturing enterprises, mostly catering for general consumption, including the production of furniture. But it is education which accounts for the largest single item of Government expenditure expected to reach $8·23 billion in 1979/80. Ten per cent of the surpluses must by law be diverted into a fund for 'Future Generations' invested abroad.

Libya has been showing an insatiable appetite for economic development ever since the new team of leaders, headed by Col Muammar Qaddafi, took power in 1969. At times in the seventies Libya almost reached the limits of its purchasing power generated by petroleum sales in her efforts to develop and modernise the country as rapidly as possible, and substantial resort was had to external borrowing. The population, now nearly 3 million, was mostly Bedouin in the past, nomadic tribesmen scratching a living from the soil, with extremely low incomes and underprivileged in every way compared to the European settlers, mostly Italian, who held the economic levers of the country and the best irrigated land along the coast. The Libyan citizen now, however, enjoys one of the highest standards of living in the world, supported by a comprehensive social welfare system and first-class education and employment opportunities.

Libya recorded progress in all sectors of national development. Such projects as the Misurata steel mill and Ras Lanuf oil refinery have absorbed huge sums of petrofunds, but they should soon be paying their way. The merchant fleet, non-existent before 1980, now numbers 11 ocean-going vessels. There have been some delays in the implementation of the ambitious plans, including the current, 1976–1980, development plan. But this is understandable given that the total planned expenditure under this plan was set at nearly $32 billion. In the first four years the growth of GDP was on average 9·5 per cent a year, compared to 10·7 per cent planned. But in 1980 development spending increased by 40 per cent compared with the previous year's level, having reached a value of about $8 billion in 1979 (or 2,400 million Libyan dinars). It was estimated that some 700,000 expatriates were working in Libya in 1980.

Agricultural and rural development is one of the priorities in Libya and Col Qaddafi is said to have declared that he wanted to make Libya as green again 'as it was at the time of the Romans'. Many imaginative crop farming and livestock raising schemes in various parts of the country, including oases deep in the desert, such as Kufra, are being implemented at a total cost of nearly $5 billion under the current five-year plan. Agricultural output has been rising by 8·5 per cent a year, wheat reaching an annual production of 110,000 tons.

Algeria provides the example of an oil-rich country spending more for its economic development in recent years than it was able to earn through its substantial exports of oil and gas. The tide turned in 1979 when revenue from hydrocarbons reached $9,800 million, or more than half as much again as in the previous year. In 1980 the revenues are expected to attain $12,000 million. With $40 a barrel Algerian crude was the most expensive in the world in mid-1980.

By 1978 external debt amounted to $19 billion and debt servicing accounted for just about a quarter of total exports which, because of the larger revenues now, could be brought down to still a very substantial 22 per cent or so in 1979.

But it is the industrial West which provides most of the tools for development and expertise even in the case of countries whose relations with the supplying nation have been consistently less than ideal.

Algeria, which in 1978 imported goods to the value of almost $9 billion, 64 per cent of this being industrial supplies and machinery, bought nearly 70 per cent of the total from western European countries, including EEC, and nearly 10 per cent from North America.

According to information supplied by the First National Bank of Chicago[6] merchandise imports of OPEC countries were estimated at $100 billion in 1979, increasing to $129 billion in 1980 and $160 billion in 1981. They represent a very substantial element of the recycling process and a very significant source of employment in the western industrial countries.

Accompanying heavy imports from industrial countries has

33

been a fast growing expenditure on services, such as fees for contractors and consultants, mostly going to industrial countries of the West, and transfer payments, including remittances of expatriate technicians and workers, to both industrial and developing countries. Other such 'invisible' payments have included profits earned by foreign companies, particularly oil concerns as well as insurance and freight costs on imports. All these items emanating from the rapid economic development in oil-rich countries amounted in 1979 to something like $45 billion according to estimates published by the Bank of England,[7] which was offset to some extent by inflows, in particular of investment earnings amounting to between $15 and $20 billion in the year concerned.

An important, if somewhat controversial, part played by development in oil-exporting countries generated by petrodollars is the very large number of immigrant workers there from neighbouring as well as more distant regions. Significant numbers have come from Egypt, Yemen and Pakistan, and there are also many Palestinians as well as people from India, Bangladesh and as far away as South Korea and the Philippines. The money sent home by these workers and technicians helps the balance of payments situation in their home countries but on the other hand, in some cases, such as those of the Sudan and Somalia, the exodus deprives those countries of much needed skills and expertise.

In the case of the Arabs, of whom there may at any given moment be anything between one and two millions working in other Arab countries than their own, the proportion of population thus involved must be very significant indeed. Dr Mohammed Imady, Director General of the Arab Fund for Economic and Social Development (AFESD), has made this interesting point with reference to the mobility of the Arab workforce: 'More than anything else, this melting pot is schooling Arab communities, that until recently had little physical contact, in the art of living together, of understanding each other and making the personal adjustments that such contacts would entail'.[8]

In view of the above and other payments and transfers the balance of current account of the oil exporting countries, according to the Bank of England Bulletin, varied greatly over these years, being even in deficit in 1978 but recording an

estimated surplus of 74 billion in 1979. According to projections
made by IMF in 1980 current balance of payments accounts of oil
exporting countries would attain $115 billion in that year.

To a large extent the surpluses depended on the price of oil
which after sharp increases in 1973/74 more or less stagnated for
some years, being in 1978 10 per cent down on its previous peak.
Overall in 1979 the weighted average price of an OPEC barrel
was 50 per cent higher in nominal terms than the average for
1978 and by the end of 1979 the real price of oil was some 40 per
cent higher than at the 1974 peak. There were substantial
increases in 1980 whose impact will be discussed later.

The fluctuations of the current account surpluses were little
influenced by changes in the oil production levels in petroleum
exporting countries and, except for a drop of about 9 per cent in
1975, remained in the range of 31 to 32 million barrels a day up
to 1979, but fell somewhat early in 1980, according to the Bank
of England Bulletin.

A significant part of capital transfers from oil-rich Arab
countries has consisted of lending to other developing countries,
that is aid for the Third World development in broad terms.
Pointing out that the oil exporting countries 'have maintained a
steady flow of lending to developing countries, even when their
surpluses have been reduced', the Bank of England Bulletin, to
which reference has already been made, adds that in 1978 such
lending accounted for just under half of the total identified cash
surpluses and included aid on highly concessional terms'.[9]
Initially such aid was mostly in the form of balance of payments
support and programme assistance but more recently there has
been an increasing share of project aid.

According to the Bank of England oil-exporting countries' aid
to developing countries, not including grants and contributions
to international institutions such as IMF and IBRD, amounted to
$7 billion in 1977, $6·2 billion in 1978 and $6·9 billion in 1979.

In 1978 this aid was worth nearly half the total identified
deployed net cash surplus of oil exporting countries of $13·4
billion.

In 1979, in the year when oil prices rose substantially, total aid
to developing countries was $6·9 billion, compared with the total
identified deployed net cash surplus of $53·8 billion.

Again, according to the Bank of England, whose Bulletin

covers data referring to all the members of OPEC and in addition to the oil exporting Trinidad and Tobago, Bahrain, Brunei and Oman, capital flows from all these oil-exporting countries to the Third World as well as the IMF and IBRD amounted to $46 billion in the period 1974–1979, out of the total identified deployed net cash surplus of $236 billion achieved by those countries during that period.

Further reference will be made to data supplied by the Bank of England as the information substantially helps to explain the elusive movements of petrofunds over an entire period, beginning with 1973/74 when the first large increases in oil prices occurred. But here something must be said about Arab aid given to developing countries, and part, including to non-Arab Africa, on concessional terms, that is aid in the narrow sense of the word, the subject of much of this book.

Information on Arab aid is far from complete. Some Arab Governments seem to be secretive about it and do not publish comprehensive accounts of it, partly, I am told, because of an Arab tradition that one should not talk too much about what one does for others. Recipient countries too, especially in Africa, often fail to reveal the exact amounts of Arab assistance they have received.

There are also wide variations in the way various organisations and institutions define aid although this is always understood not to include military assistance.[10] Information supplied on external aid flows by the Paris-based Organisation for Economic Co-operation and Development, made up of leading capitalist countries, is widely accepted. One of the merits of this information is that it covers not only official commitments to aid, which is what most Arab sources do, but also the actual disbursements in any one year. However, OECD statistics tend seriously to underestimate the flows of Arab aid, which I have been able to establish myself in the case of such assistance supplied to non-Arab Africa as will be explained in the next chapter.

Yet until such time as the Arab agencies improve their statistical services, especially in regard to aid disbursement, world media and others are bound to accept the OECD as the best available guide on the matter. However inadequate, the OECD statistics also provide a basis of comparison between concessional aid supplied by OPEC countries as their Official Development Assistance (ODA) and such aid coming from other sources, including free market economy, or capitalist, countries and international organisations.

TABLE I

Total Resource Flows to Developing Countries by Donor Sources

NET DISBURSEMENTS

	$ Billion		Percentages		
	1978	1979	1970	1978	1979
ODA	26·4	29·6	47	33	36
1. DAC (a)	21·5	24·2	40	27	30
2. OPEC	4·3	4·7	2	5	6
3. CMEA countries	0·6	(0·7)	5	1	1
Non-concessional Flows	54·5	52·3	53	67	64
1. DAC (b)	53·0	50·9	51	66	62
2. OPEC (c)	1·4	1·3	2	2	2
3. CMEA countries	0·1	0·1	—	*	*
Total Resource Flows	80·9	81·9	100	100	100

(a) Including grants by private voluntary agencies.
(b) Including offshore bank lending.
(c) Official sector only.

Source: OECD.

37

TABLE 2

Concessional Assistance by OPEC Members 1975–1979

NET DISBURSEMENTS

Donor Country	As per cent of GNP					$ million	
	1975	1976	1977	1978*	1979*	1978*	1979*
Algeria	0·28	0·33	0·25	0·18	0·14	44	45
Iran	1·13	1·13	0·27	(0·33)	(0·03)	278	21
Iraq	1·65	1·44	0·32	0·76	2·94	172	861
Kuwait	8·12	4·36	10·61	6·35	5·14	1268	1099
Libya	2·31	0·63	0·65	0·93	0·58	169	146
Nigeria	0·05	0·25	0·16	0·08	0·05	38	28
Qatar	15·62	7·95	7·93	3·65	5·60	106	251
Saudi Arabia	5·40	5·73	4·32	2·76	3·15	1470	1970
UAE	14·12	11·02	10·22	5·60	1·58	690	207
Venezuela	0·11	0·33	0·14	0·28	0·18	109	83
TOTAL	2·71	2·27	1·96	1·35	1·28	4344	4711

*Figures for 1978 and 1979 are provisional.

Source: OECD.

Further, according to OECD statistics, net disbursements of concessional aid by OPEC donors, which had fallen in 1978 by some $1·5 billion to $4·3 billion, are estimated to have recovered to $4·7 billion in 1979. As a share of the GNP of OPEC countries, however, this implied a decline from 1·35 per cent in 1978 to 1·28 per cent in 1979.

But for the higher income OPEC countries—Kuwait, Qatar, Saudi Arabia and United Arab Emirates—the ODA/GNP ratio was much higher in 1979, at 3·48 per cent. Disbursements by Saudi Arabia, the largest OPEC donor, increased by $0·5 billion to $2·0 billion. Kuwait maintained its disbursements in excess of $1 billion. Iraq became the third largest OPEC donor with disbursements of $0·9 billion compared with $0·2 billion in 1978.

As regards the components of OPEC assistance, bilateral grants increased by $0·5 billion to $2·7 billion between 1978 and 1979. Bilateral loan disbursements increased marginally while contributions to multilateral institutions declined to $1·2 billion.

Among the 13 countries which are members of OPEC are also Ecuador, Gabon, Indonesia, Algeria and Nigeria which all have low or modest per capita incomes and are themselves heavy importers of capital. The inclusion of these countries brings down the average aid in terms of GNP, as these countries cannot afford to give much assistance to others. But net disbursements of four Arab countries, Kuwait, Qatar, Saudi Arabia and UAE, in 1975 amounted to 12·3 per cent of the combined GNP of these countries. In 1976 Saudi Arabia and United Arab Emirates ranked among the six largest bilateral aid donors in absolute terms, Saudi Arabia being second only to the USA.

As Table 1 shows, the bulk of capital flows to the Third World continues to be provided by the traditional donors, that is the non-communist industrial countries. Net disbursements of Official Development Assistance by Development Assistance Committee (DAC) countries in 1979 amounted to $22·3 billion. This was an increase in current dollars of $2·3 billion over 1978, or 11 per cent. After taking account of increased prices this corresponds to an increase in real terms of the order of 2 per cent, slightly below the trend value in recent years. But with DAC members' combined GNP expressed in current dollars being some 13 per cent higher than in 1978 their ODA declined marginally as share of GNP from 0·35 per cent to 0·34 per cent in 1979.[11]

It was particularly disappointing that the world's richest country, the USA, contributed in 1979 only 0·19 per cent of its GNP for Official Development Assistance to the Third World, which represented a drastic slump from 0·27 per cent in 1978, a level that was in itself far below the minimum of 0·7 per cent pledged by donor countries at the UN and urged more recently by the Brandt Commission.

Arab concessional aid, about which we shall have to say a great deal in subsequent chapters, with special reference to Arab–African economic co-operation, has been both substantial and generous by any yardstick. It is particularly impressive when related to GNP of the respective donor countries, or for that matter to the per capita income in Arab countries. On a per capita basis Arab development assistance amounted in 1975–1977 to more than $800, with over $1,600 for Kuwait, as against $25 for the DAC countries, a ratio of 32 to 1.[12]

Arab aid, which is based on a depletable resource and thus represents loss of asset in real terms as distinct from western aid which derives from renewable wealth, also has the additional advantage to developing countries that it is not tied to the purchases from any particular country, as much of the western aid is, although it is on the other hand true to say that DAC aid usually has a larger grant element than the Arab.

One should also mention the high concentration of Arab aid on least developed and most seriously affected countries. While most of the Arab bilateral aid was initially destined for other Arab countries, or 96·3 per cent in 1973, this later became less pronounced and in 1976 the proportion was 64·5 per cent in favour of the Arab countries. But it should be pointed out that some of the Arab, or technically Arab, countries are among the world's poorest and least developed; think of the two Yemens, Mauritania, Sudan and Somalia.

When comparisons are made between the Arab and DAC performance in regard to aid it is also necessary to challenge the widespread myth of a fabulous wealth of the oil-rich Arab world. In fact, Arab revenues from oil in 1976–1978 were no more than 78 per cent of what West Germany earned from her merchandise exports and 20 per cent of the total value of EEC exports during that period. Cumulative GNP of the 21 Arab countries with a total population of some 150 million is no more than 10 per cent of that of the USA and half of that of France. Even the Netherlands has a somewhat higher GNP than the combined GNPs of the five major Arab oil-exporting countries, Saudi Arabia, Kuwait, the UAE, Qatar and Libya, which together also have a population of comparable size. The truth is that despite the pockets of relative affluence in the region the Arab world as a whole remains a relatively low income area with an average per capita GNP of no more than $1,200 in 1979, as Dr Mohamed Imady, Director-General of the Arab Fund for Economic and Social Development (AFESD) has explained.[13]

It is further important to consider the erosion of the exchange value of the US dollar and world inflation which have played havoc with nominal revenues from oil. According to a calculation made by the Organisation of Arab Petroleum Exporting Countries which takes 1970 as the base year the total revenue from oil sales of 10 Arab exporters, including Bahrain, Syria and Egypt in addition to Arab members of OPEC—amounted nominally to $86,462 million in 1977, of which $42,384 million was accounted for by Saudi Arabia. But in real value the figures were $33,254 million and $16,301·5 million respectively.

Finally, as Dr Imady has pointed out, the accumulation of surpluses on the part of the Arab petroleum exporters itself 'clearly indicates that the oil producers are extracting oil at rates beyond those dictated by their development needs and, in a sense, such a course constitutes a sacrifice on their part'.

It is really quite right to ask why the Arabs should be so generous. Various reasons and motives have been advanced to explain the phenomenon, including the Islamic religion and humanitarian traditions. But there has, of course, also been self-interest, however enlightened.

Much of the Arab aid has benefited non-oil Arab countries and their development. Charity begins at home, of course. There again, aid provided to non-Arab Africa, including that channelled through the Arab Bank for Economic Development in Africa (BADEA) has often served specific purposes of solidarity and partnership of the two communities in what is fundamentally a political concept.

But beyond that, the self-interest of the Arab petroleum exporting countries and individual members of this group dictates an active, positive and substantial involvement in the pursuit of an objective of great importance to mankind— improvement of life in the Third World and its economic emancipation. Here the Arab contribution does not only come from the money they provide for the cause but also from the active support they are providing in other fields, the Arabs regarding themselves as part of the Third World and sharing its claims and anxieties.

In this manner the Arabs can give their financial power and influence in world affairs a new dimension. With their aid record they can much more plausibly argue the case for a world-wide partnership of the developed and developing nations in which the

41

interests of the two are inextricably intertwined. Thus the Arabs re-emerge as a factor in the progress of mankind—to which they contributed so much in the distant past, something of which they have remained aware all through the ages of their decline and poverty.

But having said that we must return to more mundane matters and consider what actually happens to the money that the Arab and to a smaller extent other oil-exporting countries accumulate after they have met their expenses and provided help for others. What stands out in the Bank of England Bulletin is the high proportion of these surpluses being invested in the United Kingdom and the United States of America as well as the importance played by short-term bank deposits in euro-currency markets.

According to the Bulletin[14] out of some $240 billion that could be identified at the end of 1979 as outstanding foreign assets owned by oil-exporting countries 80 per cent were in industrial countries, and half were in UK and USA.

Over half the investment in industrial countries was in the form of bank deposits, of which about 77 per cent was in the euro-currency markets, slightly over half of this in the United Kingdom. By the end of 1979 the proportion of bank deposits held in US dollars was about 68 per cent, much the larger part being in euro-markets. About 20 per cent of total euro-currency deposits were probably denominated in German, Japanese and Swiss currencies. But the high proportion of the money held in dollars of course meant that oil exporting countries have been in recent years recording very big losses because of the erosion of the international value of the American currency. In 1980 a trend appeared showing increasing investment by oil-exporting countries in currencies other than US dollars, notably yen and various European currencies, including sterling.

Apart from bank deposits, long and short term Government and private securities accounted for a large part of the assets. In spite of considerable publicity surrounding certain Arab purchases of property abroad, including hotels in London, direct investment was small, although it was increasing in 1980. Some 10 per cent of the surpluses of the oil-exporting countries by the end of 1979 were in gold.

After the first major increase in the oil price it was widely feared that persistent surpluses would present intractable problems of adjustment and financing. As it turned out the surpluses could be efficiently recycled, mostly through a number of large, so-called money centre banks in the USA, Britain, Germany and Japan. Much of the money served development in the Third World. According to an IMF report of August 1979 less than half the aggregate capital flow from non-communist industrial countries originated from their national savings, the remainder being a recycling of national savings originating in the oil surplus countries.[15] In turn this led to considerable imports by the developing countries, using money borrowed from the West. According to an OECD study this recycling was responsible for an equivalent of perhaps 900,000 jobs in the industrial countries each year from 1973 to 1977.[16]

Thus, the increases in oil prices and the surpluses of the oil-exporting countries provided the industrial countries with large opportunities for greater exports, both to the oil-rich and to non-oil developing countries. Some have been able to grasp these opportunities better than others, but that is life. In most cases there have been time lags between deficits due to higher priced fuel imports and export earnings generated from recycled petrofunds.

But on the whole, the western countries have done very well out of the deal, except for the problems of inflation and recession for which the higher prices for oil cannot really be blamed.

The challenge now is much greater as the surpluses of the oil-exporting countries are expected to go up to $115 billion in 1980 and some $100 billion in 1981. Another problem is that several banks, particularly American ones, have already exceeded their permitted or prudent exposure in developing countries.

But other institutions may now come in to share the burden to a greater extent than before and new agencies might appear. The role of international banking consortia has much expanded in recent years, with the Arabs often taking the lead. The most important of these has been the Union de Banques Arabes et Françaises (UBAF) based in Paris, in which 60 per cent of the capital is owned by nearly 30 Arab banks, including a number of central banks, while the remainder is shared by French, American, British and other western and Japanese financial houses. With group assets worth at least $6 billion the

43

consortium has been diversifying in geographical and business terms. It played a leading role in 1979 in the first syndicate loan to China of $300 million following a visit by several Arab bankers to Peking.[17]

The new sharp rise in oil prices, estimated by IMF to have increased from a little under $13 a barrel in 1978 to $31·25 a barrel on average by mid-1980, certainly created further problems for oil-importing nations, in a general setting of world-wide recession, while restoring the benefits which the oil exporters had reaped with the first large jump in petroleum prices in 1973/74 and subsequently lost.

Yet the very considerable shifts that were now taking place in trade balances were due to a number of complex causes and by no means only to petroleum prices.

While oil prices were now an important reason for the improvement in the trade balance of the oil exporting nations this change was also due to a general reduction in imports on the part of these countries following the boom in the trade marking the preceding few years.

For industrial countries as a whole the higher prices of fuel meant that this item in the import bill represented a net increase from $130 billion in 1978 to $184 billion in 1979. But at the same time the industrial countries continued to expand their exports of manufactures, the value of which rose to $170 billion in 1979, or nearly as much as the new fuel import bill. Industrial countries' exports of manufactured goods, mostly engineering products, more than trebled between 1973 and 1979, reflecting the greater purchases of capital goods on the part of the Third World, including both oil-exporting and non-oil-exporting nations. By the end of 1980 there was little doubt that most of the industrial countries were able to cope with the problem of higher prices for fuel. The main economic problem in many of those countries remained inflation, but several Governments were now adopting monetarist policies designed to restore price stability, and generally these policies proved successful, albeit at the cost of higher unemployment, especially in Britain.

Problems facing the non-oil developing countries were different, and for many of them extremely grave. According to IMF these countries as a group faced in 1979 a current account deficit of $52·9 billion compared to $35·8 billion in the previous year and might face one of $74 billion in 1980.

The higher cost of fuel imports certainly played a part in this dramatic deterioration. But not the most important part, which remained that of the increasing costs of importing manufactured goods from western countries and higher payments from non-oil developing countries to the West in the form of investment income, especially interest payments on non-concessional loans.

According to the office of the General Agreement on Tariffs and Trade (GATT) in Geneva, the overall trade deficit of the non-oil developing countries grew steadily from $15 billion in 1973 to $40 billion in 1975, the largest part of this increase resulting from the greater imports of higher priced manufactured goods from the West. The rise of the deficit in fuel, while substantial, was relatively less important. Between 1974 and 1978 the overall deficit of the non-oil developing countries levelled off, a further rise in the manufactures deficit being offset by a higher surplus on trade in non-fuel primary products. In 1979, however, the deficit in the trade balance of the non-oil developing countries worsened again as the deficit on trade in manufactures grew to $71 billion and that of fuel to $21 billion, or $35 billion if Mexico and other net exporters of fuel were excluded.[18]

While GATT statistics demonstrate the relatively small importance of the higher petroleum prices in the deficit of the non-oil producing Third World as a whole there are other important considerations that must be taken into account in this emotionally charged subject.

Most of the developing countries only import relatively small amounts of oil and its products. According to information supplied by an Arab Executive Director of the World Bank, Said E. El-Nagger,[19] 45 developing countries imported oil worth less than $100 million each in 1978/79, and in the case of 30 of these countries the cost was less than $50 million. The 45 developing countries only accounted for 5·6 per cent of the total import bill of the Third World, but they included virtually all of the least developed countries and all African net importers of the fuel except Ghana and Zambia. Only 10 non-oil developing countries had import bills in excess of $1 billion per annum each at 1979 prices while accounting for as much as 74·3 per cent of the entire fuel import bill of the group of countries. Those high importers of fuel were in descending order of importance, Brazil, South

45

Korea, Turkey, Taiwan, India, Yugoslavia, Philippines, Thailand, Cuba and Singapore.

Arab oil exporters in this context also point to the fact that they as a group still have little control over the refining and marketing sides of the petroleum business. As Dr Imady[20] has pointed out about 94 per cent of Arab oil exports are in crude form. Before 1973 oil-producing countries receiving only 9 per cent of the value of the refined product; the rest was shared between taxes levied by the importing countries, company margins and refining costs. At present—1979—the ratio is still biased in the interest of the importers and intermediaries who receive 67 per cent with the producers receiving the remaining 33 per cent of the proceeds.

The oil-exporting countries and the rest of the Third World seem to agree that the primary responsibility for helping the developing nations rests with the industrial countries, in the West and East. When the Arabs are criticised for not doing enough to help the Third World they point to the puny percentage of the production in the advanced countries, notably the USA, going for aid to the Third World. Yet the Arabs have frequently made plain that they regard themselves as part of the developing world and bound with it in solidarity. They will therefore not stand idly by, one hopes, when many of the poorer developing countries might be crumbling under the weight of oil bills. There is urgent need for international consultation and action. But the oil-exporting countries want such discussion to cover a wider range of economic problems and also the need to move nearer to the New International Economic Order and not to confine the talks to the problems of oil prices and supplies.

On this I would like to quote what is probably a typical Arab view on the subject, that of Said E. El-Nagger:

'There can be little doubt that a substantial increase in both concessional and non-concessional flows is necessary if developing countries are to cope with rising deficits and mounting debt burden, maintaining at the same time a reasonable rate of growth.

'But the responsibility for such increase should fall on all donors: OPEC as well as DAC countries. However, the inordinate prominence given to the oil-price increase and its supposed impact on inflation, deflation and the external balance of the poorer developing countries, would seem to imply that OPEC countries are uniquely responsible for a good deal of the problems besetting the world economy.

'Such an implication, to repeat the words of GATT, is both wrong and dangerous. It is wrong since total oil imports, even at prices expected to prevail in 1980, account for less than 20 per cent of total world imports and not more than 2 to 3 per cent of GNP in the oil-importing countries. It is dangerous since it shifts the responsibility to where it does not belong.'[21]

NOTES

1. *North-South : A Programme for Survival*, Pan Books, London, 1980, p. 162.
2. GATT: *Prospects for International Trade*, Geneva, September 1979, p. 12.
3. *Financial Times*, London, Saudi Arabia Survey, 28 April 1980.
4. Ibid.
5. Saudi Arabia Monetary Agency (SAMA) Annual Report 1979, Jeddah, pp. 53–104.
6. First National Bank of Chicago, World Report, May–June 1980, p. 2.
7. Bank of England, Quarterly Bulletin, June 1980.
8. *The Prospects for Economic Growth in the 1980s. Energy as a Source of Wealth for the Middle East*. Paper delivered at the Athens Seminar, September 28–29, 1979, p. 11.
9. Bank of England, op. cit. p. 158.
10. Apart from OECD the most comprehensive set of data on flows of resources from OPEC members to the Third World is supplied by UNCTAD. The major difference between the two sources seems to lie in estimates of non-concessional multilateral flows: OECD does not consider payments to the IMF oil facility as part of the relevant flows while UNCTAD does. See 'The Opec Aid Record', by Ibrahim F. I. Shihata and Robert Mabro, OPEC Special Fund, Vienna, June 1979 pp. 4–13. Also useful in this context is *The UNCTAD report on OPEC aid : A Summary*, published by The OPEC Special Fund, Vienna, July 1979.
11. OECD, Press/A (80) 39, Paris, 19 June 1980, p. 3.
12. *The Prospects for Economic Growth*, etc. p. 15.
13. Ibid. pp. 2–3.
14. Bank of England, op. cit. pp. 158–9.
15. IMF Annual Report, Washington, August 1979, p. 22.
16. *North-South : A Programme for Survival*, p. 67.
17. *Financial Times*, London, 16 July 1980, p. 16.
18. GATT/1271/6 September 1980, p. 10–11.
19. *The Impact of Oil Prices Increase*, by Said E. El-Nagger, February 1980, pp. 23–5.
20. *The Prospects for Economic Growth*, p. 6.
21. op. cit. p. 25.

2

Arab Aid to Africa

The motives, ranging from political self-interest to humanitarian altruism, which prompted the oil-rich Arab countries to open their purses wide for the benefit of the rest of the developing world after 1973, applied in a special way to the African continent.

Of course Africa includes many Arab countries, which now all benefited from greater Arab financial assistance. But geographical and cultural ties between the Arabs and Africa also include the non-Arab parts of the continent, quite apart from the fact that many of these countries have substantial Arab ethnic minorities and that Islam, a religion brought to the continent by the Arabs, is practised by many millions of non-Arab Africans.

As will be explained in a later chapter, the ability of the Arabs to furnish aid to the poor and developing countries, so many of which are in Africa, coincided with the growth of closer political understanding between the two communities represented by the League of Arab States and the Organisation of African Unity respectively. By the end of 1973 most of the Black African countries had broken off diplomatic relations with Israel, as the Arabs had wished them to do. This created a basis of trust between the two communities upon which a more systematic Arab aid effort for the benefit of Black Africa began to take shape.

Acting under the auspices of the Arab League the Arabs now established three institutions for aid to non-Arab Africa, the Khartoum-based Arab Bank for Economic Development in Africa (BADEA) for long-term development aid, the Special Arab Aid Fund for Africa (SAAFA) for emergency assistance, and a smaller Fund for Arab Technical Aid to African and Arab Countries (FATAAAC) concerned with such matters as the supply of facilities for Arabic studies in Africa.

At the same time previously established Arab aid agencies now

49

became available to non-Arab Africa and new institutions were set up whose scope included assistance to the region.

The oldest Arab aid agency, the Kuwait Fund for Arab Economic Development (KFAED), could now with a substantially increased capital offer its services to non-Arab developing countries. Similar action was taken by the recently established Abu Dhabi Fund (ADFAED) while Saudi Arabia created its own, Saudi Fund for Development (SFD). Other Arab countries also began to increase their aid to Africa, including Iraq with its Iraqi Fund for External Development.

Two multilateral institutions became important channels for Arab aid to non-Arab Africa, the OPEC Fund—to which the Arabs contribute more than half the capital—and the mostly Arab-financed Islamic Development Bank (IDB). Also set up now was a multilateral Arab agency for development assistance only to Arab countries, the Arab Fund for Economic and Social Development (AFESD) based in Kuwait.

Special attention is paid in this chapter to what have become known as the 'seven sisters'—BADEA, KFAED, ADFAED, SFD, IDB, OPEC Fund and AFESD. All of these have been active in non-Arab Africa with the exception of the latter, but as will be explained later the AFESD also has a certain relevance for our region.

Endowed with substantial capital resources—with subscribed or declared capital of the six institutions directly assisting Black Africa amounting by the end of 1980 to well over $14 billion the seven sisters deserve special consideration as typical instances of the new Arab commitment to international aid supplied on concessional terms.

Each of these agencies, all having their own legal personalities and independent administrations, has developed its specific philosophy and approach to development. Placed on a long-term footing and suitably organised and structured they testify to the serious and continuous involvement in development of the areas of their activity. They mark a new departure in institutionalised development aid as significant sources of concessional finance existing within the Third World itself. Mostly administered by Arab experts, they have in the past few years already made a significant impact in the regions of their activity. To look at them more closely both as individual agencies and as a group is all the more appropriate in view of their increasing mutual co-ordination of their systems and activities.

The Arab Bank for Economic Development in Africa

The decision to create an Arab agency specifically designed to assist economic development in the non-Arab part of Africa was made at the sixth Summit conference of the League of Arab States meeting in Algiers on 26–28 November 1973. The initiative was a response to a mission sent to the Arab League by an extraordinary meeting of the Ministerial Council of the Organisation of African Unity to examine with the Arab League the possibility of reaching a common policy for closer co-operation between the Arab and African communities.[1]

Shortly before, the Council of Ministers had shown its support for Arab causes by equating Zionism with imperialism and colonialism at its extraordinary meeting on 19–20 November and calling on all OAU member States to sever their relations with Israel. Only four African countries, of minor importance, continued their diplomatic ties with Israel. It was this striking display of solidarity with the Arabs which no doubt prompted them to reciprocate in a positive and concrete fashion and set up for the first time an Arab aid institution entirely designed to serve a non-Arab region. It was also the first major instance of one region of the developing world deciding to assist the development in another developing region in a systematic way.

While being a manifestation of Afro-Arab solidarity the new institution was yet to remain firmly in Arab hands. The Arabs did not agree with an African view that the new Arab aid should be channelled through the agency which the Africans themselves, including the Arab countries in Africa, had been operating since 1963, the Abidjan-based African Development Bank (ADB).

There was a good deal of argument about this. Should Arab aid for Africa be subject to joint decision-making? What was to be the degree of consultation between the two communities in respect of such aid? A resolution was passed at the OAU Summit in Monrovia in July 1979 recommending closer mutual consultation between the Arabs and Africans in these matters.[2] The dialogue on the topic has continued.

While the question has not been resolved by 1980 the new financial support supplied by the Arabs had as one of its major objectives the encouragement of friendly attitudes towards them in the non-Arab part of the continent, to strengthen the ties of solidarity between the Arab and African communities. There was therefore much need for tact on the Arab part, for good diplomacy and an intelligent grasp of African interests and views as well as of opinion in the Arab world. It was also important to put in the right perspective the role to be played in this by industrial countries as these would necessarily have to supply most of the technology and expertise for the development projects to be financed by Arab money.

A major responsibility to explain the meaning and purpose of the new institution fell on the chief executive appointed on 1 January 1975 when the Arab Bank for Economic Development in Africa (BADEA) was formally set up at an Arab League meeting in Cairo (it began operations in Khartoum in March 1975).

The man chosen for this task, which involved the duties of the Bank's President and Director-General and Chairman of the Board of Directors, was Dr Chedly Ayari of Tunisia. Born in Tunis in 1933 Dr Ayari had a distinguished career as academic and scholar, development expert and politician. He had received a degree in law and a doctorate in economic and social sciences at the University of Tunis and passed the highest French examination for teachers and researchers (aggrégation) at the University of Paris. He was an executive director of the World Bank Group in 1963–1964 and later became Professor of Law and Ecomonic Sciences at the University of Tunis. He had been Minister of National Economy, Minister of Planning and Minister of Education.

Closely involved as a student and young man in his country's struggle for independence, Dr Ayari later played a significant part in shaping Tunisia's pragmatic international and development policies. After gaining its freedom in 1956 Tunisia became something of a model among developing countries. A high level of economic growth was based on a balanced development of different economic sectors, such as agriculture and manufacturing industry, as well as between various regions of the country. The financial viability of an economic enterprise was regarded as important, but so was its broad social impact. The State was allocated a wide field of activity and intervention but at the same time co-operative and private sectors were encouraged. One was to find echoes of these eclectic and pragmatic approaches in the philosophy of BADEA as explained and practised by its chief executive.

When BADEA was constituted in 1975 a total of eighteen Arab States, that is all with the exception of North and South Yemen and Somalia, became members, subscribing an initial capital of $231 million, with Saudi Arabia contributing nearly a quarter, followed in order of importance by Libya, Kuwait, Iraq, the UAE and Qatar. The voting power in the Bank is in proportion to the amount of financial contribution of the respective country.

Each member country has one representative on the Bank's Board of Governors, normally its Minister of Finance. The authority of BADEA is vested in the Board which meets once a year in regular session. It is alone responsible for any changes in the capital stock, which eventually rose to $738·25 million. It is also the prerogative of the Board of Governors to interpret or amend the provisions of the original statutes of the Bank and to lay down broad principles for the policies to be pursued.

The Board of Governors retains the overall responsibility for the supervision of the Bank's management and procedures while delegating the powers of current decision-making to a twelve-man Board of Directors. Any member country subscribing at least $20 million to the capital automatically receives a seat on the Board. This accounts for seven of the eighteen members. Four members are elected jointly for four-year terms by the Governors representing the other eleven member countries. The twelfth member of the Board of Directors is its Chairman, sitting ex-officio and having a casting vote. Appointed for a five-year term, with renewable mandate, the Chairman of the Board of Directors is also the Bank's President and its chief executive.

The most important role of the Board of Directors is to approve and allocate BADEA's financial aid, which consists mostly of concessional, medium- and long-term loans, although exceptionally free grants have been made. The Board of Directors meets three times a year in ordinary session. In the meantime the chief executive is responsible for the day-to-day running of the institution.[3]

'BADEA is not a profit-making institution designed to recycle petro-dollars', Dr Ayari recently told an audience of British businessmen in London. 'It is a development agency with a political purpose—and which international development institution is not political?

'It serves the political purpose of Afro-Arab solidarity and co-operation. Its primary objective is not to invest in profitable ventures but to help development in non-Arab Africa on a broad front, taking account of economic as well as social considerations', Dr Ayari explained.

BADEA is not a charity either. There would have been no need for the Arabs to create a new institution to dispense charity. Most of the facilities provided by the Bank require repayment although on terms which in effect mean that a large proportion of the loan is a free grant. Loans approved by the end of 1979 carried interest rates of between 2 and 7 per cent and maturities from 11 to 25 years with grace periods of between 2 and 10 years. The overall 'grant element' was 39·20 per cent.

BADEA, which is designed for development project aid, does not provide balance of payments or budgetary support to individual countries. But balance of payments support was the purpose of the sister institution, the Special Arab Aid Fund for Africa (SAAFA), which started operations under the auspices of the Arab League in 1974. The Fund was created to help African countries which found themselves in temporary financial difficulties owing to the higher cost of oil imports or other circumstances affecting their balance of payments.

SAAFA, which was administered by the Arab League itself from 1974 till 1976, was in that year placed under the control of BADEA and remained so till 1977, when it was wound up and its capital, $350 million, added to the ordinary stock of the Bank. Because of this close connection with the Bank SAAFA's operations, which involved the distribution of a total of $221·744 million in loans, with a grant element of 75 per cent, to 37 African countries, are usually considered as part of the Bank's work although most of the loans had been approved and disbursed at a time when SAAFA was administered by the League.

BADEA has endeavoured to help every eligible country, that is every non-Arab member State of OAU, of which there are now, with Zimbabwe added in 1980, 41. By providing aid for the first time BADEA may open the door of that country for other Arab donors to come in. This has been the case with Angola, a country little known to the Arabs and somewhat controversial on account of its professed Marxist ideology. But true to its general principle of non-interference in the domestic or foreign affairs of recipient countries BADEA chose to help Angola as well as Mozambique, with the result that other Arab Funds, including the OPEC Fund, moved in as well, providing aid of their own.

No African country, however, maintaining ties with Israel or South Africa can receive BADEA assistance. Countries with surpluses of their own as oil exporters, including Nigeria and Gabon, have also not received any BADEA support and indeed have not asked for it.

By the end of 1979 a total of 32 eligible countries received direct aid from the Bank. Twelve countries received aid for one project each—Angola, Botswana, Comoros, Congo, Ivory Coast, Ethiopia, Mauritius, Uganda, Sao Tomé and Principe, Sierra Leone, Togo and Zambia; twelve—Benin, Burundi, Cameroon, Cape Verde, Guinea-Bissau, Kenya, Lesotho, Liberia, Rwanda, Tanzania, Chad and Zaire—benefited twice each; seven others— the Gambia, Guinea, Upper Volta, Madagascar, Niger, Senegal and Ghana—were helped on three occasions; and one country, Mali, received four loans. This does not include the lines of credit granted to the Development Bank of Central African States, emergency aid for 11 countries in 1978 and help for the Pan-African Telecommunications Network.

By the end of 1980 a total of $383·630 million was committed by BADEA, not counting the $221·744 million approved and disbursed by SAAFA.

In the geographical distribution of its aid BADEA has been concerned that a fair balance should be observed between the two parts of non-Arab developing Africa, East and West, into which the region is divided for the purposes of operations.[4] The division follows broadly the practice of the World Bank, except that Mauritania in West Africa and Sudan, Somalia and Djibouti in East Africa are not eligible for BADEA aid as they are all members of the Arab League. But some of the countries covered by BADEA were not members of the World Bank in 1980, including Angola and Mozambique.

By the end of 1980 57·7 per cent of the total commitment of $383.630 million benefited West Africa and 41·9 per cent East Africa with the rest not being specified. The difference is largely explained by the fact that there are more countries in West than in East Africa and that the population of the former is substantially larger than in the latter.

TABLE I

Annual Commitments by Region

	1975		1976		1977		1978		1979		1980		Total	
	in $ m	%	in $ m	%	in $ m	%	in $ m	%	in $ m	%	in $ m	%	in $ m	%
West Africa	51·60	72·1	27·80	44·9	40·24	60·7	40·463	59·6	33·60	76·2	27·5	38·2	221·203	57·7
East Africa	20·00	27·9	34·00	54·9	26·00	39·3	25·898	38·2	10·47	23·8	44·45	61·8	160·818	41·9
Unspecified	—	—	0·10	0·2	—	—	1·509	2·2	—	—	—	—	1·609	0·4
TOTALS	71·60	100	61·90	100	66·24	100	67·87	100	44·07	100	71·95	100	383·630	100

Source: BADEA Statistics

A very important consideration however in the geographical distribution of BADEA aid has been the relative need for such help on the part of the recipient countries. The so-called Least Developed Countries (LDCs) and the Most Seriously Affected Countries (MSACs) as well as the Sahel Zone have been accorded priority.

Out of the world's 31 Least Developed Countries[5] as defined by the United Nations 20 are in the African continent and 18 in the non-Arab region of which 15 had received direct BADEA aid by the end of 1979. As far as the MSACs[6] in non-Arab Africa are concerned all of them except two were granted BADEA project aid and all the seven non-Arab countries of the Sahel Zone were given such assistance by the end of that year.

In regard to the economic sectors to which BADEA aid goes it is for the applicant country to decide on its priorities. But it will be up to BADEA to choose, out of a number of projects submitted for finance, such schemes as seem to it most suited for economic development in that country and region.

In other words, BADEA has its own scale of priorities in respect of the sectors that need to be developed in any particular African country. As the experience and expertise of the Bank's operational staff—42 professional people were employed in Khartoum in 1980—grow, the influence that BADEA can bring to bear on the choice of priorities in Africa will correspondingly increase. Apart from the importance to the country concerned the Bank takes into account broader and regional applications. An industrial project capable of serving several countries in the region may well be preferred to one benefiting only one country, other things being equal.

'We cannot impose our views on the recipient country', Dr Ayari has said, 'or the priorities to be followed in regard to different sectors of the economy. We do express our opinion and try to persuade the country concerned if we feel strongly about the case, but in the end the decision must always rest with the Government.'

Over the past five years over 40 per cent of the money committed by the Bank for development went for infrastructure projects, which included transport communications, tele-communications and communal works, such as sewerage and drainage. It is not only that such projects are particularly needed in Africa and any further economic development may depend on their construction but it is also normally difficult for most African Governments to find finance on acceptable terms for a project that will not pay its way for many years to come. Concessionary long-term loans are particularly suited for such projects.

Much of the money committed to this sector was for roads, railways, ports and airports. Many African countries, desperately in need of such infrastructure projects, have been assisted by BADEA.

Nearly half the total amount allocated by April 1980 for the transport sector went for the construction and improvement of roads, notably in Burundi, Guinea, Lesotho, Madagascar, Mali, Niger and Zambia. Altogether the Bank has been helping in the building of 700 kilometres of roads, rehabilitation of 2,301 km and maintenance of 7,267 km of roads.

An example of this aid was a loan of $6 million to land-locked Burundi in 1978 for the building of a new two-lane asphalted road linking the country's capital city, Bujumbura, with the town of Cibitoke in the north-west, over a distance of 66 km, including the construction of several bridges. Other roads, over a distance of 370 km, are also being improved in Burundi under this project. Another component was maintenance of equipment and training of local mechanics and drivers.

The Bujumbura-Cibitoke road, running parallel to the border of Zaire, was to traverse an important agricultural area, mostly producing cotton, maize, rice, bananas and coffee. The road, which allows a daily traffic of up to 300 vehicles of over three tonnes each, would thus improve access to an important farming area and thereby help further economic development. Another expected benefit of the project is to reduce substantially the internal transport costs and thus raise the scheme's economic return.

Total estimated cost of the project is $24 million. BADEA's loan of $6 million is to be repaid over 20 years, including 5 years of grace, with a rate of interest of 2 per cent. The other sources of finance are the Government of Burundi, International Development Association (of the World Bank Group), the Federal Republic of Germany and the United Nations Development Programme.

The construction of the road was inaugurated by the Burundi Minister of Works in 1979.

Among the loans approved by the BADEA Board of Directors in 1979 was one of $10 million to enable another land-locked country, Mali, to construct a new road of 228 km between Hombori and Gao and improve the existing highway over a distance of 328 km, the total being Mali's section of the important Trans-Sahara Highway which will eventually link Algeria and Nigeria over a distance of about 2,900 km. In further justifying the grant of the loan the Board of Directors pointed to the benefits which the project would bring Mali itself. It would serve an area rich in uranium and phosphate deposits. It would help farming and animal husbandry and general economic development and employment. Various development projects planned for the area would, because of the new road, have a higher economic return.

The project, scheduled for completion in 1984, would cost a total of $78·66 million, with the Islamic Development Bank, OPEC Fund, Kuwait Fund for Arab Economic Development, Saudi Fund for Development, Abu Dhabi Fund for Arab Economic Development and the Government of Mali providing the rest of the finance.

BADEA's loan of $10 million was to be repaid over 20 years, with 5 years of grace and an annual interest of 4 per cent.

BADEA has financed two railway projects, representing just over 14 per cent of the total number of projects financed in the transport sector and involving nearly 20 per cent of the loans approved for the sector. The two projects are in Angola and Congo.

Maritime transport has been helped by extension and modernisation of ports in Cameroon and in Benin where the Cotonou Port scheme is also designed to serve other countries in the area.

Nearly 20 per cent of the total allocated for transport by mid-1980 went towards airport projects in Botswana, the Gambia and Lesotho.

In granting a loan of $6 million towards the cost of constructing an international airport at Maseru in Lesotho BADEA's Board of Directors pointed out the political significance of the project for a country which is now heavily dependent on South Africa for international traffic. It would provide considerable employment for local people during the building, and when operational would give opportunities for advanced technical training and employment in a high technology area. It would serve tourist development and generally facilitate business contacts and export trade.

Most of the transport communication projects co-financed by the Bank have been directly relevant to agricultural and rural development, which is understandable, given the great importance of these activities in Africa. 'Better communications improve internal marketing conditions and transportation of food supplies as well as access to rural areas, boost employment and promote more equitable distribution of incomes,' BADEA has said. But many BADEA-assisted schemes are directly concerned with farming and some of these by 1980 already contributed significantly to food production in the respective countries. So far over one fifth of all the aid allocated by BADEA has been for agricultural and rural development.

BADEA has helped finance four projects of food crops production. A cocoa scheme in Ghana will not only benefit 10,000 farming families and contribute to cocoa production but also improve productivity by introducing high-yield varieties on farms extending over an area of 30,000 acres. A sugar project in Guinea-Bissau, for which the Bank has financed pre-investment studies, is designed to develop sugar cane plantations, create many new jobs and contribute to economic integration of a wide area in West Africa. A maize-growing project in Tanzania has led to significant expansion in the production of the staple food, as will be explained later. In Zaire the Bank is involved in supporting a palm oil production venture to substitute for a significant import item. All the four projects directly concerned with food crop production have in common the purpose of improving the balance of payments in the countries assisted, either by helping to increase exports or by saving on imports.

A significant part of BADEA's allocations so far has been for rural development, with a total of five operations, in the Gambia, Kenya, Mali, Rwanda and Upper Volta. As the Bank has explained:

'It should be pointed out that rural development is not normally favoured by external investors because such components as the improvement of peasant home life, water supply, health service, storage installations and building of rural tracks are generally not regarded as attractive to money-lending institutions. And yet without a dynamic strategy to develop the countryside the rural masses cannot be brought into the development process and would become disillusioned with farming, a disillusionment that leads to rural exodus and slum-style urbanisation.'

An example of BADEA work in this field is a very large beef production and integrated rural development project in Rwanda, which like the neighbouring Burundi is situated right in the heart of Africa. A loan of $5 million was approved in 1976 to serve an area in the south-east of the country of over 300,000 hectares, with some 270,000 inhabitants. Centred on improvement of local animal husbandry, the project is designed to eradicate the tse-tse fly from an extensive area; set up agro-veterinary units and demonstration farms; plant tree nurseries for reafforestation; help the peasants with credits for the purchase of fertilisers and other inputs; improve the marketing and processing of agricultural produce; construct or improve access roads; and set up two cattle ranches, an irrigation project, schools, health centres, veterinary training centres and a national laboratory for the production of vaccines.

I saw the project in 1979, when it was more than half way through its implementation. It was already playing an important part in the economy of Rwanda. The project costs a total of $25·8 million of which BADEA's contribution is one fifth, the rest being supplied by Rwanda interests, the Belgian and French external aid agencies and the International Development Association (IDA) which itself contributes over half the total in the form of an interest-free loan. The project is managed by the Rwanda Government with the help of a team of French technicians supplied by the French Government.

Projects of this nature can help transform the face of Africa and solve the problem of food supply in the continent. It should be pointed out that several BADEA-assisted projects listed under other headings than those of agriculture and rural development are relevant to farming. We have mentioned roads, but hydro-electric projects too may include provision for the irrigation of farmland.

An example of this is the Kpong hydro-electric dam on the river Volta in southern Ghana for which the Bank has approved a loan of $10 million. Apart from generating power the project will provide irrigation over an area of some 6,000 hectares and thus substantially ease the country's food problems.

The dam is scheduled for completion in 1981 and will generate 140 MW and 970 GWH of electric power to enable Ghana to maintain a balance between demand and supply till 1985 when additional power sources will be needed. In addition to the dam and power station a double network of high tension transmission lines and a new transmission centre at Kpong will be built.

The total cost of the project, which is being implemented under the supervision of the Volta River Authority, was estimated in 1977 at $238 million. The Saudi and Kuwaiti

61

Funds, the World Bank, the European Development Fund, the European Investment Bank and the Canadian Government agency, the CIDA, are all contributing finance to this important scheme, which is one of the largest of its kind in Africa.

BADEA and Arab donors generally regard the construction of hydro-electric projects as a priority, as it is particularly important for non-oil developing African countries to expand their sources of energy in order to save on fuel imports. The alternative in Ghana would have been to build a thermal power station, but given the high cost of imported oil the hydro-electric plant has been chosen instead. Similar considerations have applied to Mauritius, to take another example, where much of the present electric power supply is generated in thermal stations, but a BADEA loan of $10 million will enable the island to construct a new hydro-electric scheme.

Some 15 per cent of the total money loaned by the Bank for development over the past five years was for new power generating plant, mostly hydro-electric.

Construction of new manufacturing industries has also been regarded as important, particularly because of the impact these will have on employment and import substitution. The Bank has favoured industries which can help other activities. It supported, for example, the manufacture of building materials that can be used by construction industries.[7]

An example of this is a project in Tanzania for the construction of a plant to produce brick, tiles and hollow clay units used for flooring, roofing and similar purposes and an adjacent complex for the production of concrete for road and house building, sewerage pipes and drainage blocks. The entire project is based on locally available materials and will represent a very substantial saving on imports. The initial purpose of the scheme is to help construct Tanzania's planned new capital city, Dodoma, in the centre of the country, and it is regarded as a top priority by the Dar-es-Salaam Government.

The loan of $5 million for this project was approved in 1977 and when I visited Tanzania in 1979 I was told by the local manager that the project was well on time and that a pilot plant was already operational. Eventually the plant will turn out 290 tonnes of materials a day. The project manager seemed particularly pleased with, as he put it, 'prompt and efficient disbursement operations by BADEA', which were paying for the machinery and equipment. Unfortunately, such praise was not universal in regard to the BADEA-assisted projects I had visited in Africa. Delays are frequent, although they may often be caused by administrative problems in the recipient country.

TABLE 2

Sectoral Breakdown of Total Commitments (1975–1979)

	$m.					%					TOTAL	
	1975	1976	1977	1978	1979	1975	1976	1977	1978	1979	$m.	%
Infrastructure	52·0	29·1	13·20	17·60	36·67	64	47·0	19·9	24·1	74·7	148·57	44·8
Agriculture	11·6	17·8	12·20	19·65	2·40	14	28·8	18·4	27·0	4·9	63·65	19·2
Industry	18·0	—	24·84	9·70	10·00	22	—	37·5	13·3	20·4	62·54	18·8
Power	—	15·0	16·00	10·92	—	—	24·2	24·2	15·0	—	41·92	12·7
Emergency Aid	—	—	—	15·00	—	—	—	—	20·6	—	15·00	4·5
TOTAL	81.6	61·9	66·24	72·87	49·07	100	100	100	100	100	331·680	100

Source : BADEA, Annual Report 1979.

According to Dr Ayari, BADEA is likely to give manufacturing industries greater priority in the following decade, particularly those capable of serving exports.

A recent development which will no doubt be repeated and expanded in future is assistance to regional or national financial institutions that in their turn lend money for development projects, particularly in manufacturing industries. The first case of such intervention was a $5 million line of credit granted in 1978 to the Development Bank of the Central African States (BDEAC) which caters for five countries in the region, Cameroon, Central African Republic, Congo, Gabon and Chad.

Explaining the new departure in their Annual Report 1978 the Board of Directors pointed out that BDEAC was concerned with support for small and medium-sized industries of regional impact, in a pursuit of economic integration and regional development. Specially favoured were industries for processing raw materials and manufactured products useful to all member States as well as export-oriented industries of these countries.

'The basic goal of regional economic integration in Africa, equally shared by BADEA and BDEAC and instrumental in the process of economic development and independence, justifies appropriate financial support.'[8]

Indirect aid was also extended to the Industrial Development Bank of Kenya—a semi-public corporation—in the same year, 1978, in the form of a $5 million line of credit. In justifying the aid the Board of Directors explained that 'in its role of promoting industrial development the IBD (Kenya) blends consideration of good financial return with the concern for Kenya's development'. The line of credit is redeemable over a period of 12 years, including 3 years of grace, at an annual interest rate of 7 per cent.

The IDB (Kenya) which had received similar assistance from the World Bank, the African Development Bank and European Investment Bank, specialises in helping medium- and large-sized industries.

Another move which has marked a widening of the normal field of activity was an emergency aid programme approved in 1978. This exceptional step was taken following an appeal by the OAU to the Arab world to help countries facing drought and other natural calamities and a decision of the Arab League that BADEA should be entrusted with the supply of such assistance. The cost of the programme was $15 million to be used for irrigation, food storage and similar projects designed to prevent or alleviate the consequences of drought and other natural calamities, including cyclones that had hit the island of Madagascar. Eleven countries in the Sahel and other parts of Africa benefited from the Special Emergency Programme as well as three regional locust-control organisations.

This programme was designed for speed of operations and normal disbursement procedures were shortened while repayment terms were made exceptionally easy, with a grant element of 75 per cent. But BADEA management has made clear that this operation was regarded as quite exceptional and due to abnormal circumstances.

The Bank has not infrequently extended technical assistance by financing feasibility studies or other pre-investment work, examples of which have already been mentioned. This service is particularly valuable for newly independent poor countries as it enables them to identify viable development projects.

It will have been noticed that in a large number of cases BADEA has not financed a project by itself, or merely in co-operation with local interests. Limited by its rules to the ceiling of $10 million[9] for any one loan and 40 per cent of the total cost of a project the Bank has entered co-financing arrangements with a wide range of institutions and Governments, in the Arab world and elsewhere.

The Board of Directors explained this increasingly significant aspect of the Bank's policy in the Annual Report 1978:

'It stands to reason that co-financing is vitally important in case of very large investments, such as the Sélingué Dam in Mali ($142 million), the Pulp Mill in Cameroon ($235 million) or the SONICHAR complex of coal mining and thermal power generation in Niger ($135·9 million).

'In fact, most aid institutions have ceilings to limit their financial commitments per project. Hence the advantage of co-financing which allows co-lenders to share not only the costs but also the risks and hazards entailed in large-scale investment. Moreover, co-financing helps a young aid-giving institution to take advantage of associating with older, better equipped and more experienced agencies in order to take short-cuts and speed up the pace of operations.'

Of course, co-financing and co-ordination among donor agencies help avoid duplication and accelerate development in Africa. It is also very important that they enable a concerted supervision on the part of the co-financing agencies of project implementation, making the ultimate success of the scheme more likely.

On the other hand, project implementation may be delayed when difficulties arise in reaching agreements among the parties involved in co-financing. As BADEA has explained: 'The procedure of cross-ratification of agreements, according to which no disbursement of funds is carried out before the agreements between the beneficiary countries and the different donors have been ratified causes, in certain cases, delays that may adversely affect the implementation of the project.'

From the start of its operations BADEA established close ties of co-operation and co-ordination with a large number of international institutions, such as the World Bank, the United Nations Development Programme and the European Development Fund, regional agencies, particularly the African Development Bank, and its sister, the African Development Fund, and national institutions in industrial countries, such as the CCCE, the French Central Fund for Economic Co-operation; the CIDA, the Canadian International Development Agency; the SIDA, the Swedish International Development Agency and the KFW, the German Credit Institution for Reconstruction.

Co-ordination with the Development Assistance Committee (DAC) of the Paris-based Organisation for Economic Co-operation and Development (OECD) began in 1975, particularly in respect of the following:

—exchange of information and experience on the various stages of projects as well as on regional and sectoral aid programmes;
—undertaking joint on-site missions;
—reciprocal periodical visits for co-ordination of aid programmes;
—co-financing and concerted action in providing technical assistance to recipient countries.

By the end of April 1980 co-financing by BADEA and DAC agencies reached a total of $907·51 million, covering 32 projects. In fact, about two-thirds of all BADEA operations concerned projects co-financed with DAC members. Conversely, BADEA has been involved in the financing of about 30 per cent of all development projects co-financed by DAC countries and agencies in Sub-Saharan Africa between 1975 and April 1980.[10]

As a matter of preference, however, BADEA enters into co-financing arrangements with other Arab Funds, including the Islamic Development Bank and OPEC Fund.

In this way Arab agencies between them may co-finance a given component of the project, as was the case with the joint Arab financing of the civil engineering component in the

Sélingué Dam scheme. Such co-operation of course also enables the Arabs to exercise a close control over the portion of the scheme they finance, an important consideration, for example, in regard to boycott rules applying to trade with Israel and South Africa.

While co-financing with non-Arab agencies is on a 'parallel' basis that with Arab institutions is on a 'joint' footing, signifying a closer degree of mutual co-operation and co-ordination in project implementation.

By the end of April 1980 the total amount of co-financing by BADEA and other Arab development agencies and Governments, including the IDB and the OPEC Fund, came to $463·83 million, contributing to the financing of 21 projects costing a total of $1,544 million. Thus, the share of Arab co-financing amounted to 30 per cent of the development cost concerned. About 40 per cent of BADEA's operations, in numbers or in value, have been undertaken in joint financing with other Arab aid institutions.

Co-financing is one of the subjects discussed at regular biannual meetings attended by BADEA and other Arab aid agencies concerned with development in non-Arab Africa. Standardisation of general terms and conditions for aid commitment, as well as procedures for allocation of resources, disbursement of funds and contract awards are among other matters usually on the meeting agenda. By 1979 a total of 11 Arab aid organisations attended these meetings.

When Arab agencies select a project for possible co-financing, a joint mission may be sent to the site of the scheme. Monitoring of project implementation may also be done on a joint basis as Arab aid institutions now tend to give representative powers to one among them for supervising a given co-financed project. This helps lessen the costs of the management of Arab aid programmes while increasing their efficiency.

BADEA has been given a special role where Arab aid to non-Arab Africa is concerned. For example, the Arab Funds meeting in Kuwait in April 1977 asked the Bank to prepare an inventory of projects from the region suitable for Arab finance. This request was carried out. The Bank, in close consultation with African Governments, prepared a pipeline of 410 such projects in various economic sectors, 346 of these being of national scope and 13 regional, with the remaining 51 concerning technical co-operation on both national and regional levels, incuding the Pan-African Tele-Communication (PANAFTEL) and Trans-Sahara Highway projects. Out of this list a shorter and more select inventory, the so-called 'integrated pipeline', was drawn up of projects which BADEA itself was considering for aid.

In regard to inter-Arab co-operation for aid to non-Arab Africa the practice followed over the past five years has been largely pragmatic and flexible, as Dr Ayari explained to the writer:

'If BADEA has a special role to play as far as Arab aid to non-Arab Africa is concerned this does not mean that other Arab Funds will not use their own initiative. We have been "fishing" for suitable projects to assist Africa, but so have other Arab Funds.

'Arab funds are absolutely free and in no way restricted by any special role entrusted to BADEA as a co-ordinator of aid. There have been many cases when an African project was brought to the attention of the rest of us by an Arab Fund other than BADEA. An example of this was the Maseru airport scheme in Lesotho which Abu Dhabi had first discovered and sponsored. BADEA then came in and we helped to get things arranged.

'We are not the only source of information about Africa for the Arabs. We cannot be that. Arab countries have bilateral relations with African States which may lead to Arab interest being aroused in respect of a project. But the good thing is that we get together and arrive at a common decision.

'There have also been cases where BADEA took second place to some other Arab Fund because at the time we lacked the expertise required for the particular venture. For instance, in the case of the Sélingué Dam in Mali, to which we had committed an exceptionally large loan of $15 million in 1976, BADEA did not have any experts on dams. We then agreed that KFAED, which had such experts, should take the lead among the Arab Funds co-financing the project and act as leader in the course of implementation.

'But we had been promoting the Sélingué Dam. We had been talking about it at our meetings with other Arab Funds, we were able to raise money for it—and that is the most important part of co-ordination. When we play the role of co-ordinator this above

all means organising finance so that the project can get off the
ground.

'In other cases we had not only introduced the project to Arab
Funds and sponsored it, but also administered the entire Arab
contribution, as with the Cement project in Guinea which we are
co-financing with the Abu Dhabi fund and the Islamic
Development Bank.

'Our role has been particularly important in respect of African
countries which were not very well known in the Arab world,
such as Mauritius and Seychelles, or even might have been under
some suspicion for their policies, such as Angola and Mozambique. We first brought these countries to the attention of the
other Arab Funds. In Angola we now co-finance a railway
project with the OPEC Fund which specially requested us to
administer their loan.

'In Cape Verde we helped organise the ADFAED assistance for
a fishing project which is now implemented in co-operation with
the Food and Agriculture Organisation of the United Nations.

'As BADEA is getting stronger, more expert and more
experienced, we receive more requests from Arab Funds to
administer their financial contributions to development schemes
in Africa and our role as co-ordinator becomes more important.'

Being a political as well as financial institution BADEA has been
closely involved in matters of Afro-Arab co-operation on various
levels, including the highest. BADEA took a very active part in the
preparations for the first Afro-Arab Summit in 1977 and has
since been co-operating with institutions set up by the
conference. Like the African Development Bank and the
Economic Commission for Africa of the United Nations BADEA
has been accorded a consultative role in the machinery of Afro-
Arab co-operation.

Although it is a creation of the Arab League, BADEA operates
independently.[11] But intimate working relations are nevertheless
maintained with the political organisation of the Arab world.

When Egypt was suspended from membership of the Arab
League in 1979 BADEA's Board of Governors followed suit,
severing relations with that country. Egypt, which had contributed $1·5 million to the subscribed capital of the Bank, or 0·202
per cent of the total, entitling her to 1·96 per cent of the vote,
was suspended from membership and BADEA office in Cairo was

closed. But the services of the Egyptian employees of the Bank were retained.

While BADEA has in this way mirrored the major shifts in Arab policies there has been little sign of inter-Arab rivalries and differences affecting the Bank's work. Indeed, the sense of partnership and smooth co-operation among the representatives of Arab countries that might otherwise have been pursuing widely diverging or opposing policies was in itself remarkable and certainly a credit to the Arabs.

There has been close co-operation with African institutions. One of the first steps taken by BADEA was to establish a working partnership with the African Development Bank and its affiliate, the African Development Fund. This partnership has continued and the institutions frequently meet to discuss current development problems in Africa and explore possibilities for co-financing of projects. BADEA has been intimately involved in OAU work and the President, or delegations authorised by him, attended all meetings sponsored by this African organisation if they had any connection with BADEA's mission and more particularly when they concerned Arab-African co-operation. This included annual meetings of the Council of Ministers and the Summit Conferences of the African Heads of State and Government. BADEA has also been participating in numerous conferences and seminars sponsored by the Economic Commission for Africa of the United Nations and other regional and international organisations.

A formal agreement binds the Bank with the World Bank Group and there is close co-operation with the three members of the Group, the International Bank for Reconstruction and Development, International Development Association and International Finance Corporation.

Close contacts have been cultivated with the United Nations agencies and organisations, some of which were formalised in specific agreements, as were those with the Economic Commission for Africa, UNDP, FAO, UNESCO and the International Communications Union (ITU). These ties often result in concrete joint activities as was the case with FAO in regard to the Special Emergency Aid Programme in 1978 or with ITU in respect of PANAFTEL.

BADEA has also concluded co-operation agreements with a

number of western countries and their development institutions and there is a formal agreement with Yugoslavia. There is active co-operation with OECD.

After five years of operations, what has BADEA achieved in terms of what it set out to do—to help economic development in Africa and strengthen ties of friendship and partnership between the Arab and African worlds? What does Dr Ayari himself regard as the greatest achievement of his organisation?

'It is too early', Dr Ayari replied to my question, 'to draw any definite conclusions. At any rate, it is not for me to say what has been our main achievement, but for others.

'But I think it is important that we have been able to create an agency of this sort from scratch. We have done this in five years. We have been able to establish ourselves as an institution designed for development which is respected throughout the African continent and the Arab world as well as in the international financial community as a whole.

'We have been able to enhance the interest of the Arab countries in Africa. This I believe is very important. More than once we have been instrumental in throwing a bridge between non-Arab Africa and the Arabs. We have been active as spokesmen of the Arab States in Africa and of Africa in the Arab region.

'We have been able to spread the message of Afro-Arab co-operation so that this is now better understood by the public opinion in Africa and in Arab countries than it had been a few years ago.

'Thanks to our contacts and our relations with the public and with the media, we have also no doubt contributed to better co-operation between the Arabs and Africans in regard to OAU and the Arab League. I think these are BADEA's main achievements.'

What about failures?

'We have', Dr Ayari went on, 'of course had our disappoint-ments and frustrations. We are very much aware of BADEA's inadequacies. Have we been financing the real priorities in Africa today? The answer must take account of the fact that often the most needy African countries have no development plans or programmes, no projects which can be assisted by outside support.

'We have certainly not done enough to promote regional

projects, to help more towards regional integration in Africa. This must be one of our priorities for the future.

'We have not been able to disburse rapidly enough the loans to which we were committed. The situation in this respect has recently improved. But we must keep working on this problem as must other donors as well as the recipient countries themselves', Dr Ayari concluded.

Disbursements represented 1·4 per cent of commitments in 1976, 4·6 per cent in 1977, 23·1 per cent in 1978, 35·5 per cent in 1979 and 45 per cent in 1980.

Where does BADEA go from here?

The Bank's lending averaged about $66 million a year over the five-year period, 1975–1979, and more than $70 million in 1980. In 1979 it declined temporarily to just over $49 million but this was due to technical reasons in the recipient countries.

A prospective plan drafted in 1979 for the following 10 years of operations has not been revealed. But it is understood that more technical assistance is likely to be provided to African countries, especially by financing feasibility studies of projects that are likely to be viable and can be presented to potential donors.

African countries themselves are now giving greater priority to agriculture, particularly food crop production, than before, which must be taken into consideration by BADEA. Dr Ayari has said, as we have seen, that the Bank might in future give a greater share of its aid to manufacturing industries than had been the case till now. More aid for industrial development will probably be channelled indirectly through development agencies, regional and national, something that would give greater flexibility to the ultimate use of a BADEA facility.

BADEA will undoubtedly wish to give greater priority to regional programmes and projects. These should generally become more important in Africa following the first economic Summit conference organised under the auspicies of OAU in Lagos, capital of Nigeria, in April 1980 when a decision was made to work for an 'African economic community' by the year 2000. BADEA played an active and important part in the deliberations of this economic conference.

At all events, the Bank's managers feel that the institution has proved its significance as an instrument for development in the region of Africa which comes within its scope and that it has substantially contributed to better understanding and co-operation between the Arab and African communities. The need to continue the work has also been amply demonstrated and accepted by the Arab States contributing to the Bank. The unanimous re-election of Dr Chedly Ayari as BADEA President for another five-year term by the 17 Governors at their meeting in April 1980 in itself testified to the good work of the Bank and the continuing faith of its founders and financial backers.

The Kuwait Fund for Arab Economic Development

KFAED's role at the birth of most of the other Arab aid agencies has been variously described as that of a father or a midwife. At all events, its experts drew up the statutes for BADEA and took the initiative with the Arab League and Arab Governments for bringing to life the new institution designed specifically for assistance to non-Arab Africa. The Fund's work in regard to other sisters has been no less significant and consequently KFAED is considered with something like special respect and appreciation by the rest of the family.

When preparing this book I was told by Dr Chedly Ayari that it was vitally important for a proper understanding and appraisal of Arab aid to talk to Mr Abdlatif Youssef Al-Hamad, Director-General of the Kuwait Fund for the past 17 years.

To see him I had to travel to Kuwait, but this in itself was valuable as the book was to contain personal impressions as well as facts and figures. Kuwait, the world's richest country per head of population, displays the mood, prospects and dilemmas of a major Arab oil exporting State that can be taken as typical, at least among the Gulf States from which the major part of Arab aid comes.

Kuwait, heir to an old and proud Arab seafaring tradition, had a hard struggle to survive until quite recently. In 1946 its population was about 90 thousand, mostly consisting of im-poverished Bedouin people. In 1978 the population was 1·2 million with a Gross National Product of KD 3,672 million, or about $12·8 billion, taking the conversion rate at $3·6 dollars to the Kuwaiti Dinar.

This was KD 3,464 per capita. Soon the revenues from oil were to soar again, from nearly $10 bn in 1978 to an estimated $16–17 bn in 1979. In spite of very considerable budgetary expenditure, much of it for economic and social development in Kuwait, the net surplus in the 1979/80 financial year may have reached some $10 bn. In 1980 the Government had at its disposal up to $40 bn of reserves in foreign assets.[12] Substantial surpluses will continue in spite of the reduction of oil production in April 1980 from 1·2–2·2 million barrels a day to 1·5 million b/d. Even if production were to continue at the former rate the known reserves would last for well over 80 years.

After an absence of eight years I found Kuwait City in 1980 unrecognisable. There had in the meantime been a great expansion in the population, which continues, and the native Kuwaitis in their traditional long robes and Gulf Arab headgear were less in evidence. There were more other Arabs, particularly Palestinians, and many people from Iran and the Indian subcontinent.

Kuwait was bustling with activity, and there was clearly work enough for all. Although recent immigrants might be paid comparatively low wages, these were likely to be much higher than in the countries they had come from. At all events, there was little agitation or discontent to be observed. It was money which mattered to the immigrants more than anything else. Although Afghanistan and Iran were close geographically, their tribulations seemed very remote from Kuwait. The hierarchical structure itself seemed to ensure political stability and, being rooted in tradition, was acceptable to most people that mattered, very unlike the situation in Iran under the Shah. But relations between people of different ranks and nationalities seemed easygoing and friendly, and it was no surprise to me to see the Prime Minister joining spontaneously in a local sabre dance, in full view of everybody.

Harsh climatic conditions, marked by frequent sandstorms and temperatures in excess of 50° Centigrade during three months of the year, and a terrain consisting mainly of desert, give little scope to agriculture, less even than in most of the other countries of the Gulf.

Dependence on imports, not only of food, but of most of the other goods that the country needs, marks Kuwait's fragile economy, although some progress has been made in diversifying production, into oil refining, petrochemicals and other manufactures. Kuwait is also dependent to a great extent on expatriate skills and labour. To lessen this dependence the Kuwaitis have made massive investments in education and training facilities for the native population.

Kuwait City looked like a huge building site in 1980, as it had on my earlier visit in 1972, but it was then much smaller. It was now risky to walk about at night, metal pipes, bars and other building materials providing frequent stumbling-blocks for the unwary. Many half-completed buildings were already housing shops, some of which offered the best that the world could provide. But there were also countless little establishments run by recent immigrants selling all manner of consumer goods and trappings, every shop apparently doing a roaring trade.

No doubt there was a masterplan behind the non-stop and ubiquitous construction activity, but it was already apparent that the Kuwaitis might come to regret not having left more green spaces between the houses.

Mr Al-Hamad gives religion as the leading motive for Arab concessional aid to poor countries, an aid which in the case of Kuwait in one recent year, 1977, exceeded 10 per cent of the State's Gross Domestic Product.

Explaining what lies behind Arab aid, to an audience in Copenhagen in 1979,[13] Al-Hamad said:

'This may not seem very "modern", but the first consideration that I would like to stress here is that in a region like the Middle East, people at all levels still relate their attitudes, more or less directly, more or less consciously, to the teachings of the dominant religion, Islam: They who hoard up gold and silver and spend it not in the way of God, unto them give tidings of painful doom ... says the Quran in a verse which has a number of equivalents in the Muslims' Holy Book.

'To spend in the way of God in modern interpretation is to share with other people in whose situation (or worse) we were just a short while ago.

'Indeed, in all Arab oil countries one can easily perceive at the highest levels of responsibility a pervading sense of moral duty, or ethical imperative, not to act miserly but come to the assistance of less fortunate brethren.'

75

Thus, as Al-Hamad agreed when I interviewed him in Kuwait, even the religious motive is not entirely altruistic; after all you help save your own soul by following God's commands!

Humanitarian motives have blended with reasons of self-interest in the case of Kuwait as much as in that of other Arab countries embarking on aid programmes for the benefit of the outside world. But it was Kuwait which had begun it all, even before the country's independence in 1961.

Kuwait has often been cited by Arabs as a model of a small country, gaining influence and prestige on account of its positive and magnanimous attitude to the problem of development and poverty in the under-privileged countries.

Underlying this attitude and policy is a feeling of solidarity, of 'being in the same boat', with others, first with the Arab countries in the Gulf region, then with the Arabs elsewhere too and eventually with even wider regions of the world.

'We are all in the same boat', Al-Hamad explained, 'some of us might be in the de luxe cabin, others below deck. If the boat sinks we shall all go down, although the people below deck may be submerged a little sooner.'

A worry then, that the boat might sink. There was also the discomfort of being rich in the midst of poverty.

'I regard the world as a village. I don't like to see many poor people inhabiting the same village as myself,' he said.

Yet, he pointed out, the world often forgot that many Arab countries were still poor and developing. The Arabs must be viewed as part of the Third World.

'The only difference', he said, 'is that some of the Arab countries have a commodity which is crucially needed by the developed nations, and consequently should be used as an instrument of Third World solidarity. Without solidarity that weapon will be destroyed, nullified. With that weapon in our hands maximum advantage can be secured in the new relationship between the rich and the poor.

'Solidarity is the key factor. Once you isolate some countries, start accusing them of being responsible for this and that, you will destroy the most significant weapon wielded by the Third World today, and don't forget that the weapon will only be available for a few years.'

The situation in the world would have been different had the advanced countries heeded the appeal of the United Nations and brought up the percentage of their GNP devoted to Official Development Assistance (ODA) to 0·7 per cent a year.

The Brandt Commission, in which Al-Hamad participated, called on the advanced countries to meet the target by 1985, which would almost double the flow of that type of aid by that year, and to raise the percentage to 1·0 by 2000.

'People have criticised me for this as being politically unrealistic', Al-Hamad said, 'but at least the targets give you a yardstick by which you can measure, criticise or praise the performance of individual countries.'

But some people believe western aid as a whole is calculated to perpetuate the existing unfair international order.[14] Are the Arabs not helping to preserve this order by associating themselves with western official aid and encouraging such assistance?

'We don't want destruction', Al-Hamad replied, 'we want evolution. A destruction of the existing world order would not benefit anyone. Let's face it, we do not possess technology. We have to buy technology. The Third World cannot make progress without technology. Technology is only available in industrially advanced countries. There is no escaping this fact. But the question is on what conditions and how you buy technology. There, changes must be made.

'Look at the role international oil companies play today and the role these transnationals played some five years ago. What is important is who makes the policies and decisions and who has the authority. And that is what we are trying to do with the Third World. By making developing countries more independent, by helping them to improve and strengthen their economies, we are in fact assisting them to stand up and play the role expected of them. Realistically, they cannot play that role unless they have the tools and the instruments as well as the will to do it. That cannot come about except by development.'

Concessional assistance supplied by Kuwait has at the time of writing been provisionally estimated at $1,241·3 million in commitments and $856·4 million in net disbursements—4·54 per cent of the GNP—for 1978 compared to $1,253·1 million in commitment and $1,443·0 million in disbursements—or 10·09 per cent of GNP—for 1977.

The major part of this aid was dispensed directly by the Ministry of Finance, much of it as assistance for Egypt, Jordan and Syria. Balance of payments support was also provided for several countries as well as assistance in emergency situations. Political considerations are often important in allocating this aid, with national security, goodwill and regional stability being particularly relevant in this connection.[15] But with insignificant exceptions this aid too has been supplied without ties to any source of procurement or other strings. Multilateral organisations, international and regional, are also normally assisted through this direct Government channel.

The second channel of Kuwaiti aid is through the General Authority for the Arabian gulf and South Arabian States. But this is a relatively small operation covering mostly health, education and religious life.

The third channel, the Kuwait Fund for Arab Economic Development (KFAED), was set up in 1961 by the Kuwait government, as an institution with its own legal identity and a capital of KD 50 million. Its purpose was to be what the name implied. It was not only the first agency of its kind in the Arab world, but the first instance of one developing country setting up a special institution for economic help to other such countries, initially Arab only.

In 1974 the Fund was made available to non-Arab countries and its capital was raised to KD 1 billion. In the following year the first non-Arab African countries were receiving loans.

The link with the Kuwait Government has remained. Not only does the Government subscribe and pay in all the capital of the Fund, but the country's Prime Minister also chairs the Board of Directors consisting of eight distinguished Kuwaiti citizens which has a final decision, arrived at in meetings that take place three or four times a year, on such important matters as the allocation of loans.

But the Kuwaiti Government has itself come to recognise the importance of leaving KFAED to do its work in its own way. There have even been cases when the Fund resisted pressure from the Government Ministers in matters on which it felt strongly. The way the Fund has run its affairs, pursuing the vision of development and economic and social progress, as free as possible from political and ideological considerations, has won

it a world-wide reputation in which Kuwait and its Government
have shared.

By mid-1979 the Fund had committed a total of KD 590
million in concession loans for development projects and
technical assistance grants. In the last year for which details are
available, 1978/79, 25 loans amounting to a total of KD
100·35 million were approved compared to 14 loans worth KD
57·5 million in the previous year. Of the total new loans the share
of the Arab countries was approximately 60 per cent while Asian
and African (non-Arab) countries received 27 per cent and 11 per
cent respectively (see Appendix for details of KFAED aid to non-
Arab Africa). The Fund also began its operations in Oceania
with a first loan to Papua New Guinea.

In addition there were three technical assistance grants in
1978/79 of KD 100,000 each—the same number as in the
previous year—in which Guinea and Rwanda were helped in
Africa, for the benefit of a hydroelectric scheme and road project
feasibility studies respectively.

Whatever the organisational set-up of KFAED it is Abdlatif
Youssef Al-Hamad, the Director-General, who matters most, to
put it mildly. To many KFAED has been Al-Hamad. He has given
the organisation the unmistakable imprint of his personality.[16]

Born in Kuwait in 1937, Al-Hamad studied at the American
University in Cairo, took a degree at a university college in
California and read international affairs at Harvard. After a short
diplomatic career he took up the position of acting Director-
General of the Fund in 1962 and was established in the post in
the following year.

A few visits to KFAED, now housed in the impressive, and still
only half-completed premises, in the centre of Kuwait City, were
enough to bring home to me the significance of Al-Hamad's alert
and fast-moving personality. Al-Hamad likes to do his business
in a personal as well as informal manner. The coffee parties he
gives every morning in his office are normally attended by his top
professionals as well as people from outside. A man from Asia or
Africa may come to argue his case. While talking to the man next
to him Al-Hamad, coffee cup in hand, will occasionally react
with incisive comment to a conversation he has overheard from
across the room.

What manner of man is he? I thought, watching him at the

coffee party and remembering the interview I had had with him the day before. He certainly looks younger than even his inconsiderable age. Imaginative, with a penchant for broad ideas and generalisations, something of a visionary; also something of an amateur, perhaps, in terms of strictly banking professionalism, even if this may be to the good when bold and innovative approaches are needed, as they so often are in the development area. A man ready to give the benefit of the doubt, but who will relentlessly persist in putting the damage right if trust has been misplaced, as some recipients of KFAED aid have learnt.

He manifestly enjoys his work and influence, but wants to keep a low profile, for himself as well as for KFAED. This may be modesty, but also shrewdness and wisdom born out of experience. 'We have been in this business too long not to realise that boasting about giving aid to developing countries or even deliberately publicising such activities can be counter-productive,' he told me.

There is emphasis on flexibility and speed, which accounts for the good disbursement record.

'We have a rule in this house,' he explained, 'that every piece of paper ready to be processed must be dealt with within twenty-four hours. The second point is that by appraising your projects properly you know what to expect and are therefore able to control the process and progress and in consequence are able to build up a good record of disbursement.'

There is no specialisation among the professionals, who are economists, scientists, lawyers and administrators, many of them former university dons, in regard to geographical regions. An Asian country today, an African tomorrow. This may sometimes cause worries to the professional concerned as he will have to familiarise himself very rapidly with a country he knows little about. But it keeps him from getting too attached to any one country or groups of them. Projects must be looked at on their merits, although other things being equal the more underprivileged countries, including the least developed, get priority. Between April 1975 and June 1978 countries with less than $520 per capita GNP received 84·2 per cent of the total.[17]

Africa is particularly important, as Al-Hamad explained:

'Africa is of great importance to us as well as to many other development agencies, because it is the continent with the largest number of poor countries, not necessarily the largest number of poor people.

'But it is also the continent with the biggest potential for development. It is the continent that shows the greatest yet unexploited mineral and agricultural potential and therefore in giving special emphasis to our relations with Africa we are helping the people of the continent and in the process are helping ourselves and our own future, by releasing resources that might be needed by our children and grandchildren.'

Al-Hamad also pointed out his interest in helping regional developments in Africa, like the Senegal river development project or the Trans-Sahara Highway, both of which KFAED has been co-financing.

'We encourage regional and joint efforts whenever we can', he said. 'We have for instance joined the African Development Fund and help the African Development Bank indirectly by purchasing their bonds. We have been associating ourselves with the ADB/ADF Group whenever possible to assist Africa on regional and sub-regional basis while never losing sight of the development needs on national level, particularly in regard to infrastructure.'

Al-Hamad disclosed that it was because of the more urgent needs of Africa that KFAED had postponed the idea of extending its activities to Latin America and other parts of the Western Hemisphere.

'We wish to focus on Africa', Al-Hamad said. 'It doesn't make any sense, morally or professionally, to by-pass the countries that particularly need our help, the countries in which we still have so much to do, for the sake of the glory of saying that we are present in the entire world.'

KFAED prides itself on being as apolitical as possible. Vietnam is being helped as well as Thailand, Morocco as well as Mozambique. The Sudan, which has seen more changes in its political orientation than most African countries, from a strong pro-Russian and socialist stance to a fairly pronounced pro-western and conservative posture, has nonetheless been consistently assisted in its development by the Kuwait Fund.

Yet an exception to this principle has been the treatment of Egypt which till its peace with Israel in 1979 had ranked as the chief beneficiary of KFAED aid. Al-Hamad explained:

'Even before the Camp David agreements we had ceased considering any new commitments for the benefit of Egypt as we had too many there already and progress on most of the projects concerned was not very good. We are now focusing our attention on completing our projects in Egypt rather than committing new funds. After the Camp David agreements we said to Egypt: "We shall not be doing any more projects with you, but we'll carry out and honour all the commitments already undertaken."'

Al-Hamad then gave me his reasons in more detail:

'Your attitude to a brother when he departs completely from the family is one thing, and your attitude to a neighbour departing your neighbourhood is another. Egypt was regarded as a brother and was therefore receiving a much larger share of our aid than if it had been merely a neighbour. But then Egypt was expected to behave as brothers behave. When the Egyptians began to take decisions that were crucial to our well-being and security without consultation or co-ordination with us, then the best we could say was, "we'll not deal with you any more in the spirit in which we have been dealing with you so far."'

KFAED aid is mostly for specific development projects which are always carefully appraised by the Fund's professional staff before a decision is made to assist them, and whose implementation is then monitored. In a few cases the Fund has granted finance for a Government development programme without reference to a specific scheme. But this, as Al-Hamad explained to me, is possible only when the Government concerned and its policies are well known and mutual trust exists. Occasionally the Fund has granted loans to other development agencies, such as industrial development banks.

It does not matter whether a project is in the public or private sector, but perhaps because the aid is supposed to assist a development of national significance and the Government concerned must in any case sponsor the scheme and apply for the loan, most of the money so far has gone to help State-owned enterprise.

While assisted projects are supposed to be viable and useful it is the economic rather than strictly financial return that is decisive. In this respect KFAED's criteria, of course, do not differ from those of other Arab aid agencies.

Much of the commitment so far has been for the benefit of

infrastructure and agricultural development. In the case of non-Arab Africa these two sectors have accounted for about 90 per cent of the total aid.

Terms of KFAED loans vary according to the economic sector, a road-building or rural development project benefiting from softer conditions than an industrial scheme. On average the grant element has been about 50 per cent. But in view of the precarious economic circumstances of many developing countries at present (1980) KFAED management is understood to be trying to secure even more favourable terms, which, however, must depend on the agreement of the Board of Directors and the Kuwait Government.

To illustrate a KFAED operation the following example may be quoted from the 1977/78 Annual Report of a loan extended to the Gambia in that year for a road project. The loan of KD 4·5 million—with 2 per cent interest a year and a 25-year repayment period, including 5 years of grace—had a grant element of 58 per cent. The Annual Report described and justified the loan in the following terms:

'Out of the total road network in the Gambia no more than 190 km are at present asphalted. The project is for the construction of 112 km of asphalted road between Soma and Yoroberikunda to extend an existing road to an agricultural area in the interior of the country. Completion of this road will reduce transportation costs of agricultural exports, particularly groundnuts, through the port of Banjul. Total cost of the project is estimated at about KD 5·74 million, of which KD 4·5 million is in foreign exchange and covered by the loan. Implementation of the project is expected to be completed by 1980.[18]

As in the case of BADEA and indeed other Arab Funds, KFAED's role ought not to be viewed in isolation, but as part of the total Arab and international development activity. The Fund normally represents the Kuwait Government in international development organisations and assemblies in which the State is involved. Abdlatif Y. Al-Hamad himself is, for instance, alternate Governor for Kuwait at the World Bank and an Executive Director of the Arab Fund for Economic and Social Development (AFESD), to name just two important institutions in which he is personally active.

Personal connections can be very important as an international fraternity of like-minded people is emerging in the field of development, of men who know and can trust each other. There is also a great deal of movement of personnel as between one institution and another, especially Arab, which makes co-ordinated work all the easier. At the same time a common philosophy is growing out of this intellectual environment which in turn can exert pressure in favour of the reforms and changes that the developing nations are clamouring for.

TABLE 3

Sectoral and Geographical Distribution of Fund Loans
1.1.1975–30.6.1979

(Million KD)

Country Groups	Agriculture and Primary Sectors	Transport, Communications and Storage	Electricity	Industry and Services	Total	%
Arab Countries	47·970	90·100	31·750	71·730	241·550	55·9
African Countries	14·910	28·000	16·370	4·500	63·780	14·8
Asian Countries	17·200	8·800	80·850	16·345	123·195	28·5
Other Countries	1·200	2·130	—	—	3·330	0·8
Total	81·280	129·030	128·970	92·575	431·855	100·0
%	18·8	29·9	29·9	21·4	100·0	

Source: KFAED

What impact then has KFAED made in the countries which it has been helping to develop? Al-Hamad himself said he thought it would be presumptuous on his part to talk a great deal about what had been achieved. He said:

'Let's face it, our business is a long-term haul. We must have the patience, foresight and ability to take a long-term view of things. For me to say that we have achieved a lot would have been presumptuous, just as it would have been untrue to say we had achieved nothing. The judgement, I think, should come after two decades. It's only then that you will be able to see whether there has been an impact. Certainly, where we have been operating we have left an impression, a favourable impression I think, but an impression is not an impact. It would have been presumptuous to say that it is.'

Many observers have been more generous in their comments and praise. They pointed to the noticeable way in which the Fund has been augmenting the resources available to developing countries and to its catalytic role of mobilising domestic as well as external capital for development. All this has markedly increased the growth rate in recipient countries, especially in small African and Asian countries. The Fund's role in the fields of technical assistance, by financing feasibility studies, providing direct advice in development matters and in other ways, has been particularly valuable in the least developed countries.

What of the future? In 1978/79 financial year the paid-in capital of the Fund increased by KD 56 million, bringing the total to KD 568 million. Accumulated reserves also increased, by KD 41 million—with returns from placement of undisbursed funds and loan repayments—to an aggregate total of KD 187 million. Total resources accordingly stood at KD 775 million at the end of the year.

Although the Kuwait State was registering record surpluses in 1980 there was no suggestion of any new aid agency being set up, or of the declared KFAED capital of KD 1 bn being raised.

Al-Hamad told me: 'We are confident that we can continue lending at the rate of between $350 million and $400 million a year. But we have no intention of going substantially beyond that. We are aware of our limitations.'

The Abu Dhabi Fund for Arab Economic Development

Abu Dhabi, one of the principalities making up the United Arab Emirates (UAE), provides an almost classic case of quick progress from 'rags to riches'. The present opulence has however not erased memories of the very recent past when the country was all but destitute. Rather, the recollection, according to the Director-General of the Abu Dhabi Fund for Arab Economic Development (ADFAED), is behind the Emirate's present largesse:

In an interview in 1978 Mr Nasser al-Nowais explained:

'Fifteen years ago this part of the world, particularly Abu Dhabi, was mostly desert country. People had great difficulty in finding shelter, they had no permanent settlement and no basic constructions. In fact, they were desperately poor and illiterate.

'Affluence is new to Abu Dhabi as it is to the rest of the Gulf. But knowledge of this has been a major factor in establishing our Fund, because when you have yourself been poor you know how the poor feel and you try as much as you can to help them, wherever they may be in the world. Besides, Muslims are expected to provide charity—'zakkat'—a contribution from the rich to the poor.

'In our part of the world we always try to help people when they are in difficulties. If you have hit on hard times the head of the tribe will come to your help. He will do as much as he can, perhaps even kill his last goat.[19]

The hospitality of this desert people is proverbial and few visitors to Abu Dhabi in search of financial help have returned empty-handed. It is estimated that something like 20 per cent of UAE's Gross Domestic Product is given away as aid to other countries and people, with the oil-rich Emirate of Abu Dhabi providing practically all of it. There may be other motives for this conduct besides sheer altruism. Among such motives is no doubt a desire that the world appreciate the responsible attitude taken by Abu Dhabi to its wealth.

The philosphy inspiring Abu Dhabi's aid policies owes much to the country's ruler, Sheikh Zayed bin Sultan al-Nahyan, who is also President of the United Emirates. A man of great humanity as well as penetrating intelligence and wisdom, Sheikh Zayed has often himself made the decision about helping a country, sometimes in circumstances when other potential donors shied away. An example of this was his decision to provide invaluable help to Somalia.

According to information supplied by the Abu Dhabi Fund the UAE made loans and grants to 'brotherly and friendly countries' to the tune of DH 1·5 billion in 1979, compared to 1·2 bn in the previous year. In addition, in 1979 UAE supplied a total of DH 650 million in contributions to regional and international organisations, including the World Bank Group and IMF.

The largest part is channelled through the UAE Department of

Finance. But a sizeable proportion of the UAE Governmental aid in grants and loans to the developing world has been managed by the Abu Dhabi Fund, by 1979 a cumulative total of nearly DH 1·5 bn.

Out of the bilateral UAE Governmental aid in loans and grants administered by the Fund a total of DH 67 million benefited Black Africa in the period 1977–1979. A sum of DH 8 million was allocated to Comoros for health and education sectors, DH 40 million for a road project in Uganda and DH 19 million for hospitals in Zaire.

ADFAED in its own right signed in 1979 a total of DH 505·9 million in project aid, of which DH 402·8 million was in the form of loans and DH 103·10 million in equity participation, as against DH 840·0 million for loans in 1978 and 5·6 million for equity participation.[20]

Non-Arab Africa in 1979 benefited from loans totalling DH 24 million from ADFAED compared to DH 32 million in 1978, and the peak of DH 45·2 million reached in 1977. The total for 1974–1979 was DH 121·2 million (for details see Appendix). While aid to Black Africa has been thus declining it is interesting that out of the total of 16 projects under consideration by the Fund in 1979 10 were in non-Arab Africa.

The Fund's initial authorised capital was DH 500 million, when the ADFAED was set up in 1971, but in 1974, when it also became available to non-Arab countries, the authorised capital was raised to DH 1 billion—or given a conversion rate of 1 UAE Dirham for 0·26 US dollars, to about $520 million. Subsequently the capital was raised again, to DH 2 bn and in September 1979 a decision was announced to double this amount, to reach DH 4 bn. Paid-in capital in 1979 amounted to DH 1,565, 780.

While Arab countries received about five-sixths of all ADFAED aid in 1974–1979 the poorest countries generally were given priority in lending. But loan terms do not vary according to the economic position of the recipient, only according to the economic sector financed. Infrastructure gets the softest loans and manufacturing industry the hardest, but rates of interest usually vary between 3 and 5 per cent, with repayment spread over 12 to 22½ years, including grace periods from 18 months to 8 years. The average grant element in 1974–78 was 36 per cent—not including a DH 663 million facility for petroleum development in Oman carrying 4 per cent interest and repayment over 7 years with 2 years of grace.

The relatively low grant element is due to the very large proportion of the finance going for industrial development. No doubt it is felt that loans for other purposes, including road building and other communications may be more conveniently obtained from the UAE Government which lends on softer terms or even provides outright grants.

More than half the money loaned in the 1974–1979 period, amounting to about DH 3 bn, was to help manufacturing and extractive industries, with water and electricity, communications and storage, agriculture and rural development and fisheries following in order of importance. A small percentage of the total was also destined for housing and tourist development.

No ADFAED loan may exceed 10 per cent of the Fund's capital or 50 per cent of the total cost of the project.

An example of an ADFAED loan to Africa is a facility granted to Tanzania in 1977 for a sugar· project. This was for DH 24 million, bearing 4 per cent interest per annum with maturity of 10 years and a grace period of 5 years.

According to ADFAED's Annual Report for 1977 the project aims at increasing sugar production in Tanzania in order to alleviate the burden of balance of payments and to secure a basic food commodity.

'The project', the Report explains 'calls for the ... setting up of a new factory with annual capacity of 56,000 tons of white sugar and will include a fermentation and rectification unit for molasses.

'Total costs of the project are estimated at about DH 315 million, including DH 246 million in foreign currency. The fund will cover about 7·5 per cent of the cost and 9·7 per cent of the foreign exchange needed for the project which is co-financed by the African Development Fund, African Development Bank, the Government of the Netherlands, the Government of India and a number of Indian banks. The Tanzanian Sugar Corporation will manage and execute the project after its completion in 1982.'

While concessional loans make up the bulk of the Fund's operations technical assistance grants are also made occasionally and the Fund is empowered to guarantee loans. But where

ADFAED differs from all the other Arab bilateral agencies is that it can take equity. Capital participation assumed considerable importance in 1979 for the first time and is designed to encourage other organisations and individuals to put their money in the enterprise in which the ADFAED has acquired an equity stake. But the condition is that the venture must be important for the recipient country and the economic sector concerned.

ADFAED also acts as adviser to the UAE Government on aid and international economic and financial matters generally and represents the Union in international and Arab development institutions with which it has been engaged in lively co-operation.

Initially the Fund relied heavily on other agencies, especially Arab, for co-operation in aid administration, but it is now increasingly independent in project appraisal, follow-up and supervisory work.

The authority of the Fund is vested in a Board of Directors chaired by Crown Prince Sheikh Khalifa bin Zayed al-Nahyan. The Board, which meets six times a year, takes a close and active interest in the affairs of the ADFAED, including allocation of aid.

But the day-to-day running of the administrative, financial and technical matters is delegated to the Director-General who is appointed on the recommendation of the Board. Since 1978 the post has been occupied by Mr Nasser al-Nowais, born in 1947 in the capital of Qatar, Doha. He studied public administration at the University of New York and in the United Kingdom. He has already given proof of much imaginative and dedicated work although his loyalty to Sheikh Zayed and close co-operation with him have been particularly noted by observers.

The Saudi Fund for Development

Of all the Arab funds the Saudi Fund for Development, the aid institution of the richest oil-exporting country, is undoubtedly the most dynamic as far as aid allocation is concerned. Established in 1974 with an authorised capital of SR 10 bn—or about $3·33 bn at the 1979 conversion rate of SR3 = $1 US—it had by June 1978 already signed 130 loan agreements for individual development projects in the Third World, representing a total commitment of SR

10·31 bn. Nearly half of this was for the benefit of African countries, particularly Arab.

In the last year for which full data are available, 1977/78, a total of nearly SR 2·36 billion of loans were signed, of which three—for Gabon, Senegal and Mali—were for non-Arab Africa and totalled SR 243·085 million, or about $81 million. In contrast to this relatively small amount it should be pointed out that the Fund's commitment, as distinct from actual signed agreements, for the benefit of non-Arab Africa totalled SR 987·25 million, or about $329 million, distributed in 18 development projects, in the year 1977/78. Additional information supplied by SFD revealed that in the period from 1975 till end of March 1980 loans totalling SR 1,256·315 million, or about $418·6 million, were signed for the benefit of non-Arab developing African countries.

Apart from a significant gap between commitment of a loan and the signing of an agreement in respect of it there have been delays between the signing and the actual disbursement of money, as was noted by an OECD report in December 1979.[21] According to this report disbursement trebled between 1976 and 1977 but increased only marginally in 1978, to $200 million. The OECD report also says that the Fund signed a total of 29 new agreements in the calendar year 1978, involving an amount of $765 million, or about 10 per cent less than in 1977. The grant element however rose to 57 per cent, making SFD the softest among the Arab bilateral funds.

Even before this more recent increase in the grant element the terms were very favourable, averaging in the first four years of operations a repayment period of 20 years, including 5 years of grace, and service charge (including interest rate) of 2·6 per cent. Terms varied both according to the nature of the project and the economic position of the recipient.

In 1978, according to OECD, 18 per cent of the total commitment was in favour of non-Arab Africa, or double the percentage in the previous year, but three-quarters of the total in 1978 were for the benefit of Arab countries. Least developed countries continued to receive one third of the total, but the share of the Most Seriously Affected countries fell to 47 per cent.

The Saudi Fund is the only one of the seven sisters, apart from the OPEC Fund, to take the entire world as a potential field for its activities. Taiwan and Brazil have been helped, although preference is for countries closer to home, particularly Arab and African. Asian countries receive a large share because of the greater number of poor people in that continent. Arab and Muslim countries are clearly favoured, but others are not neglected, such as Rwanda, Burundi and Ghana in Africa.

Loans extended to African countries, 1974/75—1977/78, totalling SR 5,038·3 million.

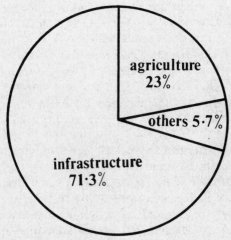

Source: SFD
Annual Report for 1977/78.

SFD has been particularly interested in assisting infrastructure development. Nearly 40 per cent of the total aid granted in the first four years of operations was for transport communications, including roads, canals, ports and airports. But the Fund regards even such basic manufacturing industries as fertiliser and cement making as part of infrastructure. Education, health and housing come under the heading of Social Infrastructure. Agriculture, much of it basic rural development, received about 20 per cent of the total by the end of 1979.

An example of an SFD loan for Africa was one extended to Senegal in 1977/78 for the Dakar-Thies road project. The scheme involved the construction of a new road over a distance of 62·4 km in four lanes of paved highway. Seventeen kilometres of connecting roads were to be rehabilitated as part of the scheme. The loan agreement signed in January 1978 was for SR 125·64 million, accounting for 50 per cent of the total cost. Maturity was 20 years, including 5 years of grace and there was a service charge of 3 per cent per annum, giving a grant element of 40 per cent.

Although the Fund has been rapidly expanding it still employs only a relatively small number of professional men at its headquarters in Riyadh. To a certain extent SFD still depends on other institutions for its aid administration, including the Arab Fund for Economic and Social Development (AFESD).

Like other Arab funds which play an important part in the overall financial and economic strategy in the respective countries SFD is directed and managed by people of the highest political and professional standing in Saudi Arabia. The Board of Directors, whose six members include a royal prince, is headed by the Saudi Minister of Finance and Economy, Mr Mohamed Abalkhail.

The Board must approve all loan commitments.

Although the Fund plays an important role in Saudi Arabia's aid effort the major part of the money destined for external assistance is dispensed directly by the Government. Few details are known of this assistance, but it is assumed that the bulk is disbursed in the form of general support grants to other Arab countries. There is also a very substantial contribution to Arab and international multilateral aid institutions.

According to OECD provisional information, concessional assistance by Saudi Arabia in 1978, including SFD, amounted to $3,417·4 million in commitment, of which $362·2 million was for multilateral organisations and the rest in bilateral aid.

Net disbursements in that year totalled $1,455·3 million, or 2·32 per cent of Saudi Arabia's GNP. This marked a sharp fall compared to the previous year when net disbursements totalled $2,400·8 million, or 4·3 per cent of GNP, although commitments in 1978 increased substantially. If these provisional figures for net disbursement are confirmed it would mean that Saudi Arabia lost its position as the second largest aid donor in the world which it had occupied in 1976–77, but it still remained one of the most important donor countries and the largest among the OPEC States.[22]

Islamic Development Bank

By the end of 1979 the Jeddah-based Islamic Development Bank (IDB) completed four years of operation with a record that inspired confidence in its future. This perhaps surprised the critics, who had doubted the viability of a financial institution refusing to either charge or take interest. Banks normally live on the difference between the interest rates on their deposits and on their loans. But the Islamic Development Bank, which is mostly financed by Arab Governments, was created with the express purpose of helping Islamic countries and communities all over the world with finance while strictly adhering to Shariah Law which bans interest as a form of usury.

In order to abide by its principles and yet avoid intolerable financial loss the Bank has been charging service expenses for its loans, amounting to between 2·5 and 3 per cent a year, or not very different from interest rates carried by the facilities extended by other Arab funds (repayment varies from about 10 years for loans serving commercial projects to 40 years for some cases of infrastructure projects, including generous grace periods).

But the Bank has been making profit by investing its non-disbursed funds in western finance houses, not directly, but via the Saudi Arabia Monetary Agency. Net income at the end of 1979 from these operations was over $90 million.

Yet there is little doubt that IDB has made the point which it had set out to make. Its own operations marked an increase of 73 per cent in 1979 over the previous year. There were 36 member countries, 9 of them from non-Arab Africa—Cameroon, Chad, Guinea, Guinea-Bissau, Mali, Niger, Senegal, Uganda and Upper Volta. Two more countries were applying for membership. Moreover, the example has proved catching. In 1979 eight banks were already in business in various parts of the Islamic world adhering to Shariah. Needless to say, one of the objectives of IDB is to encourage and assist the banks operating with full respect for the Islamic ethical principles.

The loans which IDB has been providing to its member countries mostly serve infrastructural projects, such as roads, airports and power schemes. But lending has accounted for only a small proportion of the total financing—for nearly ID 130 million out of the total of nearly ID 760 million approved in the first four years (ID, Islamic Dinar, is equivalent to 1 SDR of the International Monetary Fund and equalled $1·3 US in 1979). The rest of the financing was in the form of participation in capital, leasing, profit-sharing and technical assistance as far as, in the terminology of IDB, 'project financing' was concerned. There was another important and fast expanding item, trade financing.

The projects assisted are as a rule in the public sector and they have all been in member countries, although the Bank intends to introduce a scheme to assist Islamic communities in countries which are themselves predominantly non-Muslim.

Equity financing accounted for about ID 125 million in the four years. An example of this is the pulp and paper mill near Douala in Cameroon in which the Bank bought a holding for over $8·3 million in 1977. The mill, costing altogether $232 million, is designed to turn out 122,000 tonnes of sulphate pulp a year, with the production based on locally available tropical hardwood. When fully implemented the project is expected to have a significant socio-economic impact on the economy of Cameroon and generate substantial foreign exchange earnings for the Republic.

Dr Ahmed Mohamed Ali, the Saudi President of IDB, told me in an interview I had with him in 1979 of the importance he attached to developing countries taking industrial enterprise into their own hands and mastering the required technology. He said with reference to Africa:

'It's no use African countries buying foreign equipment and machinery and then letting these be operated by foreigners. In this way the African countries would never develop or truly emancipate themselves. It is vitally important particularly for African youth to master modern technology and skills.'

By backing an enterprise in the Third World with risk capital the Bank is encouraging other investors to move in, including those from the developed world who may bring with them modern technology.

'It is especially necessary that we should encourage the growth of such industries as are likely to help other economic development in the country concerned, for example cement-making plant', Dr Ali explained. He told me of his plans to help finance the construction of a large cement manufacturing establishment in the Sahel to serve three countries in the area. In fact, by 1979 the Bank participated in the equity of a total of four cement factories, including one in non-Arab Africa.

The Bank has also been taking, more recently, equity in industrial development banks.

Another way of helping a country acquire modern technology is by leasing equipment and machinery, such operations accounting for nearly ID 55 million in the first four years. One country, Turkey, has been helped in this manner to obtain modern facilities for the production of electronic equipment and components.

Technical assistance, although not very large in financial terms, has been important to those developing countries which, for instance, lack the facilities for identifying and preparing their development projects. Niger, for example, has been helped with a grant to pay for the feasibility study concerned with an important road project[23].

Trade financing recently grew in importance and by the end of 1979 accounted for well over half the total commitment so far. The idea is to help member countries purchase such vital commodities as petroleum, cement and fertilisers. But another purpose of this aid is to encourage trade among Muslim countries. Imports of oil from Saudi Arabia and fertilisers from Kuwait have, for example, been financed under this heading, although in some cases imports have come from developed countries. What the average concessionality of these operations is has not been revealed, but there is a mark-up on the finance supplied by the Bank. The intention is to develop the system and give IDB more of the role of trader rather than merely financier. It is also hoped that financial institutions in the member countries will deposit the funds they can spare with the Bank in order that this may finance trade support operations. In this case the mark-up will have to be maintained at a fairly high level.

Total financing approved by the Bank, 1976–1979 in ID millions

Type of financing:	Number of projects or operations:	Totals by the end of 1979:
Projects financing:		
Loans	24	127·11
Equity	24	124·82
Leasing	7	54·82
Profit sharing	1	4·27
Technical assistance	13	3·38
Total project financing		313·85
Trade financing:	45	445·68
Grand total:		759·53

Source: Islamic Development Bank

By 1979 the Bank was making an effort to mobilise further resources given the high level of commitment. By the end of the year the subscribed capital amounted to ID 780 million while the authorised capital was ID 2 bn. Total resources at the end of 1979 stood at ID 866,243,525, which included ID 750·5 million paid-up capital and various deposits and income. There was no question, of course, of borrowing in the market, given the Shariah ban on interest.

The subscribed capital of ID 780 million is divided into 78,000 shares of ID 10,000 each, giving the contributor a corresponding number of votes. Thus Saudi Arabia, with a subscription of ID 200 million, commanded 21·36 per cent of the vote in 1979, followed by Libya, UAE and Kuwait. The Arab countries as a whole had over 80 per cent of the vote in the year concerned.

The Bank derives its authority from the member countries whose representatives, in most instances Ministers of Finance, sit on the Board of Governors. This Board in turn appoints a 10-man Board of Executive Directors responsible for the administration of the Bank, including final approval of loan allocations.

The Board of Governors also elects the President for a period of five years who serves as Chairman of the Board of Executive Directors. From the start of the Bank till the time of writing this position has been occupied by Dr Ahmed Mohamed Ali. He studied commerce in Cairo and public administration in the US where he took a PhD at the State University of New York. Before taking over the post at the Bank he had served as Deputy Minister of Education in Saudi Arabia and Vice-Rector of King Abdel Aziz University.

The OPEC Fund for International Development

There is a more direct relationship between the higher world prices for oil and financial assistance to developing countries in the case of the OPEC Fund than in the case of any of the other six sisters. The OPEC Fund was created in 1976 as a facility of the 13 petroleum-exporting countries, members of the Organisation, which benefited from the steep rises of fuel prices after 1973/74. Yet this does not mean that OPEC's aid operations are to be seen as compensation for the greater cost of the imported petroleum and products which many developing countries are facing.

Dr Ibrahim F. I. Shihata, Director-General of the Fund, told me in an interview I had with him in Paris in July 1979:

'If we had wanted to compensate oil-importing developing countries we would have had to provide aid according to the amount of the oil they import. But we have never—to give an example—helped Brazil, the largest importer of oil in the developing world, but have, on the other hand, assisted Egypt, Tunisia and Bolivia, which do not import oil.'

In the first lending operations only the so-called Most Seriously Affected countries were helped—with direct balance of payments support. All these countries had an income per head of less than $250 in 1974. Subsequently other countries, including those with medium incomes per capita, became eligible when a priority list of 67 countries was drawn up.

'We try to help where aid is most needed', Dr Shihata explained. 'Our criteria are based on a combination of factors which affect the general economic and financial situation of the beneficiary country, including the resource gap, per capita

income, population, current balance of payments and debt
service ratio—as well as oil import cost since 1974.

'Each factor is given a weight and the total is added up to
provide a yardstick for the country's eligibility,' Dr Shihata said.

Between 1976 and end of 1979 about $654 million of direct aid
was committed for the benefit of 72 countries. Of this total about
$336 million had actually been disbursed. Some 37 per cent of
the commitment went to the Least Developed Countries.[25] In
October 1980 OPEC Fund reported that by that date it had
signed 210 loans with 76 developing countries worth $901
million, not including $683 million it had contributed as grants
and loans to other development agencies.

Project aid was, gradually becoming an important mode of
OPEC Fund intervention and by the end of 1978 it reached $203
million compared to $237 million for balance of payments
support.

Non-Arab developing Africa benefited by mid-July 1980: with
a total of $284·8 million in loans, of which $180 million were
balance of payments support and the rest were project and
programme aid.

Dr Shihata made clear to me that the Fund would have
preferred to give more project aid as this was more likely to
tackle the real causes of the recipient country's economic
problems. But given the present world economic recession, and
the escalating cost of manufacturing goods and technical services
as well as fuel, the balance of payments aid would gain in relative
significance in the immediate future, he said.

However, balance of payments loans too have been development oriented. Recipient countries have been expected to spend
the money on equipment and other tools of development as well
as on food. Moreover, the Fund has been encouraging the
developing countries to use the local currency counterpart of the
loan for specific development projects agreed with the donor.

Thus by the end of April 1980 a total of $242·504 million worth
of counterpart funds had been approved for utilisation, $50·424
million of it in non-Arab Africa. All these projects have been of
economic or social significance. Maturity of the loan is reduced
by five years if the beneficiary country does not agree to employ
the counterpart funds for development. Most of the countries
have agreed.

In project lending power-generating schemes have had priority, accounting for about a third of the total by the end of 1979, followed by manufacturing industry and industrial development banks, agriculture and agro-industry, transport and road building, public utilities and telecommunications.

An example of a project loan for Africa was one of $5·3 million granted for the construction of a number of tea factories in Kenya, tea growing and processing being one of the African country's growth industries.

The loan was for 20 years, after 5 years of grace, and interest-rate free. International Bank for Reconstruction and Development for its part contributed finance towards the total cost of $36 million and also accepted the administration of OPEC Fund's share. A total of 17 factories were to be built, employing eventually 2,000 people and processing 19,000 tons of tea a year, mostly for export. Leaf was to be collected from 35,000 small-holding growers. The economic rate of return for the project was given as 16 per cent.[26]

All OPEC fund loans are interest-free for low-income developing countries, but relatively richer countries are charged 4 per cent a year and in one case 5 per cent was agreed. A higher rate is envisaged for loans to high-income developing countries when such loans are concluded.

A service charge of 0·75 per cent is applied to programme and project loans and 0·5 per cent for balance of payments loans. The repayment of project loans is over 20 years, after 5 years of grace. Programme loans are repaid in principle over 10 years, after the grace period.

Balance of payments loans have a maturity of 15 years, after 5 years of grace.

The grant element for project loans was estimated at 62·5 per cent for the period ending 1979 and that for the balance of payments loans was about 58 per cent on average.

The OPEC Fund was set up by the oil-rich developing countries to help the rest of the Third World and demonstrate that in spite of the newly acquired wealth the 13 petroleum exporting countries felt themselves to be part of the community of developing nations.

In accordance with this view the Fund has conceived a strategy of co-ordinated attacks on the existing unsatisfactory state of affairs: the poor countries must be helped to lift themselves from poverty and become more independent; at the same time all developing countries must be encouraged to co-operate more closely among themselves and, finally, the present system must be challenged directly: efforts to build a New International Economic Order ought to go on in parallel with the aid provided to individual countries or groups of them.

This strategy is behind a financial grant of $435·5 million supplied by the OPEC fund for the establishment of a new international agency to help agricultural production in the Third World, with particular emphasis on improving the present, by and large disastrous food situation. After the Fund had pledged its contribution to the planned agency western nations followed suit and supplied the rest of the finance to enable the International Fund for Agricultural Development (IFAD) to start operations with a capital of $1 billion in 1977. Many agricultural and rural development projects have already been financed with the help of the money made available by IFAD in Africa and elsewhere. More recently the OPEC Fund has been working for the expansion of the financial base of the new agency.

But IFAD also provided the first instance of an international organisation in which participating developed nations have found themselves in a minority in respect of decision-making as the OPEC members and the non-oil developing countries together make up two thirds of the voting power. In this way the developing countries should be in a better position to influence development.[27]

An example of IFAD's work is provided by its participation in a major rural development project in Burundi, in East-Mpanda, where 6,000 hectares of land are being developed, 2,400 hectares for irrigation. Roads, drinking water wells, 15 schools and 15 dispensaries will also be built under the project in which OPEC Fund, African Development Bank, European Development Fund and World Food Programme join efforts with IFAD and the Burundi Government. The OPEC loan of $2 million is being administered by the African Development Bank. The project provides a significant instance of Arab, European and African development interests working together on a scheme of major importance to hard-pressed Burundi in Central Africa.

The twin purpose of helping economic development in the Third World directly and creating conditions for NIEO has been served by grants-in-aid totalling $40 million which OPEC Fund extended to UNDP, the world's foremost technical assistance organisation, and some other similar institutions by the end of 1979. Technical assistance related to Niger River Basin Project is an example of operations financed by the Fund under this heading. Another is to meet the costs of labour-intensive schemes identified by UNDP in Burundi, Tanzania and Nepal. The schemes will create employment for poor, unskilled labour in rural areas. Capital requirements are small in relation to labour input in these schemes and the Fund's contribution will meet the cost of simple items of imported equipment, such as tractors and jeeps.

The Fund also acts as transfer agency for the profits accruing to OPEC members from sales in public auctions of IMF gold holdings. The funds are transferred to a trust fund administered by IMF to provide eligible developing countries with special balance of payments assistance. By 1979 a total of $64·9 million was transferred in this way by the Fund.

In another development the Fund has pledged to contribute $100 million to the Common Fund of the proposed international agreement to stabilise prices of raw materials and other basic commodities and improve their marketing. No final conclusion has yet been reached at the time of writing in negotiations for the Common Fund, perhaps the most important single topic in the North-South dialogue. But the Fund's pledge, which is to cover the contributions made by the poorest countries to the Common Fund, should encourage all those concerned to speed up the negotiations and come to agreement.

In various ways the Fund and its Director-General have been endeavouring to help towards a better understanding between the advanced and developed nations as well as to assist the people of the Third World to improve their grasp of the problems and formulate more convincingly the propositions they wish to make in their dialogue and discussions with representatives from industrial countries.

Support for the UNCTAD Research and Training Centre serves such a purpose. It will offer specialised orientation and training courses in each of the developing regions, through their own institutions, and should help raise the level of understanding of trade and development issues. As Dr Shihata has pointed out, 'It should also contribute to the elaboration of effective action-oriented policies in the area of international economic relations and help to develop and organise programmes of research on economic questions that are of vital importance to developing nations'.[28] Another instance of support for a similar effort is the help extended by the Fund in 1977 for the establishment of the Centre for Research on the New International Economic Order, at Oxford.

Dr Shihata himself has made numerous contributions to the discussion on economic development and cash flows, some of which have been published as monographs by the OPEC Fund and other agencies. In many assemblies and organisations he has pleaded the cause of developing nations, often in unpublicised statements. A recent example of this took place in April 1980 when he addressed a meeting of the European Parliament's Committee for Development and Co-operation in Brussels, pleading for greater international support for agricultural development and food supplies in the Third World. This, of course, is a theme to which the Fund has been particularly attached, witness its help for IFAD.

The Fund has consistently used its influence to achieve better terms of international aid for the Third World and make such aid more efficient and to simplify its procedures.

At the time of my interview with Dr Shihata in July 1979 he was in Paris to take part in the annual meeting between Arab Funds and western aid agencies. At these meetings, which are held behind closed doors and are organised by the Organisation for Economic Co-operation and Development (OECD), many problems of aid to the Third World are thrashed out and technical hitches smoothed, but controversial matter is also frankly aired.

On this occasion, as Dr Shihata told me the next day, the controversy was about tied aid.

'You cannot expect the Arabs to go on co-financing with you if you persist in tying your aid to purchases in your own countries,' Dr Shihata told the western representatives.

He said that the Swiss representatives had supported him and that the Swedish delegate had expressed his gratitude, for Dr Shihata's warning would make it easier for the Stockholm Government to uphold its policy of untied aid in the teeth of opposition mounted against it by certain Swedish pressure groups. Tied aid of course restricts considerably the choice of suppliers for the beneficiary country and thereby affects the quality of aid and the speed of its implementation. Often it is just a way of subsidising an ailing industry in the donor country.

Africa as such has no special place in the world-wide purview of the OPEC Fund, but because of its problems it is a large recipient of aid. However, Dr Shihata did point out to me that 'many countries in that continent benefit from our principle that aid should not be given as compensation for balance of payments losses due to higher prices of imported fuel but rather according to general development needs.'

Dr Shihata stressed the importance of co-ordination among Arab Funds, including the OPEC Fund, for aid to Africa, particularly in the field of co-financing. He thought the role of BADEA as a co-ordinator of Arab aid to non-Arab Africa should be further strengthened.

'When we need information or analysis regarding a situation in non-Arab Africa', he said, 'we should be turning to BADEA. This is our aim, but, naturally, it takes time to realise it fully.'

He told me of his plans to have BADEA administer a loan the Fund was intending to grant Angola. BADEA was already active in the newly independent country but neither IBRD nor IMF, which might normally have been approached for technical assistance, were there. While appreciative of the assistance so often extended by the World Bank and IMF it was important, Dr Shihata said, that developing countries should rely as much as possible on their own institutions.

In January 1980 it was announced that the OPEC Fund had approved a loan of $3 million for a railway project in Angola in which BADEA was to be one of the co-financiers and would also administer the Fund's loan.

In January 1980 the Fund assumed the status of an international development institution with its own legal personality, very much like BADEA or AFESD, while before that it had been technically speaking only a special account collectively owned by contributing member countries of OPEC, the Arab countries contributing slightly over half the total capital resources. From now on the Fund would also administer its own loans while before it had to rely for that on other institutions.

In May 1980 the Fund was renamed 'OPEC Fund for International Development' and its capital resources were raised by another $1·6 billion (after an increase of $800 million in January 1980), bringing them to a total of close to $4 billion. It was also decided to keep the headquarters of the Fund in Vienna.

In practice the Fund has retained its former structure. The Ministerial Committee on Financial and Monetary Matters, consisting of the Ministers of Finance of the OPEC members, now became the Ministerial Council in which the institution's authority is vested. Like the former Ministerial Committee the Council lays down the general policies for the Fund. The Governing Committee, in which all the member countries are also represented, now became the Governing Board, responsible for administration, including the approval of loans.[29]

The Governing Board elects its Chairman, who signs the aid agreements although this task is sometimes delegated to the Director-General. In November 1979 Dr Mahsoun Jalal of Saudi Arabia, Executive Director for Saudi Arabia on the Board of the International Monetary fund and till then Managing Director of the Saudi Fund for Development, was elected Chairman of the then Governing Committee, now Governing Board, replacing Dr Mohammed Yeganeh of Iran.

Among the responsibilities of the Governing Board is also that of appointing the Fund's Director-General who is in charge of day-to-day administration of the institution. Since the inception of the Fund in 1976 the post has been held by Dr Ibrahim F.I. Shihata of Egypt, a world authority on legal aspects of international development finance. After his studies in international law at Cairo and Harvard universities he taught international law and for eight years served as legal expert of the KFAED and close assistant to Abdtlatif Y. Hammad.

The Arab Fund for Economic and Social Development

The Arab Fund (AFESD) is alone among the seven sisters not to assist directly any part of the non-Arab world, including non-Arab Africa. But a few words nonetheless ought to be said about it, for technical if for no other reasons. AFESD began operations in 1974, one year before BADEA opened for business. Well-endowed with professional staff and expertise, the Arab Fund has provided technical assistance to other Arab funds, particularly the Saudi Fund for Development, and some help also to BADEA.

Moreover, AFESD has been entrusted with the task of monitoring the entire Arab aid effort, including that which is destined for non-Arab Africa. AFESD is present at every meeting of the Arab Aid Co-ordination Committee and a representative of the Fund takes a record of the proceedings. The Fund checks the implementation of decisions taken at the biannual meetings. AFESD has also played a very active part in the efforts to standardise and simplify Arab aid procedures. Thanks to these efforts loan agreements signed by the co-operating Arab agencies are virtually identical now in their formulation.

AFESD, which is based in Kuwait, also keeps a small office in which data on all Arab aid is collected and published quarterly, although, as I was told by the person in charge, co-operation in this regard was more effective with some of the organisations than with others.

But data published on the activities of the seven sisters should be fairly comprehensive and reliable.

To students of Arab aid for non-Arab Africa a major institution financed by the Arabs, if only for themselves, is important enough to take some account of in this narrative. The great development need of the Arab world is itself inevitably a limiting factor on Arab generosity directed to others. Dr Mohamed Imady, Chief Executive of AFESD, said, when I interviewed him in Kuwait in 1980, that there was no question of non-Arab Africa receiving less aid because his Fund was to get more capital, as it must. 'Arab aid to non-Arab Africa is regarded as very important by all Arab governments', he explained, 'although the grounds for it may be almost entirely humanitarian.'

Yet even regardless of the question of money the Arabs have only a limited supply of organisational and managerial talent and skills that can be deployed in their development agencies.

On the other hand, development in the Arab region has significance for Africa as the two communities are both part of the Third World and share concern for its progress in addition to the much closer and more specific ties linking the two in the Afro-Arab movement. The importance of this aspect is all the greater in view of AFESD's interest in promoting Arab regional development, particularly in respect of transport, telecommunications and industrial development.

Generally, the Fund has financed mostly infrastructural schemes, particularly for transport communications and electric power. But agricultural development in the Sudan, designed to turn the country into a major supplier of food for the Arab region, has been the subject of a specialised activity. It was AFESD which first investigated and then promoted Sudan's huge agricultural potential. Co-operation is now based on a long-term agreement between the Fund and the Sudan Government and AFESD established a special institution, the Arab Agricultural Authority for Investment and Development, based in Khartoum, to finance farm development in the Sudan and co-ordinate outside capital investment and concessional aid destined for the same purpose.

However, AFESD showed little activity in 1978 and 1979. By the end of 1977 it had committed KD 295·3 million in loans for 46 projects and KD 3·4 million in grants-in-aid for technical assistance. By contrast, only one operation was reported in 1978, costing KD 0·407 million, and only two in 1979, in the form of loans worth a total of KD 19·40 million.

In September 1979, Dr Saeb Jaroudi, of Lebanon, who had been President of the Fund since 1972, was replaced by Dr Mohamed Imady, a former Syrian Minister of Economy (he received his Ph.D. at New York University in 1960).

Meanwhile, Egypt, which had received a total of KD 67·9 million in loans by the end of 1977, more than twice as much as the next most important beneficiary, the Sudan, had its membership 'frozen'. No further aid was to be granted but existing commitments arising for the benefit of third party suppliers would be honoured. At the same time Egypt was, although its membership was 'frozen', expected to continue contributing to the capital of the Fund according to the original commitment. While being the main beneficiary of the Fund Egypt is also the largest shareholder, accounting for nearly 13 per cent of the shares.

At the time of writing the Arab Fund had an authorised capital of KD 400 million, or about 1·44 billion dollars—with KD 385 million subscribed by the end of 1979. Dr Imady told me there was urgent need to replenish the capital resources and at a meeting in Baghdad in January 1980 suggestions for additional capital of the Arab Fund ranged from KD 600 million to KD 5·5 billion.

'I have no doubt', he told me, 'that the respective Arab Governments will see that all the viable projects submitted to the Arab Fund are implemented and that the necessary finance is made available.'

In 1980 loans for eight new projects were approved, including a major steel works development in Mauritania to which the Fund would contribute KD 10 million. Tunisia, South Yemen, Somalia and the Sudan were among the other beneficiaries.

The Fund was established in 1971 (but only began operations in 1974) as a joint venture of 21 Arab Governments. Its structure is a mirror image of the two-tier system we have seen in the case of BADEA, with the Board of Governors as the supreme authority and a Board of Directors under it with a Director-General, the Bank's President, as the Chief Executive.

The Fund lends to both public and private organisations in Arab countries but loans must always carry a Government guarantee. Interest rates are either 4 or 6 per cent, the former being charged when the beneficiary is a poor Arab country. Maturities range from 15 to 25 years, with grace periods from three to six years.

Iraq, Libya and Qatar

Iraq has recently been expanding its aid programmes, with total concessional disbursements amounting to $144 million in 1978, most of it being bilateral assistance. Commitments in bilateral aid reached $559 million in 1978, most of it for the benefit of Jordan and Syria. Chad was among the African countries benefiting from this new commitment.

Part of Iraq's assistance is channelled through the Iraqi Fund for External Development, the capital of which was doubled in 1979 to reach $200 million Iraqi Dinars, or $677·2 m.

The Fund was reported to have granted a $6·5 million loan to Guinea in 1979 for extension of a plastics factory in Conakry. The loan, co-financed with EDF, bore interest of 3 per cent per annum, with maturity of 12 years and had 3 years of grace for repayment.

With effect from 1st June 1979 Iraq had been compensating the poorer development countries, with bilateral long-term contracts to purchase Iraqi oil, for any further increase in oil prices until the end of 1979 by means of long-term interest-free loans.

Libya has for some years been a significant source of capital aid to non-Arab Africa, but no details of this are available. Libya's multilateral contributions amounted to $94 million in 1978 and in the same year the country's aid disbursements, according to information supplied by OECD, are estimated to have exceeded $140 million, or well above the level in each of the two preceding years. Bilateral commitments are believed to have reached $569 million in 1978, but the lion's share of this was general support assistance for Jordan and Syria under the Baghdad agreement.

The Libyan Arab Foreign Bank, a semi-public institution, has been playing a major part in the development of Africa, although it is difficult to assess the concessionality of this aid. There have, however, been known cases when loans were extended to non-Arab interests at times when it would have been virtually impossible for the recipient to obtain assistance from any other source. LAFB has also been involved in equity financing and a number of joint banks were established with non-Arab African agencies, including one in Niger in 1977/78 with a capital of $2 million.

Qatar has been providing some concessional aid to non-Arab Africa, but the OECD claims that the State's overall external assistance programme appears to have fallen sharply from $194 million in 1977 to $100 million in 1978, mainly on account of a very pronounced reduction in bilateral grants, which fell from $147 million to $28 million. Bilateral loan disbursements—again according to OECD—decreased by one-third to $20 million while multilateral contributions trebled to over $50 million. The reduced aid flows in 1978 resulted from the tight balance-of-payments situation, increased scrutiny of aid requests and disbursement difficulties in recipient countries. Following the reappearance of budget and balance of payments surpluses and in view of the country's large commitments made in favour of Arab countries at the Arab League Summit conference in Baghdad the volume of Qatari aid was in 1979 expected to increase substantially.

Qatar has no special fund to channel aid, the Government does it through its own machinery. The Qatar Government also takes part in the Arab Aid Co-ordination Committee for non-Arab Africa and there have been cases when the Gulf State co-financed projects with BADEA.[30]

In the period from 1973 till the end of 1979 the Arab Governments and their agencies committed a total of just over $3 billion in concessional aid to non-Arab Africa (see Appendix for details), according to incomplete data collected by BADEA. In addition, the Arabs approved nearly $1·35 billion of non-concessional aid, giving a total for both commitments of nearly $4·4 billion in the seven years.

Speaking only of concessional aid, which can be defined as aid in the strict sense of the term, this reached its highest point in 1976 when $560 million was committed. It was nearly $520 million in 1978 and nearly $530 million in 1979.

However, preliminary estimates made by BADEA early in 1981 indicated a very sharp increase of Arab aid commitment for non-Arab Africa in 1980. According to these rather incomplete data the commitment totalled $1,151·43 million in current values, or 115% over the previous year's level. There was also a very large increase in the proportion of the aid provided on concessional terms, i.e., with a grant element of at least 25%. This proportion is said to have been as much as 97·3% in 1980.

Even in terms of constant, 1975, US dollars Arab aid for the region in 1980 was very substantial at $822·45 million. The aid shot up not only in absolute but also in relative terms, with Arab ODA accounting for over a third of such aid estimated to have been approved for the region by all donors in the year concerned.

In the period from 1973 to 1979 Arab concessional aid for non-Arab Africa accounted for about one quarter of the total of such aid to the region. But it should be pointed out that such international organisations as the IDA and UNDP, a very important source of non-Arab aid, receive substantial support from Arab Governments. In 1978 for example these Governments disbursed a total of $298·8 million dollars on concessional terms for assistance to these institutions.[31]

Noticeable in the direct Arab aid benefiting non-Arab Africa are the very high proportions going to particularly under-privileged groups of countries as nearly one third of the total was allocated for the seven non-Arab countries of the Sahel Zone, about half for the Least Developed Countries and well over two thirds for the Most Seriously Affected Countries.

Much of Arab aid has been for specific projects. It is such projects that will eventually change the situation in Africa. But they usually take a long time to implement while the need for financial aid may be now and then, calling in fact for balance of payments or budgetary supports. Project aid also restricts the recipient Government to the scheme that has been agreed upon when in the meantime some other development might be given priority. That is why Governments normally prefer to receive development assistance in the form of programme aid, which is not given for a specific project but for a whole range of possi-bilities, for instance general development of the transport sector.

The Brandt Commission has recommended that programme aid should be more frequently used by the donors, but the Arabs have so far supplied relatively little of this to non-Arab Africa. Nonetheless, a substantial part of Arab aid for Africa has been in the form of balance of payments support.

According to BADEA estimates Arab aid committed in the period from 1973 to 1978—both concessional and non-concessional and totalling nearly $3·9 billion—included nearly $800 million for balance of payments support while most of the rest was project aid, with transport and communications, agriculture, social development, and support for financial institutions, leading the list in that order. Social development included the construction of schools and religious buildings, with the item as a whole accounting for somewhat less than one tenth of the total aid. The same information also reveals that approximately two thirds of the Arab aid to Black Africa in 1973–1978 was contributed by seven countries, Saudi Arabia, Kuwait, Qatar, UAE, Libya, Algeria and Iraq.

Project aid is in principle preferred by the Arab donors, for two reasons mainly. If assistance is to have a lasting effect and help remove the very causes of underdevelopment and con-straints it should go to appropriate development projects, especially for infrastructure. Then, project aid can be monitored and its results properly assessed by the donors.

Incidentally, it is not quite true to say that project aid necessarily takes very long to bring any results. Even the start of a large project, which may take years to execute, often creates important positive changes, for instance by providing employment on the construction site and opening up a hitherto closed or remote area to the outside world, as I have observed in the case of the Sélingué Dam construction, to be described in a later chapter. The decision to embark on an important development project, even if very long-term, can have immediate psychological impact on the population that will eventually benefit from the scheme, as I have seen in the case of the Senegal river development project.

Much of the technology and know-how going into projects built in Africa with Arab assistance comes from the advanced free market economy countries, i.e. from the West. This trilateral co-operation has been criticised by both Arabs and Africans when it leaves the two partners merely a passive role, because such co-operation would be far from helping the recipient country to stand on its own feet; it would on the contrary be calculated to perpetuate the dependence of such countries on western technology and expertise. We shall later be giving an Arab view on this matter.

Yet, it is, on the other hand, not entirely correct to say that the Arab contribution in this co-operation for development in Africa has been exclusively financial. It seems to me important to stress the intellectual and organisational effort and expertise that the Arabs have been investing in this development. Professional men with experience who staff and run such agencies as BADEA and KFAED are much in demand today, not least in the Arab world itself. That a considerable proportion of this development expertise has been allocated for the benefit of non-Arab Africa is in its turn a measure of the commitment the Arabs are putting into Afro-Arab co-operation.

But these experts, wherever they may be working, in Khartoum, Kuwait, or Jeddah, are also building solid bridges of understanding between the two communities, and of knowledge and appreciation of each other's potentialities and problems. This also helps to create the basis for what may eventually become a self-generating co-operation, rooted in private enterprise and investment as well as trade.

NOTES

1. *Arab-African Co-operation*, BADEA, Khartoum, December 1978, p. 9.
2. Resolution on Afro-Arab Co-operation stated inter alia:
   'Commends the Arab financial institutions, and more especially BADEA, for their positive contributions towards the strengthening and consolidation of the ties of solidarity and co-operation between the African and Arab peoples, and urgently calls on them to draw up long-term co-operation programmes by co-ordinating their action with similar African institutions;
   Urges the Arab financial institutions to define a practical and clear policy on transfer of their financial resources in the form of Arab investments in Africa, and requests the OAU Secretary-General to hold consultations with his counterpart of the League of Arab States to that effect;
   Appeals to the African and Arab Specialised Institutions, namely ADB, BADEA and ECA to co-ordinate their action regularly and harmonise their short-, medium- and long-term co-operation programmes.
   Authorises the OAU Secretary-General to establish the necessary contacts with his counterpart of the League of Arab States so as to review the co-operation and structure of the joint institutional mechanisms entrusted with the implementation of the Afro-Arab Co-operation programmes and submit appropriate proposals to the next Afro-Arab Ministerial Conference.'
3. For BADEA management procedures, including bidding for contracts connected with the Bank's project aid see *Management of BADEA Projects and Procurement Rules*, BADEA, Symposium on Business Opportunities from World Aid Projects, London, December 1979.
4. In the customary division of the Sub-Saharan Africa applied by UN agencies BADEA's East Africa covers the Eastern and Southern African sub-regions, but without the Sudan and Somalia and with Zaire added. The Sahel, Western Africa and Central Africa are part of BADEA's West Africa, with the exception of Mauritania and Zaire.
5. The list of the Least Developed Countries is drawn up by the UN on the basis of the following indicators: GNP per capita, share of manufacturing in total output and literacy rates. In 1978 the following African countries were listed: Benin, Botswana, Burundi, Cape Verde, Central African Empire, Chad, Comoros, Ethiopia, the Gambia, Guinea, Lesotho, Malawi, Mali, Niger, Rwanda, Somalia, Sudan, Uganda, Tanzania and Upper Volta.
6. The 45 MSACs in the world are listed as such by the UN on the following grounds: 1. Low income per capita combined with low productivity and wide technological gap; 2. Worsening terms of trade; 3. High debt servicing compared with export earnings; 4. Deficiency and inelasticity of export earnings; 5. Low foreign exchange reserves; 6. High transport and transit charges; 7. High dependence of the economy on foreign trade.
7. A cement factory built in Togo with the help of a loan of $10 million approved by BADEA in 1975 also serves Ghana and Ivory Coast.
8. BADEA annual Report 1978, p. 41.

9. The exception to this rule was a loan of $15 million granted to Mali in 1976 to assist in the financing of the Sélingué Dam.

10. *Development of Agriculture and Transport Sectors in Africa, BADEA Approach*, BADEA, Khartoum, May 1980, p. 48.
    See also Dr Chedly Ayari: 'BADEA's role as Co-ordinator of Arab Aid to Africa', Symposium on Business Opportunities from World Aid Projects, London, December 1979, pp. 7–8.

11. See 'General Agreement' founding the Bank, Art. 3 (1), according to which BADEA 'enjoys full international legal status and complete autonomy in administrative and financial matters.'

12. 'Kuwait', *Financial Times* Survey, London, p. IV. 25 February 1980.

13. *Perspective on Arab Aid Institutions*, by Abdtlatif Y. Al-Hamad, KFAED, May 1978, pp. 13–14.

14. *Aid in Africa*, by Guy Arnold, Kogane Page, London, 1979, p. 19 etc.

15. *The Arab's New Frontier*, by Robert Stevens, Temple Smith, London 1976, pp. 9–19.

16. Ibid. pp. 56–60.

17. *The Economy of Kuwait*, by M. W. Khouda and P. G. Sadler, Macmillan, London, 1979, p. 243.

18. KFAED, 16th Annual Report, 1977/78, p. 34.

19. *Voice*, London, 1 September 1978, p. XVIII.

20. See Annual Report 1979, ADFAED.

21. *Development Co-operation*, 1979 Review by OECD, Paris, December 1979, p. 138.

22. Ibid.

23. According to the 'Policies and Procedures for Financing Operations of the Bank', technical assistance operations will play an essential role in IDB's activities, serving three purposes: 1. transfer of technology to member countries, 2. preparation of feasibility studies and formulation of bankable projects, and 3. help supervise the projects and enterprises during construction and initial operation, pp. 5–6, Islamic Development Bank, DCD/80.36.

24. IDB 4th Annual Report, 1979, Jeddah.

25. OPEC Annual Report 1979, pp. 22, 57–64.

26. OPEC Fund Annual Report 1978, p. 31.

27. *The OPEC Aid Record*, by Ibrahim F. I. Shihata and Robert Mabro, Vienna, OPEC Fund, June 1979, p. 9; and see also *OPEC Aid, the OPEC Fund and Co-operation with Commercial Sources of Development Finance*, by Ibrahim F. I. Shihata, OPEC Fund, Vienna, November 1978.

28. *The OPEC Special Fund and the North-South Dialogue*, by Ibrahim F. I. Shihata, Third World Foundation Monograph 4, London, 1979, pp. 11–12.

29. *The OPEC Fund for International Development, Basic Information*, OPEC Fund, Vienna, July 1980, p. 5.

30. For data on aid supplied to Africa by Iraq, Libya and Qatar, see *Development Co-operation, 1979* Review by OECD, Paris, December 1979, pp. 136–138.

31. *Flows of Resources from OPEC Members to Developing Countries*, OECD, Secretariat Working Document DCD/79.31, Paris 1979, p. 20.

3

Africa,
The World's Poorest Region

The pot-bellied child illustrating an appeal for public charity will in most cases be African. Malnutrition and under-nourishment are, as it were, endemic over much of the continent. In 1975 there were about 400 million people living in developing Africa and about a quarter of these suffered from malnutrition, their intake of nutrients being below the critical minimum. Out of about 800 million people of this world said to be living in absolute poverty, 100 million are in Africa. Out of 31 Least Developed Countries 20 are in Africa, 18 in non-Arab Africa.

There are exceptions. Where oil has been struck the countries concerned are able to develop fast. An example of this is Nigeria where the gross domestic product has been increasing by over 9 per cent a year, although with the country being the most populous in Africa income per head of population is still only about $600. Nigeria does not need Arab financial support but much of the country's own resources must be devoted to help regions and populations inside Nigeria which are still very poor and undeveloped. A similar situation prevails in the other major oil exporting country in Sub-Saharan Africa, Gabon.

In 1977 crude petroleum accounted for 58 per cent of the total value of exports of developing Africa, meaning the entire continent with the exception of the South African Republic. Eighteen other primary commodities, among them coffee, cocoa, tea, tobacco, sugar, groundnuts, cotton, copper and phosphate rock, accounted for another 25 per cent of the export earnings, illustrating the heavy concentration of African export trade on a range of primary materials.

Outside the oil exporting countries economic growth in Africa has been slow. Over the past 20 years it amounted on average to only 3·7 per cent a year, according to ECA, which, with a population expansion estimated at 2·7 per cent a year, meant an increase of a bare 1 per cent a year for each African. ECA wrote in a recent report about these non-oil developing countries in Africa:

'About 75 years would be needed to double the per capita income if the past trend continues into the future, a frightening forecast indeed considering the present low per capita incomes. The prospect is even worse if consideration is given to the deceleration in the rate of economic growth from 3·9 per cent yearly in the 1960s to 3·5 per cent in the period 1970 to 1977.'[1]

What is particularly worrying is that the situation will get worse rather than better if the present trends are allowed to continue, which is particularly true of the deteriorating problem of food production and supplies. According to the Plan of Action adopted at the first African economic Summit conference held in April 1980 in Lagos: '... if the world economic forecast for the next decade is to be believed the overall poor performance of African economies over the past 20 years may even be a golden age compared with the future growth rate.'

The reasons for this deplorable state of affairs are many and complex.

There is the heritage of colonial and neo-colonial exploitation which accounts for the lopsided economic development in Africa. It has been said that Africa produces what it does not consume and consumes what it does not produce. Colonialism meant that primary production sectors were developed only to serve the interests of outsiders, with Africans being as part of deliberate policy or due to the prevailing economic system placed in the position of cheap labour or left as primitive cultivators or pastoralists outside the cash economy.

In more recent years the slow growth or stagnation of the western economies, which are the main markets for African exports and sources of development capital for Africa, greatly contributed to the problems the continent was facing. In the fifties and sixties western economies enjoyed good overall growth of some 5 per cent in real terms. Post-war reconstruction, technological advances, full employment policies and relative stability of prices all contributed to this. But world recession, which began in 1974, is still with us. African economies on the whole suffered from this as their export earnings were reduced while wild fluctuations of many commodity prices caused wide-ranging disruptions of economic life and planning.

In many African countries, particularly the land-locked and island countries, the escalating cost of fuel has produced a new dimension to economic problems. Serious thought is being given to these difficulties by oil exporting countries as the last thing these want is for their sister countries in the developing world to crumble because of inability to finance the required imports of petroleum and its products as well as manufactured goods whose prices are seriously affected by the cost of liquid fuel.

Oil consumed in Africa is only a fraction of the continent's total fuel output yet the leaders in Burundi and Rwanda told me late in 1979 how it was rapidly becoming impossible for them to finance the transport from ports a thousand or so kilometres away of most of what these land-locked countries needed to be able to live. In Mauritius the economy was being crippled on account of heavy freight costs for sea transport and the cost of oil that was consumed in the island's thermal power stations on which supplies of electrical energy mostly depended. In Tanzania,[2] to give one more example from my personal experience, the Minister of Finance and Planning, Amir Jamal, told me in 1979 that his country was facing an import bill for fuel that was 10 times bigger than in 1973 (although of course consumption of oil and its products considerably increased in Tanzania in the meantime). Much of the development, including that of agriculture, was now in jeopardy because of this high cost of fuel, Mr Jamal said.

Yet while increased costs of fuel have captured the imagination world-wide the imports of petroleum and its products have certainly not been the only or even the most important item on the balance of payments in non-oil developing Africa. Much greater imports of now higher priced food have been equally significant. Much more significant than oil has been the import of manufactures from industrial countries, particularly engineering products, whose prices have also been escalating. Finally, payments for services to western countries have represented a large and fast expanding burden.

Many of these problems in Africa can in no way be attributed to actions or omissions on the part of the Africans themselves. But the merit and historic significance of the Lagos 1980 economic conference was to focus on what the Africans could and should do to help themselves. Making, as they put it, their 'agonising and frank' reappraisal of the situation and future prospects, the African leaders gathered at this first Summit entirely devoted to economic problems showed both courage and imagination.

That the record of economic development in independent Africa had been so inadequate over the past two decades was, the African leaders said, in large part the fault of the African Governments themselves. For instance, as the Plan says, 'At the root of the food problem in Africa is the fact that Member States have not usually accorded the necessary priority to agriculture both in the allocation of resources and in giving sufficient attention to policies for the promotion of productivity and improvement of rural life.'[3]

African Governments, the Plan continued, must also take the responsibility for the poor progress in economic co-operation and integration among the African countries themselves. Intra-African trade has in fact been sharply declining as a proportion of Africa's total commerce. Africa seems to have become more and not less dependent on the outside world since independence. There is no real justification for the kind of 'divide and rule' situation that seems to be gripping the Black Continent. Only political will on the part of the African Governments themselves is needed for them to embark on the road of true economic and social emancipation, as the conclusions of the Lagos conference make plain.

The sombre message of the Lagos Summit came, ironically, at the time of what was perhaps the greatest political triumph for Africa since the start of the de-colonisation process after the last war. The conference was able to welcome Zimbabwe as the 50th member of the OAU. The outcome of the Zimbabwe people's struggle for freedom demonstrated that guerrilla warfare had been necessary, yet the actual transfer of power was based on an electoral verdict of the country's ordinary men and women under the supervision of a Commonwealth team. This was a great event of which all who took part in it could be proud. But it was above all a tribute to the sagacity and common sense of the people of Zimbabwe.

The new leader, Robert Mugabe, surprised many when he

insisted on the need for the new country to retain the services of the white minority as well as to co-operate closely with the western world. He also told Naim Kaddah, official Arab League representative in Nairobi, when the two met in Harare in May 1980, that Zimbabwe would welcome economic and financial co-operation with the Arabs. By joining OAU Zimbabwe, of course, automatically became the 41st African country to be eligible for BADEA assistance.

The outcome in Rhodesia considerably strengthened the African case for freedom of African people wherever they still were oppressed. For did the solution found for Zimbabwe not suggest that the West, if it wanted to keep the Russians and communism out of southern Africa, would be much wiser actively to support the African liberation movements in the region?

But with yet another political problem out of the way the increasingly disastrous economic situation in independent Africa is being brought in all the sharper focus. At some foreseeable stage the Africans must after all begin to enjoy the fruits of their political emancipation in terms of reasonable material prosperity. It is also clear that political independence could prove an empty shell if the continent is allowed to sink into ever greater dependence on outsiders for the physical survival of its people.

The Lagos Plan of Action, a 140-page document that was unanimously adopted at the 28–29 April 1980 Summit conference, is a penetrating analysis of the present situation and a coherent programme for the improvement of these conditions over the next 20 years, to attain a fairly self-sufficient and viable African Economic Community by 2000. Much of the preparatory work for this document, which is based on the so-called 'Monrovia Strategy for the Economic Development of Africa', had been accomplished by ECA.

It is for the first time that a strategy for African development as a whole has been adopted by the OAU in such a detailed and comprehensive manner. It now constitutes an African charter for development over the next two decades. OAU, of course, has no powers of compulsion, but the document is bound to influence the thinking and decisions of the African Governments. For the Arabs, and BADEA, it provides important terms of reference in regard to priorities the African Governments are now expected to attach to individual sectors of their economic development plans.

I would now like to give a closer look at these sectors, diagnose their problems and indicate the cure as has been prescribed by the Lagos Summit. First of all I shall attempt to survey and discuss agriculture and rural development in Africa as this is the nub of economic activity in the continent; we shall then look at the development of manufacturing which is important for many reasons, including as a source of essential materials for development such as cement and fertiliser and provider of employment; transport and communications will be referred to as they are often a pre-condition for any modern economic development; energy problems must be touched upon as they assume special significance at the time of high fuel cost and are of particular concern to the Arabs and indeed for Afro–Arab co-operation; manpower and population matters are of great importance as the people represent the greatest wealth for this young continent—as well as one of its most acute headaches; and at the end something must be said about the 18 Least Developed Countries where all the problems besetting Africa are magnified and where international action and Arab co-operation are particularly important and needed.

Agriculture and Rural Development

Some 70 per cent of the African population is rural. In 1977 65·1 per cent of the African people lived by farming and agriculture accounted for 32·7 per cent of the Gross Domestic Product in the non-oil exporting countries of the continent. The share of agriculture in the national product has, however, been falling in many African countries because of its relative decline rather than because of any improvements in the structure of the economy.

According to data supplied by FAO the annual growth of agriculture in Africa amounted to a mere 1·3 per cent in the years 1970 to 1977. Food production, accounting for 87 per cent of the total agricultural output, was also increasing by the same small percentage, which because of the growth in the number of mouths to feed, amounting to 2·7 per cent a year in the same period, represented a net and steady decline of production in relation to the average person in Africa.

Particularly worrying, according to ECA, has been the situation in West, East and, especially, in Central Africa. These three regions have been pulling down the average for the continent as a whole, which is particularly serious considering that the three regions represent over 70 per cent of the total population of developing Africa and about 66 per cent of the cultivated area (in 1977).

Three countries in Southern Africa, Botswana, Lesotho and Swaziland, have made the best progress in Sub-Saharan Africa. But out of 50 African countries only 17, with a population representing less than one-quarter of the total, have increased their agricultural production by more than 3 per cent a year, which is the rate considered to be the minimum for food supply per capita to be improved.[4]

TABLE I

Increase of output between 1970 and 1977, by product :

Food crops	11·3 per cent = 1·5 per cent a year
Animal products	8·9 per cent = 1·2 per cent a year
Mainly commercial crops	1·1 per cent = 0·2 per cent a year
All items	10·1 per cent = 1·4 per cent a year.

Source: ECA, Survey of Economic and Social Conditions in Africa, 1977–1978, p. 36

Although Africa has good and even excellent climatic and soil conditions for a number of crops, there have been only a few in the case of which output per hectare was higher than elsewhere and the only really important one was sugar cane. Average production of this per hectare in 1977 was 61 tonnes against a world average of 56 tonnes.

In the case of rice paddy and maize, for which Africa has a good climate, output figures per hectare were 67·6 per cent and 38·8 per cent respectively of the world averages in 1977, and it is interesting that in both cases the figures for Africa were significantly higher in 1970.

For two important cereal crops, which are staple food in many African countries, millet and sorghum, the figures for 1977 were 92 per cent of the world average in the case of the former and 55 per cent in the case of the latter. For all cereals the output per hectare in developing Africa in 1977 was 860 kg, the same as that recorded in 1970, but world average was 1,949 kg in 1977, or 11·1 per cent better than in 1970.

For three major cash crops exported from Africa—coffee, cocoa and cotton—the 1977 average outputs per hectare were 86 per cent, 85 per cent and 61 per cent of the world averages; in 1970 these ratios had been 100 per cent, 94 per cent and 76 per cent respectively.

Poor agricultural performance has necessitated large imports, especially of cereals and meat. Alarmed by this development African Ministers of Agriculture issued in November 1976 their Freetown Declaration with a call on FAO to produce a plan by which Africa could become self-sufficient in food supplies in 10 years. FAO then produced the Regional Food Plan for Africa which was adopted by the African Ministers gathering in Arusha, in Tanzania, in 1978, was endorsed by the Monrovia Summit conference and recommended by the 1980 Lagos conference of African Heads of State and Government. The Lagos Plan of Action itself incorporated the main ideas of the Regional Food Plan which to date remains the most authoritative and comprehensive analysis of Africa's food production problems.

FAO could not produce a plan that would make possible food self-sufficiency in 10 years time, as the Freetown Declaration called for. Instead, the FAO Regional Plan envisaged that the food self-sufficiency ratio, which declined from 98 per cent in 1962–1964 to 90 per cent in 1972–1974, might be increased to 94 per cent by 1985, provided that the massive investments and improvements suggested by the Plan were carried out. Otherwise, the self-sufficiency ratio would go on declining, probably to 81 per cent by 1985.[5]

Among the reasons for poor agricultural production one ought first of all mention the drought which frequently recurs in several areas, but most particularly in the Sahel, in western Africa. According to FAO 44 per cent of the land in Africa is subject to drought, or almost twice the world average. In addition, 55 per cent of the area is affected, or likely to be affected, by desertification against only 4 per cent in Asia and 1 per cent in South America. Desertification and drought are therefore two of the major problems affecting agriculture and rural life in Africa.[6]

Many areas in Africa have suffered from other calamities, such as locusts. Worse still has been the prevalence of trypano-somiasis: it is estimated that 21 African countries covering an area of approximately 10 million square kilometres are menaced by the tsetse fly. Other large tracts of land are affected by river blindness or onchocersiasis.

A very serious cause has also been social unrest. Agricultural production in the countries which gained independence in 1970–1977 decreased by as much as 27 per cent while in those countries which had major political upheavals it grew by only 1·3 per cent in that period. In fact, production growth per capita would have been slightly positive overall but for social unrest. In the group of countries where there was social stability the annual production growth rate was 2·8 per cent.

But, as ECA has pointed out: 'In addition to the exogenous factors such as drought or social unrest other factors more closely associated with agricultural policies such as investment pro-grammes in agriculture, incentives to farmers and the land-holding system hindering intensity of labour in farming should also certainly be held responsible for the situation.'[7]

Africa is the only developing region showing a decrease in the volume of tractor imports between 1971 and 1976. While the use of fertilisers per hectare doubled in the 10 years to the mid-70s it is still pitifully low by world standards at 12 kg of the nutrient per hectare. There has been little advance in irrigated agriculture, in spite of the great potential that exists for this in several parts of Africa, including the Sahel Zone.[8]

It is particularly difficult to improve farming methods and raise crop production when agriculture is based on multitudes of tradition-ridden smallholders, as is the case in most of Africa.

Not only are there not enough extension workers to teach better methods but many of those that there are lack such expertise as can be useful to the farmer or lack the ability to communicate with the farmer not knowing his way of life and problems. The inability to transmit to the smallholder the achievements of modern agronomy in a meaningful way has been a major failure of development in the Third World, but especially in Africa. It is however important to point out that the problem is now much better understood both by international organisations, such as FAO, and by local Governments.

One has recently seen many hopeful developments in this

respect: training courses for extension workers in which they are made to share in the life and work of the local peasantry and ordinary schools being geared to development needs as pupils and students are taught and trained in such matters as horticulture and agriculture so that when leaving school they will not only be literate but good farmers.

I have seen new concepts taking root in FAO circles over the past few years and such ideas being successfully applied in the field. In the past much too little attention was paid to the need to convince the local farmer that it is in his own interest to adopt the methods which the manager of a local farm development scheme was disseminating in the area. Many such projects, which are often run by expatriate experts provided by FAO, proved abortive and were often discarded as local people failed to take up the new ideas. In some a mistake was made by selecting a small number of exceptionally talented and eager peasants and concentrating the extension work and other assistance on them in the hope that they would act as models and would in due course be followed by others. What often happened however was that these exceptional and privileged peasants were treated as odd-men-out by their own community and may even have been driven out of the village!

It is now widely recognised that an agricultural expert introducing new and more productive ways of farming must be much more than only a good agronomist. He must have an understanding of the people around him and be able to bring them to his side, not only some of the people, but most of them, including the women and children because these can be of decisive importance as the actual workers in the field.

I have seen excellent results being achieved by this new approach in several parts of Africa recently, with productivity increasing considerably and incomes being doubled or trebled in a short time with comparatively little additional outlay. Helping this movement is an increasing awareness on the part of the farmers themselves that they must change their attitudes as otherwise they would not be able to ensure the survival for themselves and their families as pressure on land mounts and better farming methods are becoming imperative. To my mind, an important part of the battle for a reversal of the present trends in African agriculture will have been won when the farmers are truly persuaded of the need to change their attitudes to work. There is little doubt that an enormous potential exists in this respect in Africa and that one can be optimistic on this score.

Such views are also reflected in the Lagos Plan with its special emphasis on the need for new approaches and action on the part of the Governments as the main agencies for progress.

The Plan urges the African governments to set up specific annual goals for food and agriculture and recommends that an integrated approach should be taken to farming and rural life, particularly with reference to young people, in order to arrest the drift to urban areas.

'Over the years 1980–1985', the Plan says, 'the objective should be to bring about immediate improvement in the food situation and to lay the foundations for the achievement of self-sufficiency in cereals and livestock and fish products. Priority action should be directed at securing substantial reduction in food wastage, attaining a markedly higher degree of food security, and bringing about a large and sustained increase in the production of food, especially of tropical cereals with due emphasis on the diversification of agricultural production.'

Urgent measures are recommended in each of these areas. Significant progress must be made towards the achievement of a 50 per cent reduction in post-harvest losses (which at present amount to up to 40 per cent of the food concerned) by, among other things, constructing appropriate storage, processing and other facilities and training technical staff for food control work.

In regard to food security, African countries should aim as a first step at setting up national strategic food reserves of the order of 10 per cent of total food production. Agrarian reform programmes should be instituted 'consistent with the political and social conditions prevailing in respective countries'. There must be an improvement in the organisation of agricultural production.

African countries are urged to implement the FAO-prepared Regional Food Plan for Africa, but the main immediate objective should be to bring about quantitative and qualitative improvements in food crop production, including cereals, fruits, tubers, oil seeds and vegetables, with a view to replacing a sizeable proportion of the presently imported products. Besides, production of certain crops should be encouraged in countries which could grow them but as yet do not do so. In particular this should be done to reduce the increasing demand for wheat and barley by cultivating cereals such as millet, maize and sorghum.

A number of urgent measures are recommended in respect of food crops, including:

—promotion of better agricultural practices, particularly intensive use of improved input packages and plant protection measures;

—modification of the techno-economic structures of production, so as to provide the small farmers and members of production co-operatives with the necessary incentives to increase production;

—better utilisation of water for irrigated cereals on ongoing irrigation schemes and initiation of new schemes;

—soil and water conservation;

—flood control and drainage;

—intensification of the use of improved hand tools and draught animals and promotion of mechanised farming where justified;

—physical infrastructural development, including the building of small bridges, dams, access and feeder roads and the improvement of education, health and other social facilities, much of which should at this stage as far as possible be undertaken through voluntary self-help participation.

In respect of animal husbandry the Plan recommends:

—immediate support, training in animal health and establishment of specialised trypanosomiasis control units, improving the productivity of trypano-tolerant breeds, and integrated development of areas freed from tsetse, establishment of vaccine production facilities and an effective regional quarantine system and research in tick-borne diseases;

—animal breeding;

—control and eradication of foot and mouth disease;

—controlled grazing and range management;

—development of animal feeds and infrastructural development.

In regard to fisheries the annual fish production from African waters should increase by one million tons by 1985, which should permit a rise of 1 kg in the level of average annual fish consumption per person between now and 1985. Included among the proposed measures are the development of industrialised off-shore fleets and increased productivity by individual fishermen as well as better shore-based infrastructure facilities.

The Plan then specifies the following recommendation: 'It is strongly recommended that governments undertake the formulation and application of policies to ensure that prices of farm inputs and farm produce provide an adequate incentive for increasing food production particularly by small farmers, while safeguarding the interests of the poorer consumers at the same time. Efforts should be made to reduce the widening gaps of income between the rich and the poor in rural areas.'

The Plan suggests that forestry should be more closely integrated with agriculture to ensure adequate supplies of fuel wood and the contribution of forest resources to industrialisation should be increased. Among the most urgent measures recommended are organisation of inventories of national forest resources, control of soil erosion, stepping up of forestry regeneration programmes and expansion of forest reserves by 10 per cent over the next five years.

The Plan is critical of the agricultural research which has in the past addressed itself to a narrow spectrum of crops, neglecting a number of important food crops indigenous to the country. 'Yet', the Plan comments, 'such crops are grown by a large number of the rural population and constitute a major proportion of their diet.' Research in the area of root crops, tubers and soyabeans and into the improvement of production and nutritional values of all food crops should also be intensified.

Extension services should lay more stress on the spread of already existing technologies and the services must be strengthened so as to reach the bulk of the rural population rather than concentrating on a relatively small group of progressive farmers.

Training efforts, the Plan says, ought to concentrate on youth and women. There should by all means be more mechanisation but at the same time care must be taken that this should not lead to even greater dependence on industrial countries. However, special emphasis should be put on animal traction in the countries that have not yet reached the appropriate level of mechanisation.

The Plan gives a figure of $21,400 million at 1979 prices as total investment requirement for the implementation of the above measures. In addition expenditure for inputs would rise by about $560 million over the same period. This level of expenditure represents only part of the total as per Regional Food Plan which was approved by the Ministers of Agriculture in Arusha, Tanzania, in 1978 and endorsed by Heads of State in the Monrovia Declaration in 1979.[9] Additional resources will be necessary to cover the latter part of the decade.

The Plan reaffirms its support for the IFAD and the World Food Programme, appealing to the international community to place more resources at the disposal of these organisations. But it also says that it would be 'desirable' to aim at financing at least 50 per cent of the investment requirements from domestic resources.

Manufacturing Industry

Although manufacturing industry still represents only a small proportion of the total GDP—in 1977 there were only five countries in the entire continent where this share exceeded 15 per cent—fairly good progress is being made in the efforts put in by most African countries to step up industrialisation. It is particularly encouraging that the pace seems to have quickened lately and the percentage growth of manufacturing output in 1978 was significantly greater than in the previous year.

The overall average growth of manufacturing production in developing Africa in the period 1970 to 1978 was 6·7 per cent a year. This was less than the target of 8 per cent set by the International Development Strategy of the United Nations in the Second Development Decade, 1970–1980, but ECA has regarded 6 per cent growth and anything upwards from it as quite satisfactory, bearing in mind the general level of economic activity in the region and the handicaps imposed on the development of export industries.[10]

There have, as in all sectors, been marked disparities between the countries. As usual the oil exporting countries have done much better than the rest, achieving an average annual growth in manufacturing industry of 11·7 per cent. The other countries of developing Africa put together had only a growth of 5·1 per cent and those with a per capita income of less than $100 only

127

managed an annual average increase in the production of manufactured goods of 3·7 per cent.[11] Yet there was some growth practically everywhere.

Creation of employment opportunities being a very important reason why African countries want to step up their industrialisation programmes, it would be interesting to know exactly how successful the effort has been. Unfortunately no complete data are available, but according to the estimates of ECA for the period 1971 to 1976 employment in manufacturing industry rose by 5·6 per cent in West Africa and 2·7 per cent a year in East Africa. Mauritius, which has been blazing the trail of so many sound development ventures and programmes, was exceptionally successful in expanding its industries and thereby creating new employment. Setting up since 1971 mostly light industries, including clothing manufacturing, the island managed to achieve for every 1 per cent in real value added in the manufacturing industry an increase of employment of 1·7 per cent—far above the African average. The number of jobs in the industry between 1971 and 1976 rose from 9,200 to 26,400, or 25·5 per cent a year.

Yet, by 1979 it was clear that the efforts of the island to create a viable export-oriented light industry were meeting serious difficulties. The growth of production and employment declined and some plants, for instance one producing toys, had to shut down under the combined impact of competition coming from Far Eastern countries and lack of demand for the product due to recession in western countries. No African country, not even Mauritius, has yet joined that group of so-called 'industrialising developing nations', which includes Taiwan and South Korea, whose industries have been able to assert themselves in international competition. The success of these developing countries nonetheless has valuable lessons for Africa in that it shows that the Third World is by no means condemned for ever to play an inferior part in the international division of labour.

However that may be, the African countries in the earlier years of their independence—in the 60s and early 70s—directed their industrialising efforts chiefly into import substitution enterprise, but these policies often proved self-defeating as the industries thus set up only thrived behind high protective walls and thanks to other privileged treatment, all this leading to high

A 'trialogue' discussion held under the auspices of *Le Point* magazine in October 1980 in Paris. From left to right: M Claude Cheysson, EEC Commissioner for Development, Dr Chedly Ayari, President of BADEA, M Alain Dauvergne of *Le Point*, M Edem Kodjo, Secretary-General of the OAU, and Henri Jean-Baptiste, the French President's adviser for development co-operation.

Booming Kuwait City in 1980. The population increased from 96,000 in 1946 to 1·2 million in 1978.

In Burundi, where land is becoming scarce, a science-based approach to farming is particularly important. These students from an agricultural institute at Gitega are learning topographical surveying by doing practical field work.   (*Photo*: FAO.)

Road building in Kenya. More Arab aid goes towards the building of roads and other transport infrastructure than towards any other single type of development. (*Photo*: World Bank.)

River steamers moored at St Louis. The regulation of the Senegal river will improve navigation over hundreds of miles. (*Photo*: FAO.)

Weeding of rice paddy at an experimental station in the Senegal river basin. The steady supply of irrigation water resulting from the regulation of the river will facilitate yield improvements over a wide area. Arab aid has played a decisive role in the development of the Senegal river potential. (*Photo*: FAO.)

The author at the construction site of the Sélingué Dam project
accompanied by a Mali engineer.

A mosque near Sélingué in Mali, built by the villagers themselves.

Women play a leading part in agriculture over much of Africa. These ladies are learning to use a new tool under expert advice, in southern Mali. Arab aid is a significant source of the capital needed for agricultural development in the region.   (*Photo*: FAO.)

The pounding of rice is a common chore in Africa, as in this village in southern Mali.
(*Photo:* WFP.)

The author interviewing Dr Chedly Ayari, President of the Arab Bank for Economic Development in Africa (BADEA), Khartoum 1980.

BADEA's new headquarters in Khartoum, completed in 1980.

cost of production which the community as a whole in the end
had to pay for. Moreover such industries frequently required
considerable imports of spare parts and materials, so that even
from the point of view of foreign exchange there was little saving.
Later, some African countries gave preference to export
industries, but these also often had to be subsidised out of public
funds in order to survive against world competition. In some
countries industrial zones have been created in which privileges
are granted to any enterprise setting up business there for export.
BADEA has assisted such a zone in Liberia with a loan of $3·2
million approved in 1977.

At present the industries leading to linkages as between sectors
are more favoured. This tendency has also been supported by
Arab Funds, including BADEA, in such operations as assistance to
cement and brick and tile projects designed to serve local or
regional building industry. Industries linked to agrarian base
have also continued to receive favour with African countries.

Livestock, which constitutes one of the major natural
resources of Africa, is being developed in many countries on an
industrial scale. Notable examples of African countries seriously
engaged in livestock industries, comprising livestock production,
processing and marketing, are Botswana, Kenya, Ethiopia and
Liberia. The Botswana Meat Commission (BMC) in 1976 made
sales totalling $67·7 million and is regarded as the largest and the
most promising of all the country's industrial enterprises.
Currently, 50 per cent of BMC's raw material and hides and skins
are locally processed in Botswana's own tanneries. Other by-
products of BMC include bone meal, tallow and horns, most of
which are exported. BMC has established a cannery with the
capacity to produce corned beef from 300 tons of meat per
week.[12]

A healthy tendency has been noted of paying more attention
now to heavy (by African standards) industries, such as
chemicals and metal products rather than to light industries,
such as beverages, tobacco, clothing, furniture and paper
products. In developing Africa as a whole light industries
accounted for 68 per cent of the total in 1970, but this decreased
to 60·2 per cent in 1976, with the rest, or 39·8 per cent being
accounted for by heavy industries.

Decentralisation of industries seems to be increasingly the

trend in Africa. Many African countries now favour small-scale industries located in rural communities to provide employment where this is most needed and generally to bridge the gap between the country and urban centres. Particularly successful examples of this are found in Tanzania, Botswana and Senegal.

The Lagos Plan of Action thus sums up the reasons why an African country should develop manufacturing industries: 'Satisfaction of basic needs of population, utilisation of local natural resources, creation of jobs, establishment of a base for the development of other sectors, creation of the basis for assimilating and promoting technological progress and modernisation of society'.

In 1972 Africa accounted for only 0·6 per cent of world manufacturing production and 10 per cent of the Third World's. The Second General Conference of the United Nations Industrial Development Organisation (UNIDO) at Lima set the target for Africa to achieve 2 per cent of world production by 2000. The Lagos Plan now takes up this objective setting a target of 1·4 per cent of the world industrial production by the end of the Industrial Decade for Africa, 1980–1990 and urging that at the same time self-sufficiency in food, building materials, clothing and energy industries should be achieved. The Plan recommends that 'stress . . . be put on the need to establish links between industry and other sectors as well as between various industrial subsectors so as to promote interdependence among them and achieve harmonised industrialisation and overall economic development'.

The following targets are fixed in the medium term, up to 1990:
    a. creation of a solid basis for self-sustained industrialisation at the national and sub-regional levels;
    b. development of human resources to ensure that they are fully mobilised in the industrial development process;
    c. production in sufficient quantities of agricultural inputs, such as fertilisers, pesticides and agricultural tools and machines;
    d. production in sufficient quantities of building materials for the construction of decent urban and rural housing for the continent's growing population and in general to meet the economy's requirements in terms of building materials;
    e. development of the intermediate and capital goods

industries and particularly those intended for other
industries and infrastructural building;
f. on-the-spot processing and upgrading of an increasingly
large portion of the continent's raw materials;
g. satisfaction of industry's energy needs by developing the
different forms of energy available in the continent;
h satisfaction of textile requirements.

The following are the Plan's short-term objectives:
a. achieve at least 1 per cent of world industrial production;
b. lay the foundation for the phased development of the basic
industries essential for self-sufficiency since they produce
inputs for other sectors, i.e.:
        1. food and agro-industries;
        2. building industries;
        3. metallurgical;
        4. mechanical;
        5. electrical and electronic;
        6. chemical;
        7. forest industries;
        8. energy industry.

Among other specific policy recommendations the Lagos Plan
calls upon the African Governments 'to develop, encourage and
support African entrepreneurs to participate effectively in
industrial production with a view to a gradual acquisition of
control of the capital ownership in the sector by the Africans'.

Subregional and regional plans must be prepared for the
creation of major industrial complexes whose cost and production
capacity would exceed national financial and absorptive capa-
cities. African multinational industries should be established,
especially in such basic areas as metallurgy, foundry and
chemicals with high investment costs. There should also be
bilateral industrial co-operation among African countries through
joint ventures and otherwise. In order to obtain finance for such
industrial development which goes beyond the confines of any
one individual country the Plan mentions BADEA as one of the
possible sources of aid. The African countries, the Plan
recommends, should particularly try to 'obtain the additional
resources required to finance their industrial development from
financial institutions which, like BADEA, are controlled by

developing countries and in particular the oil exporting countries'.

Energy

The high cost of petroleum, which is with us to stay, has brought up rather suddenly the need for alternative sources of fuel and motive power. But Africa is very rich in these resources and it is in the interest of everyone, the Africans themselves, the petroleum exporting countries and the industrial world that these resources should be developed and utilised as fully and as quickly as possible.[13]

There are now about ten African countries which produce petroleum in any quantity although only four are major exporters. However, exploration, both on-shore and off-shore, for the hydrocarbons continues and is being stepped up in many parts of the continent. Africa is estimated to have 1·3 per cent of total world reserves of coal. A project in Niger for a thermal power station attracted a BADEA loan of $7 million partly because it was to be based on locally available coal rather than imported oil. Arab funds generally have looked with favour on projects designed to save on imported fuel. The Niger project also has some relevance to the exploitation of that country's chief resource, uranium. Africa accounts for 30 per cent of the world's thorium and uranium.

But of more direct and immediate relevance to Africa's energy situation is the huge hydro-electric potential of African rivers. It is estimated that the continent has up to 40 per cent of the world's entire hydro-electric potential, yet only some 5·6 per cent of this is presently exploited. Hydro-electric stations have indeed been among the favourites for Arab and BADEA finance in Sub-Saharan Africa, as we have already seen.

The hydro-electric project 'Champagne' in Mauritius has been singled out by UNDP[14] as an example of trilateral co-operation and a particularly felicitous development in an island suffering much from the high cost of fuel.

It may be worth while quoting the relevant passages in the document concerned, to illustrate the current thinking in the UNDP about the matter of energy and explain the problem as it is facing a country like Mauritius.

'As in the case of many other African countries', the UNDP

document says, 'most of the power in Mauritius is provided by thermal power stations fuelled by diesel oil, which is expensive and must be imported. Rising fuel costs, together with increased costs of shipping the many supplies which must be imported to satisfy the island's needs, have had a negative effect upon the country's balance of payments. The fact that sugar prices have been depressed in recent years has led to further deterioration of the island's economic situation.

'To lessen dependence upon expensive oil imports, and at the same time provide power for the development of new industries, with increased opportunities for employment, the Government is eager to make full use of its hydro-power resources. UNDP has been assisting the development of these resources since 1973 by financing hydro-power feasibility and design studies.

'Following up on initial studies, the current project has resulted in substantial investment commitments for the construction of the "Champagne" hydro-electric scheme on the Grand River South East. This river has a total catchment of approximately 65 square miles, and is the last major river in Mauritius to be developed for hydro-electric power. The scheme, which will take advantage of waterfalls in the region, will supply the island with 45 million kwh of electric power per year.

'Including provisions for inflation, the project is expected to cost a total of $45 million. $17 million of the total is being contributed by Arab Funds, the first Arab financial investment in Mauritius. $10 million is coming from the Arab Bank for Economic Development in Africa (BADEA); $5 million from the Kuwait Fund; and $2 million from the OPEC Special Fund (which comprises many Arab donors). The Arab loans are on a soft, long-term, low interest basis. The BADEA loan, for example, is redeemable over 15 years, including five years of grace, with an interest rate of 4 per cent.

'The project is an example of "trilateral" co-operation, linking an African natural resource with technical assistance from the industrialized world and financing from Arab, European and United Nations sources.'

The Lagos Plan of Action for its part provides an entire chapter on the problems of energy in Africa, urging the Governments to save on fuel and use other sources of power rather than petroleum. In this respect Africa has already built up a rich experience in various technologies for producing energy out of non-depletable sources.

Many African countries have been making progress in harnessing solar energy for pumping water for domestic supply and small-scale irrigation, for cooking, drying, water distillation and so on. Solar pumps are currently in operation in Chad, Kenya, Madagascar, Mali, Cameroon and elsewhere in Sub-Saharan Africa. Efforts are also being made in the biogas production field. In Kenya, bio-digesters produce not only methane fuel gas, but also excellent fertilisers. Wind energy is being used in parts of Africa to pump water, and work is done on the improvement of windmills by solving such problems as those related to jamming due to high winds, the best adjustment of the blades, better operation in low wind and increasing resistance to high and violent winds. Locally manufactured windmills have been installed in a number of countries, including Ethiopia, Mali, Senegal, Tanzania and Upper Volta. Cape Verde has an industry for the commercial production of windmills.

Perhaps the most exciting in these unusual ways of harnessing resources for energy has been that of utilising underground reservoirs of high-temperature water and steam to generate electricity. The idea is far from new, but it is only now, in view of the escalating cost of fuel imports, that it is being seriously considered and indeed implemented. The World Bank made history in Africa in January 1980 by granting a loan to Kenya of $40 million towards the cost totalling $89 million of the continent's first geothermal power station at Olkaria, about 100 km northwest from Nairobi.

The geothermal reservoir at Olkaria itself is believed to have a potential of 170 MW over a period of 25 years or more and there are two other known geothermal areas in the Rift Valley in Kenya. But the Rift Valley Region, which extends over a distance of 6,500 km from Turkey to Mozambique, abounds in geothermal potential.

Transport and Communications

In the whole of Africa there are only 78,000 km of railways which in a continent of 30 million sq. km represents an average of 2·63 km per 1,000 sq. km. The average in Europe is 63 km per

1,000 sq. km, with a total of 300,000 km of railways in an area of 4·75 million sq. km. Not only is the mileage negligible in relation to the demand for transport but the 38 networks operating in Africa are isolated from each other and use different gauges. To standardise and inter-connect these networks is a major task ahead, but preliminary studies have indicated that it would be necessary to construct 15,600 km of railway in order to link the isolated networks.[15]

The situation in respect to other transport communications is very much the same. Entire areas, rich in agricultural or other potential, remain sterile and undeveloped because of their isolation due to lack of railways, roads or other transport facilities. Transport communications are an essential pre-condition for any economic development and they are also a vital necessity if African economies are to be more closely integrated according to the present programme.

Understandably, African Governments generally give high priority to transport in their development plans and Arab and other aid agencies have been responding to this commitment by themselves allocating a very substantial part of their total aid for building of transport infrastructure, BADEA earmarking for this purpose nearly half of the total value of its loans approved in the first five years of operations.

Telecommunications, including telephone and telegraph, are not receiving the same kind of priority as transport on the part of African Governments. But it is nonetheless increasingly realised that good telecommunication services can be indispensable for development, especially if the intention is to attract foreign investment. Telecommunications are often a necessary concomitant of a transport system, including railways. African leaders have also been pressing for development of telecommunications in order to lessen the present dependence on European and American systems as too often communications, telephone and others, between African countries pass through the capitals of the industrial countries. In all cases communications between Africa and Europe are smoother and easier than between African countries themselves. It takes about two weeks at least for a letter to get from West to East Africa while it can make the journey in four days between the continent and Europe. More and more African countries have also been using radio broadcasting, and some even television, to reach outlying rural populations for purposes of education and general enlightenment. For this reason the Arabs have been strongly supporting the Pan-African Telecommunications Network (PANAFTEL). This originally covered some 20,000 km of transmission lines and 18 international exchange centres, but later, particularly after 1975, new needs appeared as PANAFTEL was to extend to newly independent and Least Developed Countries. In consequence, measures have been taken to carry out feasibility and pre-investment studies regarding the new links that have become necessary.

Aware of the need to concentrate on improvement and development of communications, drawing the attention of both African Governments and outside donors to the problem, the United Nations proclaimed a Transport and Communications Decade for Africa, 1978–1988.

The African Ministers of Transport, Communications and Planning defined at a meeting in May 1979 the principal goals towards which the African countries should work in the decade as: promotion of the integration of transport and communications infrastructures with a view to increasing intra-African trade; ensuring the co-ordination of the various transport systems in order to increase their efficiency; opening up of the landlocked countries and isolated regions; harmonisation of national regulations and reduction to a minimum of physical and non-physical barriers with the aim of facilitating the movements of persons and goods; stimulating the use of local human and material resources, the standardisation of networks and of equipment, research and dissemination of techniques adapted to the African context in the building of transport and communications infrastructure; promotion of an African industry in the field of transport and communications equipment; and mobilisation of technical and financial resources during the Decade with a view to promoting the development and modernisation of transport and communications infrastructures in Africa.

At the regional level ECA was designated by the UN General Assembly as the 'lead agency' with overall responsibility for the entire Decade programme, including co-ordination of the implementation of the plan at all levels and assisting in the mobilisation of the required resources.

Taking up the objectives of the Decade the Lagos Plan of Action for its part recommended a total of 450 transport and 100 communications projects for immediate implementation in addition to studies relating to 221 projects for implementation in later phases, costing a total of about $8·85 billion.

Broken down into sub-sectors the planned expenditure is as follows:

	In $ millions	%
Transport projects.		
I. Roads and road transport	1,796·19	20
II. Railways and rail transport	3,223·10	36·5
III. Maritime transport	320·04	4
IV. Ports	2,240·76	25
V. Air transport	632·74	7
VI. Inland water transport	86·2	1
VII. Multimodal transport	43·15	0·5
Subtotal	8,342·19	94
Communications projects.		
VIII. Telecommunications	223·48	2·5
IX. Communications by satellite	0·38	—
X. Broadcasting (radio and television)	169·41	2
XI. Postal services	44·35	1
XII. Manpower training in telecommunications	76·13	6
Subtotal	513·75	6
Total	8,855·94	100

In regard to 'roads and road transport' the projects are designed to promote the inter-connection of networks with those of neighbouring countries. Most of them are part of the planned Trans-African Highway—its main trunks and feeder roads—the object of which is to provide in the long run an effective network for the transportation of goods and persons which will facilitate trade and communications within and between African countries.

The 'railways and rail projects' are aimed at making the present railway services fully efficient. They deal with rehabilitation of existing tracks, purchasing of new rolling stock, and with training programmes at all levels to improve the operational and management efficiencies.

In respect to 'maritime transport' it must be said that African countries have only recently become interested in the industry. Technical assistance is urgently needed to set up various facilities needed for the development of maritime transport.

'Ports.' A substantial programme of renovation and provision of modern equipment is needed to enable the African countries concerned to cope with the fast expanding traffic they face.

'Air transport.' This calls for immediate improvement and supply of facilities and services required in African States in order to meet minimum standards and requirements needed for the desired number and type of aircraft to operate in the region, projects for extension and modernisation of airports representing the main body of the planned work. Priority is also given to training, and the setting up of a number of regional schools of aviation has been recommended.

In respect of telecommunications some African countries have expressed proposals going beyond the present PANAFTEL plan. The Secretary-General of OAU, Mr Edem Kodjo, criticised in his speech at the Lagos Conference the present system of satellite communications in Africa as 'balkanised', as some earth stations are directed, for instance, to American and others to French satellites. The Lagos Plan of Action echoed his concern and recommended that a feasibility study be made on a regionally integrated satellite system as well as the holding of seminars and workshops on satellite communications, all in the immediate phase of the project programme.

The Lagos Plan concluded: 'Transport and communications together constitute an essential tool which must be created, developed and maintained if African industry, agriculture, forestry and mining are to expand. African industries, however, which are in an embryonic stage of development and rapidly being left behind by the continuous progress of technology, and African efforts in . . . other fields, will not be able at one and the same time to satisfy domestic needs and also to generate the necessary resources for these purposes at the present rate of progress. Transport and communications are thus a prerequisite for development; with their aid, the immense potential of the continent can be rationally exploited with some chance of complete success.'

Demographic Movements

In one important respect progress achieved in Africa over the past two decades has been, as it were, self-defeating. General improvement in health services has resulted in a marked decline of mortality, but with high fertility persisting the growth of population is threatening to undermine any economic and social advance that is being made. The most serious has been the decline in production and supply of food per head of population, affecting particularly the least developed countries and the poorest sections of the population with the result that more people than ever before in Africa arc now suffcring from undernourishment and malnutrition.

The population of developing Africa was estimated at just over 401 million in 1975 and was expected to rise to 532 million in 1985 and 813 million in the year 2000.

While the death rate at nearly 20 per 1,000 is still high by international standards the crude birth rate at 46·3 per thousand (in 1975) is the highest for all the regions in the world, giving a population growth of 2·65 per cent[17] which again is the highest anywhere, almost double the world average, more than three times that of developed countries and about 14 per cent higher than the average for developing countries.

It is true that Africa is still more sparsely populated than any other continent, with 14 persons per square kilometre compared to a world average of 29, and 38 for the developing countries. But 44 per cent of the land in Africa is subject to drought, or almost twice the world average, and 55 per cent of the area is affected or threatened by desertification. Again, what is most worrying is that 90 per cent of the increment in agricultural production over the past 20 years has been obtained by expanding the area under cultivation and only 10 per cent by increasing the yields.

The population of Africa has also become younger than at any time in the past. Children aged under 15 years made up 44·2 per cent of the total in 1975. This has meant a great increase in the number of dependents. For every 10 persons between 15 and 65 years of age there are about 8·3 children under 15 years and 0·6 persons aged 65 and over, giving altogether 8·9 dependents, compared with an average dependency ratio of 7·5 in North America and Europe. In the developed countries the share of population under 15 years of age is about a quarter while the economically active group forms over 60 per cent in the developed countries compared with about 52·8 per cent in Africa.[18]

The proportion of children in the total population of Africa is likely to grow further on present trends as the youngsters reach child-bearing age. The present age structure also means that the rate of growth of population is likely to increase in the next few decades, to some 3 per cent a year. This is all having a very serious effect on economic as well as social progress.

It represents an ever increasing burden on such services as hospitals, schools and housing. It means that a higher proportion of the gross domestic production goes to consumption rather than for investment.

The growth of education in Africa has been in the words of ECA 'extremely rapid', with emphasis on secondary and higher education. In 1978 there were roughly about 50 million primary school pupils, a further 9·5 million students at secondary schools and some 900,000 in higher education. More recently many African countries have been adjusting the content of education in order to make learning of greater practical value and more purposeful in terms of economic, and particularly agricultural and rural, development. But the question is now how long the Governments will be able to sustain the present rate of education and training.

But even more worrying is the problem of finding useful employment for the young people that are in ever greater numbers pressing on the labour markets.

In Africa, where two-thirds of the world's least developed countries are found, ILO estimated in 1972 that 69 per cent of the total population of the continent were 'seriously poor', and 39 per cent were described as 'destitute'. Accompanying this was the very high rate of unemployment and underemployment, accounting together for about 45 per cent of the entire labour force. It was estimated in that year that about 10 per cent of the labour force in the urban areas were unemployed and 25 per cent underemployed whilst as many as 40 per cent were underemployed in the rural area. In other words, out of the total African labour force of 140 million in 1975 there were 10 million unemployed or underemployed in urban areas and more than 50 million were underemployed in rural areas.

Yet on present trends this situation will deteriorate catastrophically in the next four decades. It has been estimated that the total labour force in Africa will have increased to 225 million by 2000, with only about half of the number of new job seekers being able to find useful employment.

In view of the population pressure on resources in much of the Third World a great deal of thought, and some effort, have been invested by international organisations and Governments with the aim of reducing fertility by means of family planning programmes based on the supply of contraceptive material. Whatever the results of these efforts may have been elsewhere they have been insignificant so far in Africa. Mauritius is the only African country, and culturally by no means typical of the continent, known to have achieved a sharp reduction in birth rate, halving this in recent years to a level of only 1·3 per cent a year.

But in Mauritius the birth control campaign has been accompanied by general economic and industrial progress with resultant increase in the standards of living and greater employment opportunities for women as well as their social emancipation. It is questionable whether the birth rate could have been reduced without those factors which, incidentally, were the prime reason in the past for a decline in the birth rate in developed countries.

The majority of African countries have so far had no programmes for family planning. It has been estimated that only some 20 per cent of the total African population are covered by any such movement, either as part of direct Government policy, as has been the case in Botswana and Kenya, apart from Mauritius, or by voluntary organisation acting with tacit Government approval, as has been the case in the Gambia, Nigeria, Tanzania and Zambia, among others. Some countries with low population growth, including Gabon and Cameroon, have been pursuing pro-natalist policies.

But seeing the failure, by and large, of the family planning movement in Black Africa, expert opinion has been increasingly favouring an indirect approach, making limitation of family size part and parcel of a general educational and information exercise in which attempts to persuade people to practise birth control and space their children are combined with efforts to enlighten the community, particularly women, in respect of other matters conducive to a healthier and more prosperous as well as sensible and responsible way of life. Such matters include literacy, child care, nutrition, hygiene and home economics as well as improved agricultural methods. An example of this new approach has been the movement sponsored by FAO—the Programme for Better Family Living.[19]

I saw this at work in 1975 in Kenya where it was launched in 1972 with active participation and encouragement of the authorities, educational bodies and, above all, women's organisations. Yet when I asked in Nairobi, in mid-June 1980, after five years, about the results of these efforts I was told that the high birth rate in Kenya, exceeding 3 per cent a year, persisted undiminished.

It may well be true that the birth rate will go down once the people reach a higher standard of living. When people are poor, especially in rural areas, birth rate tends to be high partly because it does not matter so much to an individual family whether they have five or ten little children around. Besides, children are widely regarded as security for old age. There is also a strong tradition almost everywhere in Africa in favour of large families, a tradition that dies hard, as a man in Burundi explained to me:

'We shall need another generation before family planning can be successfully introduced here. According to our tradition it is desirable and important to have as many children as possible. In the past we reckoned that ten children were needed for four to remain alive. This is now no longer true, but it will take many years before people will draw the necessary conclusion.'

Kenya has demonstrated the narrow limits of what even the best organised rural educational programme can do when it comes to family planning. I saw in 1975 many energetic social workers in various parts of the country put in much personal effort to spread enlightenment, distribute the loop (as the favoured birth control device) and induce women to register at family planning clinics. In nearly every case I investigated the proportion of women actually visiting these establishments was very small and many even of those who had inserted the loop had later discarded it.

There is little scope for any large resettlement of African populations from areas of high density to regions where more people could be usefully accommodated. Emigration abroad, which played an important part in countries like Senegal from which many young men went to work in France and other European countries, is now becoming more difficult with unemployment and slow economic growth prevailing in the host countries themselves.

There is in other words no escaping the fact that the only solution to the demographic problem and indeed higher living standards in Africa is a vigorous pursuit of economic development, particularly in rural areas where much of the problem of high birth rate, poverty and underemployment is found. Giving priority to rural development is also necessary in order to arrest the present drift from land to towns and cities which has been causing such grave social problems in fast expanding slum and squatter areas. But urban population in Africa as a whole will, if the present trends continue, account in the year 2000 for nearly 40 per cent of the total as against some 30 per cent in the seventies.

The Least Developed Countries

The problems of Africa—poor economic growth, particularly in farming, high birth rate and attendant social difficulties, balance of payments deficits and general underdevelopment—assume a particularly sharp form in the least developed countries of the continent, with the factors retarding progress usually appearing all together and producing cumulative effects that are particularly disastrous. Out of the 31 countries in the world officially classed as Least Developed in 1980, 20 are in Africa and of these all but two are in the non-Arab region of the continent. In fact the Least Developed Countries make up about one-third of the total population of the continent.

Eleven of these countries are land-locked and have poor transport and communications links with neighbouring countries. Two are islands. The least developed countries would have to make exceptional economic progress in order to reach even the low average level of development in Africa. But instead of making faster progress than others the LDCs lag behind, widening the gap that separates them from the rest. In the period from 1970 to 1977 the Gross Domestic Product of the 20 African LDCs rose by only 3·2 per cent a year, or 1·1 per cent per head of population compared with an average growth of 2·3 per cent a year per head achieved by all the other African developing countries and 6 per cent a year, and 3·5 per cent a year per head of population, called for in the Strategy for the Second United Nations Development Decade.[20]

Most of these least developed countries depend on agriculture for their livelihood to a greater extent than is the case on average with the other African countries.

Yet it was only in two of the 20 of these countries in Africa that total agricultural production grew by the target rate of 4 per cent per annum in the 1970s. Drought and desertification, especially in the Sahel Zone, were major factors in this failure.

Efforts to diversify the economy and make it less dependent on what are in most cases primitive farming and animal husbandry have also been considerably less successful in the least developed countries than elsewhere. Growth in the manufacturing industries of these countries in the 1970s has been estimated at mere 2·1 per cent a year, compared with over 6 per cent a year achieved by the other developing African countries. Consisting mostly of consumer product output the manufacturing industries in Africa's LDCs account on average for only 13 per cent of these countries' combined GDP compared with some 20 per cent in the case of developing Africa as a whole.

Given the modest levels of manufacturing industries, transport and urbanisation the consumption of energy has been small. Moreover, much of the energy consumed comes from wood and agricultural waste products. Nonetheless the higher costs of imported energy have caused serious problems to many of these countries, particularly because liquid fuels make up a very high proportion, relatively speaking, of the total of commercial energy used by these countries, or about 80 per cent.

The problems faced by the LDCs have been subject of a great deal of international discussion and an agreement to do more for these countries is one of the few positive results of the North–South Dialogue.

According to information supplied by ECA, the transfers of capital benefiting the LDCs in Africa increased at a slower pace between 1970 and 1977 than was the case with the rest of developing Africa. Rising in nominal terms by 22 per cent a year on average the transfers to African LDCs reached a total of $2·3 billion in 1977, or less than half the average of $37 for Africa as a whole per head of population. Moreover the terms of aid supplied deteriorated as in 1977 only 44·5 per cent of the entire transfers received by LDCs in Africa was on concessional terms compared to 83·6 per cent in 1970.

As we have seen, much of Arab commitment for concessional aid to non-Arab Africa has been in favour of the LDCs, this being in 1979 well over half the total amounting to nearly $530 million.

According to estimates made by the ECA it is necessary that the developed countries should increase their concessional aid to African LDCs at constant prices in the 80s to levels four times larger than in 1977 in order that such assistance per head of population could increase threefold.

The Lagos Plan of Action has been critical of external aid for the benefit of the LDCs, commenting:

'Not only is the absolute amount of financial flows per capita to Africa's Least Developed Countries half the African average, but flows to the LDCs have grown less than for other African developing countries. In addition, conditions of aid have deteriorated with a declining proportion of Official Development Assistance and other concessional flows. There has also been a growing lag between the times an agreement is negotiated and the money actually paid. Discriminatory practices by some donors have also been putting a brake on the development effort of these countries.'

Yet the Lagos Plan places the primary responsibility for the development of their economies on the African LDCs themselves. The Plan recommends that priority should be given to the development of an agricultural base, not only for self-sufficiency but also for export, particularly of cereals. Industry must become a leading sector of the national economy with strong linkages to agriculture, and priority accorded to the processing of locally produced raw materials and production of basic inputs for agriculture. In transport and communications emphasis should be on feeder roads, transport facilities for land-locked countries and development of multinational transport systems. In energy, special attention must be paid to the development of renewable sources of energy in order to reduce dependence on external sources.

The Lagos Plan of Action deplores the present 'international environment' in which the African LDCs are required to sustain their economies. This environment has been 'extremely oppressive and indeed exploitative'. The least developed countries 'neither get fair values for their products nor receive any protection against the accelerating cost of technology and essential imports, including the cost of imported oil'.

To help improve the situation official concessional aid to African LDCs should be increased immediately and substantially in real terms, the Lagos Plan says. Assistance must be provided on a continuous and automatic basis and on highly concessional terms. Procedures of aid dispensation should be streamlined in order to reduce delays in approving projects and disbursing funds. Donors should refrain from using non-economic criteria in the allocation of aid. All debts contracted so far by the LDCs in Africa should be cancelled (these amounted to $5·4 billion in 1977). Appropriate mechanisms should be created urgently at international level in order to finance the oil requirements of these countries and reduce the existing heavy burden on their balance of payments and the uncertainty of the oil supply.[21]

The gloomy note struck by the Lagos conference was clearly meant to jolt African Governments, and the international community, out of any complacency that might still be around. The Africans were now called upon to look at themselves, to grasp the disastrous nature of the present trends and act in order to mobilise more of their own forces for development. They should also do more to co-operate among themselves and expand the intra-African trade from its present very low levels. The Conference commended such regional groupings as the Economic Community of West African States (ECOWAS) and pleaded that similar organisations should be set up in east, central and southern Africa.

Yet self-reliance does not mean isolationism. The Conference made clear the need for greater co-operation with other regions, including the Arab Gulf. Arab Funds, including BADEA, have for their part been supporting African integration, as we saw in the relevant chapter of this book. Mr Edem Kodjo, Secretary-General of OAU, mentioned the Bank in his speech at Lagos when he said that, 'BADEA...should be able on account of the important resources at its disposal to play a determining role in the financing of African projects leading to economic integration'.

The situation in Africa by the end of 1980 confirmed the need for urgent and drastic action for which the Lagos Conference had pleaded.

On the whole, things were worse in 1980 than at any time before. Agricultural production, which in 1979 rose only by 2·0 per cent, compared to 4·5 per cent in 1978, saw a further setback in 1980 as 26 African countries were facing shortfalls in food supplies owing to drought or refugee and resettlement problems. President of Mali, General Moussa Traoré, Chairman of the Permanent Interstate Committee for Drought Control in the Sahel, spoke in October 1980 of the region facing 'one of the most severe food crises in its history'.*

The countries of developing Africa were facing an unprecedented food import bill in 1980 of $6 billion, compared with only $1·9 billion in 1973. The import bill for petroleum and products was, according to information given to me by ECA in December 1980, expected to reach some $7 billion for the year. But more important in the total were payments for manufactured goods and services imported from industrial countries. The non-oil developing countries of Africa were according to projections made by IMF expected to register a deficit of $6·6 billion on their service account, in 1980, mostly for the benefit of industrial countries. Much of this was due to higher payments for debt services, the debts themselves having by 1978 reached a total of over $37·6 billion in the case of Sub-Saharan Africa alone.

Again according to IMF the non-oil developing Africa was expected to mark a deficit on the current balance of payments of $10·1 billion in 1980 compared with $8·5 billion in the previous year. But for many African countries it was now not so much the question of paying more for imports than of having to cut these, often of equipment and materials needed for development.

While Africa has been having these mounting payments problems external aid declined in real terms. According to projections made by IMF in 1980 official transfers (roughly equivalent to concessional aid) for the benefit of non-oil developing Africa were to increase from $2·4 billion in 1979 to $2·5 billion in 1980 and net capital inflows from $6·0 billion to

---

*Two Arab countries were singled out for special praise by FAO Director-General Edouard Saouma in October 1980 as Algeria and Libya promptly responded to international appeals for emergency food aid for Africa, by pledging $800,000 and $1 million respectively.

$6·2 billion. At the same time the share of official concessional assistance in the total resource flow has been falling markedly.

All these statistics must be treated with caution. I was told during my last interview with ECA officials in December 1980 that figures for Gross Domestic Product tend to give a distorted picture because of the inadequate weight given to productive activities compared with services, whose value may statistically increase if, for instance, a Government expands its civil service which in itself may not contribute to the creation of more wealth. On the other hand the figures only refer to the cash economy and do not cover the vast area of subsistence farming.

However that may be and however imperfect the data, they indicate an unmistakable trend of stagnation for most of the countries concerned and worse for many of them. They also make plain the need for greater co-operation, among the Africans, between these and the oil-rich Arabs in the Gulf and indeed with the developed countries which must shoulder the major part of responsibility for helping Africa.

Yet the value of such co-operation to the donor countries themselves must be measured against Africa's huge potential. After all this is a continent nearly half of whose population is aged less than 15 years. It is also a region exceptionally endowed with natural resources, as the Lagos Plan of Action said:

'In addition to its reservoir of human resources our Continent has 97 per cent of the world reserves of chrome, 85 per cent of world reserves of platinum, 64 per cent of world reserves of manganese, 25 per cent of world reserves of uranium and 13 per cent of world reserves of copper without mentioning bauxite, nickel and lead, 20 per cent of the world hydro-electrical potential, 20 per cent of oil traded in the world (if we exclude the USA and USSR), 70 per cent of world cocoa production, one-third of world coffee production and 50 per cent of palm oil production, to mention just a few examples.'

NOTES

1. *Survey of Economic and Social Conditions in Africa, 1977–1978,* ECA, E/CN. 14/697/Part I, February 1979, p. 4.
2. Shortages of fuel have impeded the transport of food and other commodities in Tanzania, according to *World Development Report 1980,* The World Bank, Washington, August 1980, p. 5.
3. *Lagos Plan of Action for the Implementation of the Monrovia Strategy for Economic Development in Africa,* OAU, Addis Ababa, ECM/ECO/9 (XIV) Rev. 2, p. 9.
4. *Survey,* op. cit. p. 36.
5. *Regional Food Plan for Africa,*FAO, July 1978, ARC/78/5.
6. *Survey,* op. cit. p. 38.
7. Ibid., p. 38.
8. *Regional Food Plan,* op. cit., p. 5.
9. Ibid., p. 31.
10. *Survey,* op. cit. p. 38.
11. Ibid.
12. *Application of Science and Technology to Development in Africa,* UNDP, TCDC/AF/7. 24 March 1980, p. 29.
13. *World Development Report 1980,* The World Bank, pp. 14–18.
14. *Application of Science and Technology,* op. cit. p. 47.
15. See Annual Report, 1979, BADEA, p. 8. See also *Development of Agriculture and Transport Sectors in Africa,* BADEA, Khartoum, 1980, pp. 22–31.
16. *Lagos Plan of Action,* op. cit. p. 84.
17. *Survey,* op. cit. pp. 120–121. See also *World Development Report,* op. cit. pp. 64–70.
18. *Survey,* op. cit. p. 13.
19. In 1977 the Programme was taken over by the Kenya Government Rural Services Co-ordination and Training Unit.
20. *Survey,* op. cit. pp. 129–134.
21. *Lagos Plan of Action,* op. cit. pp. 109–110.

4

Africa—Where The Action Is

I met Léopold Sédar Senghor, President of Senegal, in Khartoum in July 1978 when he was attending the Summit conference of the Organisation of African Unity. I was then trying to interview as many African leaders as possible about their views on Afro–Arab co-operation. President Senghor is regarded as one of the founding fathers of the movement. His country, Senegal, in West Africa, has been a fertile ground for Arab and Islamic influences over centuries.

When I rang his suite in the Khartoum Hilton I was hoping to contact one of his aides to arrange for an appointment. But the voice at the other end said: 'It's me, I *am* Senghor', adding in a friendly tone, 'come up here for a chat'.

He is a short, slightly built man with a professorial manner. He was most communicative, talking at length about himself and his views, about the Yugoslavs he had met in his life and how the Gestapo once had him lined up against the wall in wartime France ready to shoot him. But why was he so interested in Islam and the Arabs, being himself a Christian?

'I am a Christian', he explained, 'but a large majority of my people, the Senegalese, are Muslim. In our country the North particularly has been influenced by Islam while some of the regions in southern Senegal are mostly Christian or animist. When Islam first came to my country it was grafted on to an African and Negro culture, creating an Afro–Arab symbiosis, very typical of my country.'

We were now on his favourite ground, the cultural influences which shaped the nations of Africa and the world, conditioning human beliefs and actions.

'Already as a Member of Parliament in Paris', he continued, 'shortly after the war, I used my influence in the field of education, to bring home to the French people the importance of learning Arabic and studying Arab culture. It was in fact due to my intervention that in 1950 the French Government introduced Arabic as an optional subject in French secondary schools.

'In my own country I have since 1960 been working for the spread of Arabic in our educational institutions. It is now regarded in Senegal as an important foreign language, after English and German, with French of course being the official language and lingua franca, given that there are six native tongues in Senegal. We are now also setting up a special university to give courses in comparative language studies. Twenty per cent of the students will be Europeans learning African languages and Arabic.'

President Senghor explained to me that reading the Koran and other Islamic and Arabic scriptures at an early age, as many do in Senegal, encouraged abstract thinking.

'We seem to be the only country in Africa', he said, 'which is self-sufficient in mathematicians. But this gift may also explain why no less than 20 per cent of our university students take science-based subjects for their courses. This, I am certain, has something to do with the influence of Arabic and Arab heritage on our people through the ages.'

President Senghor then told me how in his view the Africans and Arabs resembled and complemented each other.

'We both have a passionate streak in our temperaments', he said, 'we tend to look in the same, often artistic and even poetic way, on the world.

'But the complementarity is due to the Africans being rather more earth-bound and realistic as they are mostly cultivators of soil. The Arabs, on the other hand, are heirs to a nomadic tradition. Inhabiting wide spaces they are inclined to be more imaginative and broad-minded. But a blend of these qualities produces remarkable results. In fact all great civilisations have sprung up in areas of cultural contact and interchange. We Senegalese are close to the Mediterranean influence where European races meet the Semitic and Negroid peoples...'

But how important is all this for economic and political developments?

'I believe', President Senghor said, 'that it is more important to have first a new cultural rather than a new economic order in the world. If an American takes for granted the appalling discrepancies and inequalities in the present international economic situation, for instance that the average income in America is some $7,000 a year while in many African countries it does not exceed $200, this is because he thinks in terms of his people's *cultural* superiority.

'He thinks that because of his cultural difference and alleged superiority it is quite natural and wholly acceptable that his own standard of living and opportunities in life should be so much greater than those of an African.

'We must endeavour to demolish such cultural prejudices and fallacies before starting to build a new international economic order, all the more so because the Arabs and Africans both have a great deal to offer mankind in the fields of culture and the arts. European composers and choreographers increasingly draw on African traditions. We, Africans and Arabs, can contribute a wealth of experience to a world-wide union of cultures, but more particularly to a fruitful merger of European, Arab and African traditions.'

It was not that President Senghor underestimated the significance of financial and economic co-operation, especially the former. But here again, he was looking forward to a wider concept.

'There must be more co-operation in the economic field as progress in the financial domain is already very considerable', he said, 'but here I regard it as vitally important that we Africans and Arabs should join Europe in a trilateral partnership.

'In such partnership the Europeans would contribute technology and know-how, the Arabs would supply finance and we, the Africans, can provide labour and our very substantial natural resources for development.'

I pointed out to him that his ideas seemed to be very close to those of some of my Arab friends, notably Dr Chedly Ayari. President Senghor knew of BADEA, which he said was 'blazing the trail with imaginative projects of financial co-operation' from which Senegal too was drawing considerable benefits. 'Dr Ayari is my personal friend', he added.

One can see some of the cultural inter-action President Senghor talked about in *Senegal*'s capital, Dakar. When I visited the city in 1979 Europeans were conspicuous, including young men with cropped hair and military bearing, although in civilian clothes. You saw Africans from many parts of French-speaking

Africa, Dakar being the commercial and banking as well as the cultural centre of the region, while numerous Lebanese shopkeepers added a touch of the Near East. This is a lively, cheerful city, with friendly and hospitable people always ready to discuss any conceivable subject, displaying their command of the French language and sense of Cartesian logic.

I found a bewildering multitude of views and organisations in Dakar, a free flow of many schools of thought, albeit all sharing a certain decorum, and respect, and even reverence, for the Father of the Nation.

The French way of thinking, culture and language provide a framework for the debate as well as terms of reference. It is remarkable, and significant, how many native people in French-speaking Africa identify with French culture, even though the French themselves, having learnt much after the last war, take care to accommodate local susceptibilities and pride.

In most of French-speaking Africa co-operation between the French Government and officials on the one hand and local people on the other seemed to be very good and purposeful, especially in regard to economic development and financial and monetary stability. But this in turn creates something of a problem of communication and inhibits dialogue between the Francophone Africans and the rest, including the English-speaking. An educated man from a French-speaking part of Africa usually knows a great deal more about France and Paris than about a neighbouring African country when this is not Francophone, although this is also true the other way round.

Dakar is not Senegal, just as Nairobi is not Kenya. These modern cities, with their good food, fun and amenities, are oases of essentially foreign culture implanted on African soil, but their influence radiates far and wide and some of the wealth trickles down even to the very least privileged, hence the attraction of such urban centres for the rural proletariat — and the grave social problems now accompanying the inordinate growth of many towns in Africa.

The principal reason for my visit to Senegal was to look at the conditions under which the celebrated Project for the Integrated Development of the Senegal River was emerging.[1] Although no work had yet started early in 1979 in the field of organisation, the '*Office de mise en valeur du fleuve Sénégal*', OMVS, had been in existence for some seven years, with its head office in Dakar. Administrative problems are all the more complicated as this is the case of an organisation set up and controlled by three sovereign African States, Senegal, Mauritania and Mali, with Guinea, where the 1,800 km long river actually originates, having opted out of the scheme some time ago.

The great river, which after leaving Guinea takes a wide loop across western Mali, provides much of the border between Mauritania and Senegal, and ends in a large delta near the old French colonial port of St Louis in northern Senegal.

The Senegal river provides a livelihood for some 2 million people in the actual basin and adjacent areas, but it has been estimated that the lives of about a quarter of the entire population of Mali, Mauritania and Senegal directly or indirectly depend on the river whose waters fluctuate between too much and too little. For some hundred years experts have been in agreement that to bring the fickle river under control and harness the potential resources would be to find the key to prosperity for millions of African people in the region.

It was nearly 60 years ago that a French hydrologist first worked out a coherent project to utilise the resources of the Senegal river for economic development with the help of a dam to regulate the flow and secure a regular supply of irrigation water for farming.

After that study a great amount of research followed, the most recent being undertaken with the help of the United Nations Development Programme. The Senegal river potential is probably the most thoroughly researched development subject in Africa, with all the relevant literature now available at an excellent documentation centre in St Louis.

All the studies seemed to agree that what was increasingly a vale of tears, particularly when drought hits the river basin, as it did in 1972–1973, could be turned into a region of plenty, a granary not only to feed local people but to provide for exports as well, if only the flow of the waterway could be regulated.

It was only in 1978 that progress in mobilising financial support for the implementation of the project was sufficient to turn an old dream into something of a reality, and this could not have been achieved without Arab help. In that year Saudi Arabia, Kuwait and Abu Dhabi together finalised their pledge for total aid amounting to $218 million. With several other international and bilateral agencies, including those of the West German and French Governments, committing for their part a total of $225 million, the project became feasible by March 1979. Although it was calculated that $663 million would be needed to complete the first phase of the project, enough money had now been secured to start the work, in the hope that more donors would back the project and more money become available for the subsequent stages of implementation. But it was not till May 1980 that the first stone was laid to construct the Diama dam near the river delta and it would be some years no doubt before the construction would begin of the other dam, 930 km upstream, at Manantali, in Mali.

From a vantage point at the top of a small hill I looked at the future construction site at Diama. A vast panorama offered itself, flat country with patches of green which might be paddy. But there were also spots of white, like snow melting in the spring. This was salt deposited there as sea water penetrates the delta and a long stretch of the river upstream at low ebb or in the dry season, but particularly in times of drought. One purpose of the Diama dam is to stem the penetration of sea water and prevent the intrusion of salinity onto the fields in the delta. This should enable two harvests a year to be made of rice and other crops in the delta region on the present irrigated area of 6,000 hectares. But the reservoir constructed at the Diama will make possible irrigation over an additional 30,000 hectares. The dam will also supply fresh drinking water to urban areas in a wide region.

Africa boasts 15 great rivers with large irrigation potential but the River Senegal is regarded as being particularly well suited for development, especially because it runs through the frequently drought-stricken Sahel region. But it takes a long time to move from a blueprint to actual work on a dam, and from that work to actual irrigation.

Literature provided to me by the OMVS made clear it would be well into the next century before the total irrigable area of about 300,000 hectares will in fact have been brought under water with the help of the two dams. The work on irrigation projects is expensive and takes a long time. It is estimated that at first only some 5,000 hectares will be added every year to the irrigated area in the basin, increasing to 10,000 hectares (or 25,000 acres) in later years.

This means that many of the people now living in the valley will be dead by the time the project really begins to pay its way. Yet even now when the project was little more than a plan hopes were already raised, with significant concrete results. Many people appeared to be changing their minds about leaving the valley. A young man working on five acres of irrigated land told me that he had problems getting water at present as the river supply was insufficient and erratic, last year his crop of rice had been very poor and he was now barely able to provide for himself, his wife and a small child. He had a job lined up in Paris. But now, with news of the river regulation project he had decided to stay.

One of the main purposes of the project is to arrest the drift of people away from the valley, something that has been going on through the ages. It was from this region that many of the formidable 'Sénégalais' soldiers came to help fight French wars. Many Senegalese have been emigrating to Europe, especially France. Above all, they converged on large towns, such as Dakar. Part of the French and German Government interest in developing the region is due to a desire to make people stay there and possibly induce some of those now in Europe to return home to the valley. To make a success of the irrigation schemes, hard-working and intelligent men will be needed. Unfortunately it is often the best who emigrate.

But several research stations along the river, staffed by FAO experts, have already shown how crop farming can be improved under irrigated conditions. So far these admirable achievements of applied research have been of relatively little use to the farmers, even when working on artificially irrigated land, as these are reluctant to experiment and bring in new or improved varieties of crops for fear that lack of water might jeopardise any additional outlay of money or effort needed for innovations to be carried out.

In one of the stations, at Guédé, some 150 miles up the river, a Rumanian agronomist showed me a variety of maize he himself had developed, which gave yields seven times bigger than the local sort. He also introduced a special variety of wheat—at present a little known crop in the basin—with grains protected by hair-like thorns against birds, which cause a great deal of damage to such crops in the region. Across the river, some 50 miles further upstream, at Kaedi in Mauritania, a Turk developed rice which matured weeks before any other variety of the crop known in the region.

In developing these crop varieties the researchers always took account of the need to make the plants particularly resistant to insects and other pests abounding in the region. Rotation patterns were fixed to take maximum advantage of irrigation; one involving two harvests of rice and one of wheat a year, resulting in the cultivating family's income becoming incomparably higher than it would have been had they relied on traditional farm practices. It was possible, by introducing the improvements under suitable conditions of regular irrigation water supply, to achieve higher incomes for people involved in farming than they would have had for a relatively well-paid job in town.

This ingenious and of course costly work of research along the river, however, seemed to me somewhat misguided, because it was not really utilised by the neighbouring farmers. But the main reason for this failure was that near perfect irrigation conditions are needed to achieve good results from better crop varieties. So that the wealth of experience patiently accumulated in these research stations, now operating under the auspices of the OMVS, should be a great help when the river is finally regulated and sufficient irrigation water is assured all the year round.

However, many of the people in the basin will benefit from the scheme as soon as the dams are built, both of them, it is hoped, by 1985. Farmers relying on the traditional form of irrigation, the 'oualo', when the river directly floods the adjacent fields, on a total of some 100,000 hectares in the region, will no longer suffer deprivation as they did in the terrible recent drought. Until all the planned modern irrigation is introduced, which may take well into the next century, the additional water made available by the river can be used by the 'oualo' farmers.

Profiting from the new development in the river basin will be also the distinct race of herdsmen, the Peuls. Those tall, handsome people are the traditional pastoralists, fitting into a time-honoured division of labour with their settled neighbours, the Oulofs, Toucouleurs and others. They will be able to receive more and better feed for their animals as agriculture improves in the valley. They will also be paid more for the animals they sell off. The hope is that some of these semi-nomads will eventually modify their way of life and settle permanently along the river, which would make it much easier to provide them with health and veterinary services, schooling and other facilities. But development in the basin will also help agro-industrial ventures to emerge, as some have already. For a number of years a plant has been operating to export frozen meat to Libya, another is making tomato paste. Yet another which I saw was turning out 30,000 tons of sugar a year based on locally grown cane.

It needs pointing out that conditions along the Senegal river are far from primitive, or even typically African, in much of the region. I travelled more than a hundred miles from St Louis on an excellent asphalted road. The villages through which I passed had brick-built houses and nearly every settlement had a mosque, many of them new and fairly elaborate, with the characteristic twin-minaret architecture. They were probably built with the help of money sent by emigrant workers. Others were simpler, constructed by the villagers themselves. The people, dressed in their respective national costumes, usually featuring long robes of vivid colour, and women wearing large turban-like headgear, had a natural dignity and seemed confident, although many of them still suffered from the consequences of the 1972–73 drought. Several of them told me they could only survive thanks to the extended family system, whereby everything is shared and nobody is consequently left in absolute need.

There can be no question of these people not being motivated by money or not understanding the importance of cash, as may be the case in some other parts of the continent. But poverty and under-development become more pronounced as one goes further upstream, with traditional African mud-and-wattle huts beginning to prevail and knowledge of French rare. At Manantali, roars and noises of wildlife disturb the night.

Mali, a vast country between the Sahara and tropical Africa, formerly known as the French Sudan, is one of the world's poorest countries, combining the problems of the under-privileged under the headings of the Least Developed, Most Seriously Affected and Sahel Countries. Mali is heavily dependent on outside assistance. Almost the entire five-year development plan, 1974–1979,[2] costing about $1,000 million, was financed from external aid, with Europeans, including particularly the French and the Germans, the Arabs and international agencies, providing the bulk of the assistance. After independence in 1960 Mali had a reputation as one of the most radical and pro-communist countries in Africa, but this regime, which was also marked by severe repression at home, was replaced, following a coup d'état in 1968 by military rule headed by the popular and pragmatic President Moussa Traoré whose government in more recent years has acquired a broader, politically organised base.

Mali, a country of nearly 6 million people, had a Gross Domestic Product in 1977 amounting to a mere $110 per head. Yet Mali seems full of promise and I found the Government and the people bent on lifting their country from the present state of poverty and excessive dependence on foreigners. The Malians are, on the whole, a serious people, hardened through suffering caused by natural and man-made calamities. One is impressed by their patriotism and positive purpose.

The Malians have a keen sense of history. Many of them identify with past glories of an empire of long ago when remarkable levels of civilisation and sophistication were attained. Names like Keita or Moussa, are very common in Mali. They are names of the country's rulers in those times and many local people claim to be direct descendants of those strong men of the past. Islam is a powerful social force in the country and the great mosque recently built with Saudi help in the capital city of Bamako is now perhaps the most striking building in town and a centre of social as well as religious activities. Relations with the Arabs have been close for centuries.

In a conversation with me President Moussa Traoré spoke of these close ties with the Arabs going back to ancient times, but becoming more important with the spread of Islam whose message radiated from Timbuctu far over western Africa.

'Our Emperor (or Mausa) Moussa', he told me, 'made history in the Middle Ages by his celebrated pilgrimage to Mecca on which he took one thousand camels laden with gold. There were a thousand men in the caravan carrying as much gold as the weight of each multiplied by their total number. On his return the Emperor brought with him Arab scholars, engineers and architects who then constructed many important projects, buildings and monuments in my country, some of which can still be seen.'

I cannot vouch for the historical accuracy of this story, but I think it is significant, as most of the Malians I met knew similar tales from their country's past. But this awareness of historical roots undoubtedly now plays an important part in the Mali nation-building process. The glory of the past is contrasted with the misery and deprivations of the present, but memory is acting as a spur to work for a brighter future.

Indeed, some of the precious metals and other minerals which played an important part in the country's economy a long time ago are being rediscovered. President Traoré did not think that close relations with the Arabs in the past, or for that matter the Islamic heritage in Mali, played any significant role in the present close ties with the Arab world, ties which he himself had done much to promote.

While Mali, he said, was poor and needed help his country also had exceptional potential for development. It was in the long run in the interests of the Arabs to help develop this potential. He hoped particularly to attract Arab private investment as the new legislation in Mali now encouraged and protected such flows.

'Mali has great irrigation possibilities', President Traoré went on, 'particularly along the river Niger, nearly half of whose length of 4,700 km flows through our country. Anything up to 20 more dams can be built to harness these resources in various parts of the country, to serve farm irrigation and hydro-electric development. Our first aim is to become self-sufficient in food and we want to increase the output of rice, wheat, sugar cane and cotton for export as well. Eventually we should become significant exporters of these commodities in Africa. Besides, Mali is very rich in such minerals as iron, bauxite, uranium, gold and diamonds.'

To the dynamic Minister of Industry, Lamine Keita, whom I interviewed in Bamako, which is in southern Mali, in 1979, when I arrived there from Senegal, hydrology was the key subject.

It was much due to his drive that the Sélingué Dam project,[3] some 150 km south of the capital, the most important single development scheme of the current five-year plan, could take off, with the help of western expertise and finance, but also thanks to substantial Arab financial assistance.

The construction of the Sélingué Dam was about half-way

through its implementation when I saw it in 1979. All the work was due for completion in August 1980. I was told by the management that the project had already won fame in world development circles, among engineers and economists. Delegations from as far as China and Russia had come to see the site. The scheme was an excellent example of trilateral co-operation. The implementation was well on schedule and there was no appreciable cost overrun.

Estimated cost in March 1979 was $142 million for the completed scheme, of which $60 million was contributed by grants and soft loans from the Arab Funds and Governments. BADEA itself contributed an exceptionally large loan of $15 million.

The Sélingué Dam project, situated on the river Sankarani, a tributary of the Niger, includes a power station to generate 181 GWh of electricity, mainly for the supply of Bamako, and a reservoir to provide enough irrigation water for some 55,000 hectares. The reservoir will be about 50 km long, covering an area of 45,000 hectares and suitable for fishery development and tourist recreation. Among other benefits brought by the project will be an improvement of navigation on the river Niger.

As the work on the project started in 1976 life began to change in the surrounding area. Some 1,200 local men soon found employment as labourers and in certain cases as skilled men and technicians, a few of them top-grade.

Neighbouring farmers were now able to sell their vegetables and other produce to the workmen on the building site. Many of these were for the first time in their lives earning cash. A 53 km hard surface road built with a grant from Saudi Arabia to link the project area with a national highway opened up a remote area. People from far away could come here now in their vehicles and purchase farm produce and fire wood.

Villagers in the neighbourhood of Sélingué told me how their lives had improved thanks to the new commercial and other activities that came with the project. This, of course, may change again when construction work ends, as very few people are needed to run a hydro-electric station. But having acquired a taste for greater purchasing power and seeing that this could be had in the village itself, without any need to move to an urban centre, the people here will no doubt find other jobs as the area is now open to the outside world. Many villagers told me they would prefer to stay where they were and take advantage of the extended family system which provides good protection and security, whilst in town they would be in most cases on their own when ill or destitute. An important lasting benefit of the project will also be the training and experience of working on the construction of a power station and dam for many Malians. When the work is completed at Sélingué these can be moved elsewhere, perhaps to Manantali, where the construction of a hydro-electric station as part of the OMVS scheme had to be dropped to the chagrin of Mali, from the present phase of the project, because of the escalation of cost estimates. But the Malians are determined to build the power station, in co-operation with their neighbours or on their own.

Shortly to benefit from the project will be the numerous villagers along the River Sankarani. Life in the past has been very hard indeed for these people because of general lack of opportunities, under-development and natural calamities, including drought. But to all these problems has been added another: onchocersiasis, river blindness. It was sad to notice blind young men being led around by children with the help of a stick. I was told in several villages along the river that two out of three people were affected by the disease and about 10 per cent on average of those affected lose their eyesight, while general debilitation occurs in every case. Onchocersiasis, which is only one of a number of major scourges affecting the health of the people in Africa, is transmitted by blackfly. This only survives along fairly fast flowing rivers. The dam will slow down the Sankarani and thus help eradicate the vector.

Another important development project in which BADEA has participated with a loan of $5 million, which became effective in 1978, is the so-called Mali-Sud Project involving nearly 350,000 economically active people and a cultivated area of nearly 700,000 hectares.

This project grew out of a cotton scheme and the cash crop still plays a pivotal part. A very important objective of the project is to combine agricultural production with livestock raising in such a way that one industry helps another, for example cotton seed providing an important supplementary feed for livestock.

BADEA assistance is mostly being used to improve veterinary

facilities, and when I visited the project, which was some 100 miles from Bamako, I was told of the successes that had been achieved by vaccination of cattle against bovine plague, bovine pleuro-pneumonia, trypanosomiasis and other diseases. This was a clear case where massive vaccination brought the most damaging diseases practically under control. But more equipment was needed and I was told of delays in the procurement of items paid for by BADEA.

The project Mali-Sud began to be implemented in 1974/75, prompted by the bitter experience of the drought two years earlier. By 1979 one could feel that if the drought came again its consequences would no longer be as disastrous, thanks to this project.[4]

It is always difficult for a passing stranger to assess a development scheme, and its success or otherwise, although one does acquire a certain instinct for these matters. Project managers will usually want to show you the best, but often there is nothing good to show. Clearly in such cases the project has been a failure. If some good can be shown, even if it is not typical of the whole project, the hope is there that things will develop in a positive direction, unless the apparent success is the result of deliberate concentration on a few individuals. In such case success is a misleading term as ultimate results may often be counter-productive.

I had no reason to think that the farmer I was introduced to was in any way held up as a model to others. He was just a man with a fairly substantial amount of land, industry and intelligence, ready to take advantage of what the project was offering him. He now owned 110 head of cattle, selling between five and ten a year, and he grew cotton on eight hectares and other crops on a similar total area. His family, including two wives and ten children, numbered 30. He said that if he had more money he would give more and better feeds to his cattle.

Yet now he was thinking for the first time in his life of making a pilgrimage to Mecca. The project had changed his life. He had no idea before how important cotton seed could be as supplementary feed for his cattle, how much the yields of food crops and cotton could be increased by relatively little additional effort; he had little idea of the importance of good manure; his animals had in the past often been sick while now the project guaranteed their health; and he had learned to make silage. All these matters he had learned, he told me, from the project extension workers and put them to good use as he did with other services provided for him. He may not have been typical of his kind, but there was undoubtedly a general improvement of standards in the area. The project, assisted by FAO expertise, was well thoughtout and successfully implemented.

If Mali is a staunchly Muslim country *Burundi*, or for that matter neighbouring *Rwanda*, former Belgian dependencies and before that German colonies, can be taken as examples of Christian, particularly Roman Catholic, impact in Africa. In Kigali, the newly constructed capital of Rwanda, undoubtedly one of the most successful and attractive urban ventures in the continent, with fine, modern buildings well spaced between areas of luscious vegetation and all spread over a number of hills, the beautiful Roman Catholic church attracts large multitudes of people of both sexes and all ages, their singing filling the air over a great distance.

On Sunday church bells are to be heard across the hills as people rest outside their houses, many listening to transistor radios. In Bujumbura, the capital of Burundi, the Roman Catholic cathedral, again built in attractive modern style, is unquestionably the most impressive building in the city, after the magnificent hotel called Source du Nil.

I found both Rwanda and Burundi, in which I travelled extensively to look at a number of development projects, mostly assisted by UNDP, rather advanced and well supplied with schools, hospitals and services and people reasonably well-dressed and healthy looking. This outward appearance must be contrasted with what we know about the very low income per head of population and other economic problems. Yet the problems were less in evidence than a certain order and well-being. This no doubt owes a great deal to Christian missionaries who are appreciated and popular in both countries.

Christianity generally has not taken such a strong hold over the parts of Africa where it spread as has Islam. Christian churches and institutions in Africa evidently still depend considerably on their ties with Europe and America. Their relatively recent establishment in wider areas of the continent coincided with the drive of colonialism and they therefore shared the opprobrium and condemnation of the system on the part of the native people, particularly during the run up to political independence and for some time after.

But right now other problems in Africa seem to have somewhat overshadowed the anger over colonialism, except in regard to areas where white racialism still prevails, of course. Most African leaders and other educated people from Black Africa I spoke to were now particularly concerned to develop as well as improve ties with the industrial world. In this context one hears less than one used to in the past about Christian missions being the thin end of the wedge of imperialism, and more about them playing a positive role in development and national and social emancipation of the communities in which they are active.

But a major reason why Christian missions are by and large no longer regarded as an extension of European imperialism and colonialism by African nationalists is the remarkable way in which these priests and nuns have been practising what they preach, not only caring for their neighbour but often positively sharing in his fate as far as this is humanly possible.

While Christianity and Islam may remain mutually incompatible and irreconcilable as religions there is no doubt that men, or women, inspired by either of the two great faiths, or for that matter by any other creed, can do a great deal of good in a region where help is so desperately needed. There is certainly no more convincing, credible and effective way of practising one's religion than by demonstrating the practical significance of one's belief by improving the quality of life of the underprivileged.

There is little doubt that in the past both Christians and Muslims erred by arrogance and intolerance, and Christians in particular have been associated with the imperialist drive of the 19th century in Africa. This drive sought to suppress and discredit the much older influence of Islam and the Arabs. Under colonial rule and some time after, being Christian in Black Africa generally carried social advantages (and in some of the countries still does) just as being Muslim was socially a minus. This had important political, economic and social consequences for the people of the two communities concerned.

But in more recent times, and in the wake of greater financial power and general influence of Arab countries and a renaissance of the Islamic world, Muslims living in predominantly Christian

African countries are recovering their self-confidence and are becoming more vocal and articulate in their claims for social equality and fair sharing. It would not be surprising if a public census carried out now found a far greater proportion of Muslims in the population of non-Arab Africa than it would have done some 50 years ago. It is also understandable that such a rebirth of religious awareness should be looked on sympathetically by the Muslims elsewhere, including Arab countries.

Yet many Arabs agree that nothing could do worse service to the idea of Afro–Arab co-operation and give greater comfort to the enemies of this movement than blatant discrimination in favour of the Muslims, to the disadvantage of the non-Muslims, in the area of financial and economic co-operation, save where an institution, such as the Islamic Development Bank, is specifically designed to help Muslim communities.

Burundi indeed is a good example of a non-Muslim African country discovering recently the utility of co-operating with the Arabs. This will certainly not work to the detriment of the country's ties with Europe or Christianity. It was interesting to see at a conference I attended in Bujumbura in November 1979, on rural development in Burundi, a Papal Nuncio as well as representatives of BADEA, the Abu Dhabi Fund, and other development institutions, including the World Bank and UNDP, taking part in a fruitful debate on what could be done to help this particular African country by joint efforts.[5]

The Minister of Finance and Planning, Mr Donatien Bihute, spoke to me of the importance his country attached to co-operation with the Arabs, particularly in regard to balance of payments support and project aid.

'We are now receiving Arab finance for development at the rate of between $30 and $40 million a year, but I see no reason why this should not be doubled or trebled in the near future,' he said.

He had recently visited a number of Arab countries and was just about to travel to Saudi Arabia to sign more long-term loan or grant agreements. Saudi Arabia, he told me, was helping with the balance of payments, in the rural development, re-afforestation and road building. Construction of a large new hospital was about to begin in Bujumbura with Saudi support.

The Kuwait Fund was the first Arab agency to help Burundi

by granting the country a soft loan for a coffee growing project in 1976, the crop being Burundi's most important export. Egypt, Libya and Algeria have been among the Arab countries active in Burundi. BADEA has supplied three project loans by mid-1980, totalling $20 million, one for a sewerage and drainage scheme in the capital city, another for road development and the third for a sugar scheme. In addition, SAAFA, the emergency fund merged with the Bank in 1977, provided $2 million as balance of payments support. According to information supplied by BADEA total Arab aid, concessional and non-concessional for Burundi in 1973–1978, in terms of commitment, amounted to $50·304 million.[6]

A good road network will be particularly advantageous for landlocked Burundi and this is now being constructed, to a large extent with Arab finance. I travelled from Bujumbura to and along the Lake Tanganyika to visit an important fishery development scheme. While the road on which I drove had only just been completed, with the help of Kuwait Fund, fisheries were being developed with financial aid from the Abu Dhabi Fund (ADFAED) and the International Development Association, an affiliate of the World Bank. The road, whose construction had been delayed because of the recent war in Uganda, over whose territory most of the Burundi, and Rwanda, imports arrive, is now of direct importance to the fishery industry emerging on the lake.

The fishery project, administered entirely by local experts, is showing promise. Well-conceived and studied by UNDP, the scheme centres on help to small-scale fishermen. These artisans receive boats with outboard motors as well as other equipment and training, on a loan repayable in 60 months. In 1979 120 boats had been supplied to fishermen-artisans. Each boat had room for four or five men and total catches were about 2,000 lb a month, but steadily increasing. By 1981 another 338 fishermen were to be equipped and helped. At the same time small harbours and fish-handling centres were being built along the shore where catches are unloaded.

I was told that Lake Tanganyika had considerable unutilised potential in fish stocks, which indeed is the case with many African lakes and rivers. At the same time demand for fish is growing fast, especially in Bujumbura which is only a very short distance away from Lake Tanganyika. Tourist trade and traffic seem negligible at present, but the lake itself, with its towering mountain range on the other side of it, close to Zaire, is one of the most beautiful I have come across. There is something vaguely romantic as well as mysterious about this lake and its distant shores, still and empty most of the time, save for an occasional paddle-steamer.

There is little doubt that both Burundi and Rwanda, with their fresh climate and mountains and considerable infrastructure and friendly and intelligent people could be profitably developed for international tourism although both countries are far away from any sea. But several local men to whom I mentioned the idea dreaded the thought of seeing their pretty country invaded by foreign tourists.

Tanzania has won fame, and aroused some controversy, by virtue of her social and economic system based on small, self-relying communities, the celebrated ujamaa villages, a concept devised by the country's leader, Dr Julius Nyerere. The idea is very sound in principle as indeed most of the African people are rural, living in villages and small settlements.

There have traditionally been few differences in wealth and status among these people and a collectivist way of life, based on co-operation and mutual sharing, seems a reasonable system. The problem arises when freedom of the individual and of his small community conflicts with the wider organisation of the State, whose interests are overriding.

These problems are all the greater when there is a lack of good administrators, or when many of these are keener on pushing other people around than on the idea of common good and respect for the individual. Power-hungry bureaucracies are the curse of all socialist experiments, especially when no dissent is allowed, and Tanzania has been no exception to this. But the Dar es Salaam Government has shown remarkable flexibility in adjusting itself to realities and recent concessions to the interests of independently farming peasantry have brought remarkable results.

This is no place to discuss the merits of the ujamaa village system, though the way the Africans arrange their lives and institutions, political, social and economic, is relevant to their outside friends, including Arabs. However, to label African countries with epithets such as 'socialist', 'Marxist' or 'capitalist' can be highly misleading. Although Tanzania is often described as socialist while neighbouring Kenya is said to be capitalist, or even 'neo-colonialist', the grains of truth in these descriptions should not be allowed to obscure the very much wider areas of the opposite.

Underlying all political life and government in Africa is the tradition of family and tribe as the most important social groupings in which the role of the individual and his responsibility and decision-making power are considerable. Traditions of personal freedom, individual responsibility and mutual consultation in regard to public affairs are much stronger in Africa than they are in Europe where our civilisation has involved a very high degree of regimentation and subordination of the masses of people to small élites and authorities.

For better or for worse it is proving very difficult in Africa for anyone to try and regiment people and impose on them a system that runs counter to the natural feelings of the community. Moreover, the Africans have a great sense of humour and ability to laugh at themselves, which makes it difficult for any totalitarian ideology to be accepted.

Even in Ethiopia which now boasts of its Marxism-Leninism I was told during a visit to Addis Ababa in 1980 of the great problems the young, mostly western-educated men faced when trying to carry through political indoctrination and regimentation in the image of the USSR. Returning to Addis after one year I saw huge, identical portraits (evidently imported) of the three bearded fathers of communism topping many large buildings, the man in the middle, Engels, being particularly unfamiliar to the Ethiopians. Slogans exhorted the workers of the world to unite and even quite ordinary men and women were being dragooned into political meetings and discussions in order to make them absorb an ideology that to many of them seemed to have little relevance to the situation in Ethiopia.

No resistance could be offered to these measures in towns like Addis but I was told that in the countryside the peasants, still much under the influence of Coptic priests, would have nothing to do with this propaganda while attempts to set up Soviet-type collective and State farms were now a contributing cause of the disastrous food situation.

Yet Addis was putting up a brave face in adversity and foreign visitors continued to be well served by the facilities provided for them and the hospitality of the locals, hotel prices being much lower than anywhere else in Africa. The two most important African institutions, OAU and ECA, retained their well-staffed headquarters in the Ethiopian capital and were able to function smoothly in spite of the upheavals and problems that surrounded them.

The underlying similarity of social attitudes all over Black Africa may, perhaps, also explain the apparent paradox that in spite of their quarrels and separate ambitions there is a good deal of consensus among the Africans on matters of importance.

But to continue with my fleeting impressions of socialist Tanzania, I found the country surprisingly easy-going, free and outward-looking. To be gregarious and sociable may be a common trait in Africa, but it was particularly noticeable in Tanzania, as was a readiness to talk and an absence of pomposity and pretence in the highest political circles—in contrast to what one sometimes reads in the world press about the East African country. Things can be arranged quickly and at short notice with understanding and a happy smile—from finding a room in crowded Dar es Salaam to interviewing a Cabinet Minister.

Amir Jamal, one of the most eminent and influential financial and economic experts in the Third World—he was a member of the Brandt Commission—and currently Tanzania's Minister of Finance and Planning referred in an interview I had with him in November 1979 in his unostentatious office in Dar es Salaam to the Indian Ocean as a bridge between the Arab and African worlds in the past. The name of the capital city was an Arabic word, meaning House of Peace, and Arabic was at the origin of the main language spoken in Tanzania and much of the rest of East Africa, Swahili.

'History', Mr Jamal continued, 'had taken a new turn, to restore a process that was interrupted by colonial adventures. We are the Arabs' natural partners, as we have been across the Indian Ocean and the Gulf throughout history.

'The Arabs too have in the course of the 20th century emerged from various degrees of colonial subjection and are developing their own identity. But the Arabs now also have great financial power in their hands and the question is how this is going to be used. I hope it will be used to create a new power equilibrium in the world, as at present it is too much tilted in favour of technologically advanced nations.

'Personally I have no doubt that it would be in the interest of the Arabs to side and identify with the rest of the developing world. If they sided with the advanced nations the oil-exporting countries would not come on top, because they would still be dependent on the West for technology. And oil will run out in due course... We now have a historic opportunity to bring about the New International Economic Order with the help of Arab financial power. But will the Arabs grasp this opportunity? I hope they will, I trust they will. We might find on the other hand that there has been an error of judgment, because we are facing a time factor and urgent action is needed.

'If the non-oil and oil-rich developing countries hold their front together and develop complementarity in a serious way over the next 25 years, the world equilibrium will be more stable and secure. Otherwise we shall have problems that will benefit neither the non-oil nor the oil-exporting members of the Third World.'

What did he think of the economic and financial co-operation with the Arabs so far?

'We are very grateful for and appreciative of the Arab aid, whether it helps our balance of payments or our economic development. Arab project aid in Tanzania has been very well selected.

'The Kuwait Fund was the first to grant a development project loan in 1975. This was for a textile factory based on local cotton and producing essential garments for ordinary people. From every point view this KFAED-assisted scheme has been very positive.

'I can say the same of the brick and tiles project assisted by BADEA or of the other project partly financed by the Arab Bank, the maize development. This has been very important as it concerns our staple food.[7] I could give other examples of extremely useful Arab aid extended to Tanzania.

'Project aid is all to the good. But it takes time to bear fruit. There is another problem, arising from our present financial and economic difficulties, caused particularly by the high cost of oil imports. In the past it has been taken for granted that normal economic activities would continue and that project aid would be channelled into a steadily developing economy. The situation as it is developing now no longer allows such assumptions to be made. Recurrent needs of the economy can no longer be covered as a matter of course. We are facing a crisis situation, in which special measures are called for. What is needed are specific arrangements in regard to oil imports, for an intermediate period, so that the necessary adjustments can be carried out in due course.

'Oil in the past had been grossly underpriced. It was only fair that prices should have been increased. The Arabs can certainly not be blamed for the present problems.

'When I was Tanzania's Minister of Industry in 1973 when we faced the first large increases in petroleum prices I said thank God that this is taking place at a time when our industrial development is still at an early stage. We can now begin to move away from the internal combustion engine which has done so much for the critical importance of oil, and use other means of traction and transport.

'But at present we are under dual stress. We vitally depend on a technology that comes from outside and is costing more and more and we operate this technology by means of imported oil at prices we shall soon be unable to afford.'

Kenya. When I revisited Nairobi in mid-1980 after an absence of two years I was, as I had been on previous occasions, amazed at the progress made in the meantime in the construction of yet more splendid buildings, mostly serving commercial and administrative purposes and local as well as international companies. Nairobi is a well-planned, beautiful, salubrious and fast improving city.

If ever Kenyans wanted to make Nairobi a showpiece of their achievement, as the Russians do with Moscow and Leningrad, they could not choose anything better. But the Kenyans have no desire to confuse the foreigner and conceal from him the less attractive parts of the country. They frankly admit that Nairobi is rather exceptional, because it is after all the capital and the business and administrative centre of the nation.

One is free to travel anywhere one likes in Kenya, if one has transport, of course. For some outlying areas, like the Turkana land in the northwest, at the Turkana (formerly Rudolf) Lake, a small aircraft, like the Cessna in which I travelled, may well be by far the best mode of transport, perhaps the only one. But is this land the 'true' Kenya? The Turkana people wear only skins of wild animals and carry bows and arrows as a matter of course, for protection and hunting. But they are as much an exception as Nairobi.

Yet travel on the excellent roads to Nakuru, along the magnificent Rift Valley, or to Mount Kenya in Kikuyu country, and you see that Kenyan peasants are more advanced and prosperous than most in Africa, with nearly every house or hut covered with corrugated iron instead of straw, and other signs of progress.

Kenya, dominated by the towering personality of Jomo Kenyatta from the country's independence in 1963 and until the great man's death in August 1978, chose a way that was not typical of Africa. Close ties with the former colonial power and other western countries and interests as well as a frankly free enterprise system and explicit rejection of Marxism gave Kenya something of a bad name in more radical African circles.

But this was often ill-informed as the Kenyan Government never really departed from the African consensus on vitally important matters of common concern. What is also often overlooked is that Kenya has made remarkable progress in emancipating its African people and creating opportunities for them. The proportion of Africans, as distinct from Asians, let alone Europeans, in the country's administration and economic activities has been growing steadily. This remains a declared policy and institutions like the Kenyan Industrial Development Bank (IDB), for the benefit of which BADEA granted a soft loan of $5 million in 1979, are designed to strengthen the native entrepreneur.

It had been widely expected that Kenya would look very different after President Kenyatta's departure. Up and coming young men, who felt their talents were not properly appreciated in a system in which favouritism admittedly played a role had spoken to me about the inevitable social changes and reforms that would follow the death of Kenyatta.

'But we can do nothing as long as the old man is alive,' one such man commented in the mid-seventies. I had heard similar remarks from people in Ethiopia when the Emperor was in power. But in Ethiopia changes came suddenly, like an avalanche, when Haile Selassie was still alive, in 1974, sweeping him and his throne away and his entire system of government. In Kenya, however, the death of Kenyatta produced no such revolutionary changes.

Evidently the Kenyans, witnessing the tribulations in the neighbouring world, saw no need for such upheavals in their own country. From what one could see in mid-1980 President Daniel Arap Moi, 55, quiet-spoken and urbane former schoolmaster and himself of an insignificant tribe was able to maintain an equilibrium among the rival tribal forces in Kenya, steering a careful, but enlightened course, which involved freeing of political prisoners and a fairly unfettered general election, even if the monopoly of power was retained by his party, KANO.

Sentiment was markedly pro-Arab in Nairobi in mid-1980.

Although the Kenyan Government had in the past always been careful to toe the general OAU line in respect to the Palestine issue this was not, ostensibly, to curry favour with the Arabs, let alone in order to obtain money from them. In 1973 Kenya broke with Israel, together with a number of other African countries. But this was done as a matter of principle, the Kenyatta Government insisted, because of Israel's disregard for UNO and OAU resolutions.

In Kenya, with its strong Zionist lobby, the Government's position did not go unchallenged. A campaign was immediately mounted against the official policy, on the grounds that the loss of Israel's support was not compensated by aid supplied by the Arabs who should have been doing much more, the critics argued, to help Kenya in her financial problems arising from higher prices of imported oil.

The Minister of Finance and Planning, Mr Mwai Kibaki—a leading Kenyan financial expert and currently No 2 in the country's political hierarchy—restated the Government's position in the Nairobi Parliament in June 1974.

Kenya, he said, broke off her diplomatic relations with Israel as a 'matter of principle', because the Republic did not 'support taking other nations' territories by force of arms'. He reaffirmed Kenya's continued support for the resolutions of the UN and OAU on this matter. Replying to those in the Parliament, including some Assistant Ministers and a full-blown Minister, who had

174

been attacking the Arabs for not rendering Africa sufficient assistance in the face of inflation (allegedly caused by increase in oil prices), Mr Kibaki said Kenya did not 'break off relations with Israel so as to be compensated by the Arabs'. He added that it was 'a great pity' that members of the Kenya Parliament should air their views on this matter in the way they had, giving an impression that Kenya had broken relations with Israel for the sake of Arab aid.

There has in fact been a consistent stand on the part of the Kenyan Government, under Kenyatta as well as under Moi, in regard to the question of the Arabs and Israel. Early in 1975 Kenya received balance of payments support of $3·6 million from SAAFA, when this was still under the administration of the Arab League. In September 1976 BADEA signed a loan of $5 million to help an integrated agricultural and rural development project.

Yet at the same time discordant voices continued to be heard in Nairobi, and the Kenyan press, perhaps the liveliest, best informed and most articulate in Black Africa, could scarcely be described as pro-Arab.

In September 1979 President Moi visited Saudi Arabia amid reports that he was negotiating with Saudis a loan of $50 million. But in Kenya itself controversy flared up later in the year regarding the activities of the Arab League Mission in Nairobi, accused by the Kenyan Government of 'spying' on Kenyan companies suspected of trading with Israel and thus interfering in the country's internal affairs. The Arabs were rejecting these charges.

Soon Kenyan–Arab relations were on the mend again, attaining a kind of delayed honeymoon by 1980 when President Moi visited Iraq and Abu Dhabi. Kenyan papers, including the two dailies, the *Standard* and the *Nation*, seemed to be going out of their way to give favourable publicity to the Arabs and their causes, highlighting the prospects for Kenya which closer relations with oil-rich Arab countries would bring. A pro-Arab weekly, *Voice of Africa*, made its appearance in Nairobi and the Kenyan–Arab Friendship Society was born. President Moi's visit to the Gulf in that month was hailed as a triumph by Kenyan media and Arab pledges of soft loans and other assistance, including a promise by Iraq to supply the country with oil on privileged terms and Government-to-Government basis, were lead stories.[8]

The Kenyans now also seemed to have discovered that excellent opportunities existed for export of their agricultural produce, including meat, and other goods to Arab countries. The country's fast expanding industries had been hit hard by the collapse of the East African Community and continued closure of the frontier with Tanzania. Arab countries might now provide outlets. But the Kenyans also found that the Arabs were interested in investing capital in Kenya's profitable ventures and the political stability of the country manifestly impressed potential Arab investors. It was moreover clearly in the political and strategic interests of the Arab Gulf countries that Kenya should remain stable and prosperous.

Mauritius is 1,250 miles east of the African coast, in the middle of the Indian Ocean. Why it is an African island State and member of OAU may not be entirely clear. It has not a great deal in common with Africa. Most of the one million or so inhabitants of the island originate from the Indian sub-continent and are largely of the Hindu religion although about a quarter are Muslims. There is a strong community of Chinese. A few thousand descendants of French settlers still exercise considerable economic power as owners of sugar plantations and mills. The rest of the people are mostly of mixed race; there are few Africans as such.

A racial mixture of this kind may not be surprising in an island like Mauritius. What is impressive is the apparent harmony and goodwill prevailing among the races and religions. Roman Catholic churches will be found close to mosques and Hindu temples, and it is not unusual for a church congregation in deep prayer to hear the call of the muezzin next door, in this rather small and heavily populated island.

But the art of good government is to keep the different communities in peace with one another while developing a sense of belonging to Mauritius, a local nationalism which can transcend and may eventually replace the older loyalties. Several people told me they already felt Mauritians first and Hindus, or Chinese, second. The success of communal policies in Mauritius no doubt owes much to the sagacity and good sense of the leadership, headed by Sir Seewoosagur Ramgoolam, 80 years old in 1980. Affectionately known as the 'old fox' he has been in charge of the island's affairs since independence from the British in 1968 and many years before that in actuality.

Mauritius had demonstrated that the best way to racial harmony is to treat each constituent community with respect and allow it enough stake in the national set-up to make it will the preservation of the existing equilibrium rather than its demolition. The recipe may sound simplistic or self-evident, but it requires enormous tact and flair to carry it out successfully.

The island is charming, with its fields of sugar cane turning silver in the breeze, volcanic hills and mountains clothed in ever-fresh green, profusely flowering bushes and trees (exports of flowers being a growth industry) and graceful bays. It is summer all year round and the number of foreign tourists now exceeds 100,000 a year. One thing spoils the idyll: frequent cyclones, which ravage the island's crops and wreck its buildings.

Mauritius has been dubbed 'a sugar lump in the middle of the Indian Ocean'. Some 90 per cent of the cultivable land is given over to cane. The sugar industry is the largest employer of labour and earner of foreign exchange. Some 90 per cent of all the sugar refined in the island is exported: 831,000 tonnes in 1977, an increase of 23 per cent over the 657,000 tonnes recorded in 1970.

The Mauritians have no intention of replacing sugar by other crops; for one thing few alternative crops would survive the cyclones as well. But they have made remarkable progress in their efforts to diversify their economy and make it less dependent on one commodity whose world prices are extremely fickle and totally outside the island's control.

A trebling of expenditure on capital formation in real terms between 1970 and 1977 was reflected in a lively construction programme and all manner of other activities. A manufacturing sector was created practically from scratch, based on the Export Processing Zone enjoying fiscal and other privileges. Between 1970 and 1977 the manufacturing sector grew on average at 13·5 per cent a year in constant prices. External trade from the Export Processing Zone industries expanded from nothing in 1970 to some $50 million worth of product in 1977, accounting for 19·2 per cent of the total exports in that year, compared to 68·8 per cent earned by sugar and molasses.

Standards of living in the island improved rapidly, including education and health, and women became more emancipated as well as better organised. The role of women's organisations in the development of Mauritius has been remarkable. Employment went up by about 5 per cent a year on average in 1970–1978. A good indicator of general progress was the increase in the number of television sets, from 14,000 in 1969 to over 50,000 in 1978. The overall growth of GDP from 1970 to 1976 averaged 8·9 per cent a year, a very high rate indeed.[9]

Any Third World country would have been proud of statistics like these. Indeed, there would soon be no problem of poverty and under-development, or North–South dilemma, if progress of this magnitude could be made universal. Mauritius has undoubtedly demonstrated what a Government based on popular will and dedicated to the welfare of its people, and the hard work and discipline of this people, can do to overcome even some of the problems that seem most intractable elsewhere.

Yet economic achievement in Mauritius has been fragile. By mid-1979 the country was in a sombre mood. For the first time after many years there was industrial unrest, threatening to degenerate into communal strife and radical political agitation. Workers struck, protesting against diminishing opportunities of employment and declining living standards.

This was due to circumstances beyond the control of Mauritius. The prosperity now apparently ending owed much to the exceptionally high price of sugar, which after reaching its peak in 1974 began to slide downwards. Industrial ventures, on which so much hope had been placed, found themselves in difficulties because of competition from cheaper manufacturers in the Far East. A toy factory had to close down because similar products could be made at lower cost in South Korea. The cost of oil imports added to the balance of payments problems in an island so much dependent on sea and air transport. Mauritius registered a heavy balance of payments deficit and sank deeper into debt. Two-thirds of the development budget in 1978 was paid for by external sources, mostly borrowed money.

The case of Mauritius shows how an island economy, dependent basically on the fortunes of one commodity, may face disaster because of external factors—regardless of the very intelligent and consistent policies pursued by the authorities and good response to such policies by the people at large. This also demonstrates that countries like Mauritius need and deserve external assistance, although the island's per capita income may be high at $760 in 1977 compared to Kenya's $270 and Tanzania's $200 in the same year.

The relative success of Mauritius and the pioneering role it has played in many development ventures can, however, be of great use to the rest of Africa, making this another reason why Mauritius deserves international financial and economic support. The Sugar Research Institute at Reduit, assisted by UNDP and FAO, is probably the best of its kind in Africa and is now being made a regional centre at which courses are offered to African students in both French and English (every educated Mauritian speaks the two languages fluently). In 1979 a group of Sudanese sugar men began training at the Institute.

Not only has Mauritius been in the forefront of the development of sugar technology, including both cultivation and refining, but interesting work has been done in using sugar cane tops and molasses as feeding stuffs in livestock raising. Another development has been inter-cropping, the cultivation of food crops between the lines of sugar cane.

When I visited the island in 1979 I was told by its Government of the high hopes they were placing now on relations with the Arabs which had recently begun developing, following the intervention of BADEA. The Minister of Finance, Sir Veerasamy Ringadoo, told me the Champagne hydro-electric project, in which BADEA and other Arab Funds were involved, was only the first step in what he confidently expected to become a continuous and increasing financial and economic co-operation between the island and the Arab world.

Sir Veerasamy told me that his Government had now submitted ten major development projects to Arab Funds for their consideration. He himself had already visited Iraq, Kuwait, Abu Dhabi and Dubai earlier in 1979 while other Mauritian officials had been to Saudi Arabia.

'We have been extremely well received in the Arab countries we visited and were given assurances of sympathetic consideration in respect of the projects so far submitted', Sir Veerasamy said.

'As I have not been in Saudi Arabia myself I plan to go there shortly as we hope that the Saudi Fund for Development will help finance one of our large irrigation and food crop projects. We also expect a Saudi mission here whereas the Kuwait Fund for Arab Economic Development is sending in the near future a delegation of their experts to examine the possibilities of further co-operation with Mauritius', the Minister said.

'We realise, however', he added, 'that many countries are now seeking Arab assistance. Naturally, the Arabs have to apportion their aid accordingly. We may have been a little late in joining the queue, so we must be patient and await our turn.'

Arab aid could particularly help Mauritius to become self-sufficient in food and reduce its present dependence on South Africa, especially in regard to meat supplies.

But concessional Arab aid to Mauritius should also pave the way for Arab public and private investment in the island. The planners in Port Louis told me of considerable prospects for profitable placement of Arab petrofunds in the island.

In particular, I was told the Mauritians hoped to attract Arab capital for further development of the hotel industry. There are possibilities for joint ventures to set up shipping lines. There is scope for export-oriented manufacturing industries to be established in the island with Arab participation.

The Minister of Agriculture and Natural Resources, Sir Satcam Boolell, told me there was scope for profitable joint investment in the export of exotic flowers. There were also opportunities in deep sea fisheries. But the Mauritians, I was told by several officials, particularly wanted to arrange barter deals with petroleum-exporting countries, perhaps to exchange sugar for oil.

With its good infrastructure, fine technical skills and manpower and political climate favouring private investment, Mauritius should be a good target for Arab surplus funds seeking profitable placement.

It is believed that the Arabs may have been the first to discover the island, in the Middle Ages. But they certainly had little to do with it later. It was first occupied by the Dutch, who gave it its name, in the 17th century but was subsequently abandoned by them. The French moved in, to be replaced by the British in the Napoleonic wars. Today the island's strategic importance is generally regarded as very great in the Indian Ocean and close to vital sea routes. A stable and prosperous

Mauritius is clearly in the interest of the Arab nation. An added reason for this is the vocal role played by the Mauritius Government in inter-African and OAU affairs.

NOTES

1. Technical data given here are based mainly on '*Project of the Integrated Development of the Senegal River*', Organization for the Development of the Senegal River, High Commission, Dakar, May 1978, and '*Projet de développement intègre du bassin du fleuve Sénégal*', OMVS, Dakar, December 1977.

2. For details of the Plan see, *Plan Quinquennal de développement économique et social, 1974–1978*, Présidence du Gouvernement, Republique du Mali, Bamako, August 1974.

3. *Barrage et centrale hydroélectrique de Sélingué, Mali, Autorité pour l'aménagement de Sélingué*, Ministère du Développement Industriel et du Tourisme, Republic du Mali, Bamako, 1979. For BADEA's participation see Annual Report 1976, BADEA, p. 33.

4. See Annual Report 1977, BADEA, p. 40.

5. *Table ronde des aides extérieures pour le secteur rural*, Bujumbura, 13–15 November 1979. Copious literature on economic and social development was made available by the Burundi Government for the occasion under the code T.R. 79. AGRI.

6. Annual Report 1979, BADEA, p. 67.

7. For details see Chapter on BADEA, Annual Report 1975 and 1977, BADEA and BADEA Quarterly Review, Issue No 4.

8. See *Sunday Standard*, Nairobi, May 18, 1980, and *Voice of Africa*, May 29, 1980. *The Standard*, June 5, 1980, p. 4.

9. See *Mauritius Economic Review 1975–1977*, Ministry of Economic Planning and Development, Port Louis, 1978, and *The Fruits of Political and Social Democracy*, the Government of Mauritius, Port Louis, March 1978.

5

Political Ties Need Revitalising

People have wondered why there should be a special relationship between the Arab countries and non-Arab Africa, different, for instance, from relations between Arab and some Asian countries, such as Pakistan, many of whose people now work in the Gulf. There are also many institutions and assemblies, particularly those of the United Nations and of the non-alignment movement where Arabs and Africans co-operate anyway.

Yet there are valid grounds on both sides for a special relationship. Many centuries ago Arabs became part of Africa. Two-thirds of the Arab people now inhabit the continent and about one-quarter of Africa's population is Arab. This geo-political fact has important implications for African unity for which most Africans are striving. Such moves for unity, across the Sahara, must take account of the Arab countries' double loyalty, one to the Arab and the other to the African worlds.

Both these loyalties are very real and gaining in strength. The Arab world, for its part, is becoming more unified and homogeneous, given the general economic development and improvement of communications. A very important factor here are the millions of Arabs working now in other than their native countries. In spite of manifest differences and disputes among the Arab countries there is a constant centripetal movement, based on the desire shared by most Arabs that political unity should be restored while mutual economic and financial co-operation is all the time being made stronger.

Africa too is becoming more united, in spite of frequent appearances to the contrary. The Organisation of African Unity, set up in 1963, after much discussion, prevarication and disbelief, may not be what many had hoped it would become. But it is what its members make it. It can only work on consensus. But to deny the importance of OAU as an institution would be to misunderstand what in fact has been achieved in Africa over the past two decades or so for freedom and unity. OAU may not have many 'teeth', but its moral influence has been very great. It articulated the feelings of the African people on many issues of key importance, thus helping the Africans themselves as well as the outside world to understand the situation and act accordingly. The recent liberation of Zimbabwe and before that of the Portuguese colonies have been, of course, primarily due to the armed struggle of the African people concerned. But consistent and vocal stands taken on these and many other issues by the OAU assemblies have certainly made their contribution and impact. Attempts to impose the so-called 'Bishop Muzorewa solution' in Rhodesia itself as well as elsewhere—meaning the continuation of minority racist rule behind a black-skin façade— would no doubt have been persisted in with greater determination if public opinion in Africa and in the world were not made aware of the African consensus on these matters.

What is perhaps more important than anything else is that the Africans themselves are clearly taking their organisation seriously and Heads of State and Government do not spare efforts to either go personally to the agreed city every year or send their deputies in order to justify and explain their Governments' policies. There is now an unmistakable trend, clearly apparent at the three latest annual assemblies, at Khartoum, Monrovia and Freetown, that individual Governments can no longer escape criticism and significant pressure in the OAU by hiding behind the principle of sovereignty and territorial inviolability. When making their political decisions most African leaders today take account of what the reaction to their moves would be elsewhere in the continent, and the best barometer for such reaction is precisely the OAU.

But it would be difficult to continue to develop and strengthen the consensus of African peoples, and widen the scope for such consensus, if the loyalty of the Arabs in Africa to the Arab world were in conflict, or could land in such dichotomy, with their commitment to Africa. It is obvious that any such conflict of allegiance would make the position of Arab countries in Africa and their co-operation with non-Arab people in the continent more precarious and difficult. The interests of the Arab States in Africa are in fact best promoted and protected if there is a wider forum of co-operation, between the Arab community as a whole and non-Arab Africa.

Such inter-linking is more complicated when it involves certain communities inside the Black African region, or non-Arab Africa. This is not a homogeneous area like the Arab world, but a kaleidoscope of cultures and races with the colour of the skin being a very rough, and often highly misleading, mark of identity.

Two communities within this region are particularly relevant to Afro–Arabism. One is that of the numerous Arabs living in Black Africa since times immemorial or as more recent arrivals. There are important Arab minorities along the East Coast of Africa and many are found as far into Western Africa as Lake Chad, in close tribal settlements. Many of these Arabs play a significant part in the lives of their host countries, often as traders and shopkeepers. Their welfare depends on good relations with the people in the midst of whom they live, but also on the relations of the country they inhabit with the Arabs outside. Blood after all is thicker than water. The Arab world can never remain indifferent to the fate of these communities, but their interest will best be promoted when the country concerned and the Arabs generally have close relations of partnership and interdependence, as the modern Afro–Arab movement has been envisaging. In this case these Arab communities will be regarded by their neighbours as a bridge between their host countries and the Arab world, rather than a kind of fifth column.

In the distant past these far-flung Arab communities might have been seen as advanced parties of Arab penetration in the African continent. There may even now be some romantically-inclined Arabs who would like to take up the process of arabisation which was interrupted by European colonisation.

This, of course, is one of the favourite themes of those forces which are bent on crushing the basis of Afro–Arab co-operation and partnership. The spectre of the slave-trading, imperialist Arab has been conjured up often enough. It would be naive to think that such propaganda has not found at least some fertile ground among the more gullible in Black Africa.

After all, European colonisers have consistently sought to justify their conquest of Black Africa by claiming to have saved the region precisely from such alleged Arab danger. There is no need to probe into history to find out who enslaved whom. History in fact has been full of iniquities and exploitation of man by man. The most extreme form of this was slavery and slave-trading in which many races took part, the worst being undoubtedly the Europeans and Americans, but also Arabs, mostly as middlemen, and indeed Africans themselves.

But insinuations of Arab imperialism bear little relationship to the present reality. Even if they wished to subjugate the continent the Arabs have no power to do so, although they may have large financial resources. What they are seeking in Africa are friends and allies in the common struggle for political, economic and social emancipation. But this mutual help and solidarity can only be sustained on the basis of respect for separate identity and equality of rights for all participating countries, including the right to administer ethnic and cultural minorities with an eye on the need to square the public interest of the country as a whole with the claims and welfare of the minorities concerned.

In a sense the same applies to the question of non-Arab Muslims in Africa and their relationship with the non-Muslims. Probably about half Black Africa is Muslim, or some 150 million people. In some cases entire countries, like Mali, are staunchly Islamic. In other cases Islamic communities are a majority, in most African countries they represent important minorities.

These Muslim communities in Black Africa have tended to feel closer to the Arabs and their causes than others have in Africa, although some of the Islamic countries, including Mali, have had relations with Israel in the past.

It was the Arab traders who brought Islam to Africa where it is still spreading and gaining in confidence. It stands to reason that such Islamic countries as Saudi Arabia or Kuwait, where religion is taken very seriously by practically everyone that matters, will have a special interest in the welfare of their co-religionists in Africa. But it again stands to reason that in the countries where Muslims are in a minority their interests will best be protected when their Governments maintain close working relationships with the Arab Governments, including machinery for settling any disputes with these Governments, as has been envisaged by the Afro–Arab movement.

There is, of course, no unanimity on these matters and false ideas as well as unjustified fears still abound, but this is mostly because the reality of the situation has not been properly analysed and understood by everybody concerned. There is, on the other hand, a clearly discernible and very positive trend gathering momentum, as it has found expression in such institutions as BADEA and various joint organisations established by the two communities.

One has to bear in mind that Afro–Arab political alliance and partnership are of very recent date, indeed the political independence of the countries concerned is in most cases of recent date too.

It had taken some time for independent Africa to begin realising that the interests of Arabs and Africans converged. This realisation was prompted by the movement for African unity, which was universally popular and regarded as very important by most Africans, especially because so much of the continent still remained under colonialist or racist regimes and had to be liberated. Another important factor was that of the non-alignment movement, to the progress of which Afro–Arab solidarity can be directly traced.

The movement for Afro–Arab solidarity has been considerably influenced by the problems of Israel and Palestine which acted at certain times as a catalyst and other times as a constraint on better co-operation between the two communities.

There is a solid basis for Afro–Arab partnership even when the Middle East problems of Israel and Palestine are finally solved one day, as they must be. But there is little doubt that to many Arabs African co-operation in the struggle against Zionism has been of primary importance and they measured the professed friendship and solidarity on the part of the Africans by the way they reacted to the existence and policies of the Jewish State. But many Africans have believed that the problems of Israel and Palestine were not African problems and that attempts to drag these matters into African assemblies even made any collaboration with African Arabs undesirable.

The problem of Palestine strongly affected the very first moves of independent African countries for greater mutual co-operation and unity, in which the charismatic personalities of Gamal Abdel Nasser, President of Egypt, and Kwame Nkrumah, President of Ghana, played such important and pioneering roles. Neither of

187

the two great men, one Arab, one African, could be said to have been strikingly successful in their lifetimes, but they are both still widely regarded in their respective communities as men of vision, genius and courage.

I remember watching the two men, together with Jawaharlal Nehru and Marshal Josip Broz-Tito as the four of them dominated the proceedings at the first conference of the non-aligned nations in Belgrade in September 1961. Both Nasser and Nkrumah (in a well-cut suit and twirling his walking stick with panache to reinforce his oratory) were formidable speakers, if somewhat bombastic and looking perhaps slightly absurd to anyone, like myself, who then knew or suspected little of the non-alignment movement.

Gamal Abdel Nasser was by far the most influential as he bestrode the Arab as well as the African scene. His popularity among his own Arabs was not easily perceived by outside observers. But I remember being in northern Yemen at the time of his death in September 1970 and seeing old men weep: the entire population seemed grief-stricken at the death of the hero. Yet not many years before he had sent an Egyptian army to intervene in the affairs of northern Yemen, a move that was highly unpopular locally, to put it mildly.

Again, another occasion reminded me of his strange charisma. I was in Zanzibar, off Tanzania, very pretty in its deep green colours and fragrant with the smell of cloves (the island's main crop), but also terribly hot and humid at the time, shortly after a revolution in 1964 in which almost the entire Arab population, formerly the ruling class, is believed to have been put to death. I could not believe my eyes seeing a huge portrait of Nasser rising from behind the immigration official's counter at the ramshackle old airport. 'How come?' I asked a local man. 'He is a good man and we black people in this island all love him,' he replied.

There was rivalry and distrust between the two great men, Nasser and Nkrumah. Their political philosophies and strategies differed although they both strove for the unity of Africa. Nkrumah had good relations with Israel, which he wanted to keep and he was, at least for some time, rather pro-western and anti-communist. Nasser's main plank was to alert the Africans to the dangers of western imperialism and neo-colonialism. His great success was that he managed to persuade a group of African countries, gathered in Casablanca in January 1961, from which town the group took its name, to endorse a resolution identifying Israel as a 'tool of imperialism and neo-colonialism'.

Gamal Abdel Nasser, who had fought Israel unsuccessfully in 1956, sought to bring under his leadership wider circles of friends, the first of these circles being the Arab world proper, the next the Muslim and then the African. He showed deep concern for the Africans still struggling for their freedom when he wrote his famous book, *The Philosophy of Revolution*:

'We cannot...stand aloof from the terrible and terrifying battle now raging in the heart of that Continent between five million whites and 200 million Africans. We cannot stand aloof for one important and obvious reason—we ourselves are in Africa. Surely the people of Africa will continue to look to us — we who are the guardians of the Continent's northern gate, we who constitute the connecting link between the Continent and the outside world. We certainly cannot . . . relinquish our responsibility to help to our utmost in spreading the light of knowledge and civilisation up to the very depth of the virgin jungles of the Continent.'[1]

Nasser was as good as his word. Cairo became a home for African exiles and a political base for African freedom fighters who were offered material, logistic and moral support by the Egyptian Government. Radio Cairo developed special programmes to encourage the nationalist struggle, and Islamic teaching was used to expand the African 'circle', though it was much less of a political factor than is often thought, according to an eminent Nigerian scholar, Adeoye Akinsanya.[2]

Various aid and technical assistance programmes, consisting of training technicians in the UAR and providing experts, doctors and teachers for African States, were launched. The UAR signed commercial, cultural and loan agreements with a number of non-Arab African countries and thousands of Egyptian scholarships were awarded to African students to enable them to complete their studies in Cairo. Such work was to be taken up by other Arab countries, including Libya, in later years, but Egypt played undoubtedly a pioneering role.

However, Africa as a whole was not yet ready to accept an Afro–Arab political partnership. Not only was there no agreement on who the enemies were that the two communities were facing but there was considerable dislike and distrust of Nasser's somewhat paternalistic attitudes to the African 'circle'. He sometimes made the impression as if he wanted to shoulder 'the white man's burden' in Africa.

The Casablanca group of African countries, which comprised Egypt, Libya, Ghana, Guinea, Mali, Mauritania, Algeria and the Provisional Government of Algeria was challenged by two other groups, both much larger, which also advocated greater African unity but refused to accept Palestine as an African issue. They also tended to be more pro-western and generally less radical than the Casablanca group in which Nasser and Nkrumah were the two leading figures.

The larger of the two, the Monrovia group, comprised 17 countries, as they signed a joint declaration in Lagos in 1962. The other group, that of Brazzaville, formed in 1960, consisted of 12 States, all of them former French dependencies and anxious to keep on good terms with France whose policies they thoroughly endorsed, including the war in Algeria. There was some overlapping between the two groups, Ivory Coast, for example, being a member of both, but neither included any country of North Africa.

It was significant for the prevailing mood in Africa at the time that the two groups made the dropping of the Palestine issue a condition for their agreement to work with the Casablanca group with the view to creating a joint African organisation. This was duly set up at a conference of the African Heads of State and Government in Addis Ababa in 1963. President Nasser did not even mention Palestine at this inaugural meeting of the OAU. For some time his policy remained one of self-control and low-profile in Africa as far as the problem of Palestine was concerned.

Meanwhile, Israel was making further gains in Africa, establishing diplomatic relations with most of the countries and providing technical assistance, including military training as well as agricultural help, to a large number of them.

From 1958 to 1971 a total of 2,763 Israeli advisers and experts were sent to Africa while 6,797 Africans were trained in Israel. By 1966 eight African countries had been granted loans worth approximately $25 million. This co-operation totalled 80 per cent of all Israeli aid granted to the Third World. In addition to assistance in military training and in the equipment of armed forces and police, which was given to 10 African countries, including especially Ethiopia, Uganda and Tanzania, Israel succeeded in setting up para-military youth organisations in 17 countries.

Joint ventures were established in a great number of countries ranging from a shipping company in Ghana and water resource development firms to a large number of construction companies. The volume of orders handled by the latter amounted by the end of 1972 to about $300 million. Israeli firms had by that time invested $54 million dollars in Africa, including more than $20 million in Nigeria. Arab relations with non-Arab Africa were then still very meagre, only Saudi Arabia, Syria and Lebanon, among non-African Arab states, having ties with any non-Arab African country.[3]

It must be said that for Black Africans the advent and existence of Israel, a state recognised by the United Nations in 1948, was never a great emotional issue, one way or another, although Islamic countries on the whole felt stronger about Israel's policies, particularly after 1967 when the problem of Jerusalem, a holy city to all Muslims, became acute.

In fact, many non-Arab Africans felt a degree of sympathy for the Jewish State, as indeed they had felt for the long-suffering and oppressed Jewish people whose fate reminded them of their own. The Israelis, for their part, were not slow in backing up any sign of sympathy with offers of efficient technical assistance. It is important to understand this in measuring the sacrifice the Africans eventually made in severing their relations with the Zionist State.

At some stage the Israelis even offered assistance to African liberation movements, although this was declined.[4] If the offer had been accepted this might have strained Israel's relations with South Africa, an important source of financial aid for the Jewish State. Elsewhere, the Israelis did not hesitate to support an African armed struggle if this promised political benefit, as was the case with the limited help Israelis provided to the Black African rebels in southern Sudan.

But it would have been very difficult for Israel to keep up the pretence of supporting African liberation struggles, due to the close partnership with the United States and other western Governments and interests whose official policy was to support the Portuguese Government in Africa until this was toppled in April 1974. By and large Israel voted against the interests of independent Africa in the United Nations and votes of independent African States were often hostile to Israel.

It soon became apparent to most people in Africa that even technical assistance and economic co-operation provided by Israel for Africa was really a tactical manoeuvre, designed to alienate the Africans from the Arabs. It is difficult to visualise a basis for any very significant long-term economic co-operation between Africa and Israel, and the aid that was being extended to the Africans was certainly something that the Zionist State could ill afford.

It is therefore misguided to say, as some do, that any African country might be seriously thinking of resuming ties with Israel as an alternative in case of disagreement with the Arabs over the amount of money it might receive from them or other disputes. The question has only been raised by politically unimportant individuals. In all official assemblies and Government statements of recent years, including particularly those of the OAU Summit conferences, Afro–Arab co-operation and solidarity have been emphatically stressed and reaffirmed.

Whatever the importance of Israel and Palestine for the Arabs, the true and positive roots of Afro–Arab solidarity must be sought in the increasing awareness of the two communities of belonging to the same group of historically underprivileged, exploited and oppressed peoples. This awareness grows as the nations concerned begin to emancipate themselves and assert their claims and interests. On a world scale this feeling of solidarity among the underdogs has found its political expression in the movement of non-alignment, which is sometimes misunderstood as a policy of neutralism, an attempt to keep away from great power entanglements, a flight from reality. Non-alignment, which also used to be called 'positive' or 'active' neutrality, is on the contrary a device by which developing countries seek to assert themselves and redress their grievances in a world dominated by great power blocs, a form of struggle for justice and freedom from exploitation, political as well as economic. Non-alignment, in spite of its tribulations, is likely to endure and indeed become stronger as long as the world seems to such disadvantaged peoples to be arranged for the benefit of a minority of privileged and economically and militarily powerful nations.

Yugoslavia and its leader Marshal Josip Broz-Tito took a prominent part in bringing together countries of most disparate social and political systems in this non-alignment movement and giving it its content and direction. Without the bitter experience of the short-lived alliance with the USSR and profound disillusion with Soviet-type communism the Yugoslavs would not have thought of non-alignment.

But for the rest of the Third World it was the memory of colonial oppression and the struggle for greater equality with the former masters, who continued to play a dominating role in the economies of the developing countries, that made the new orientation particularly attractive. Besides, the West continued to support various colonialist and racist regimes in Africa and elsewhere, unwittingly creating the impression of fighting rearguard actions in order to prolong the lives of social bodies that had been doomed by history.

This accounted for the anti-western tilt of the non-alignment movement from its very start. When the Soviet Union in her cavalier fashion announced resumption of nuclear testing on the very eve of the first conference of non-aligned nations in Belgrade in September 1961, there was no formal protest from the gathering, although some delegates, including Kwame Nkrumah, said they were 'shocked'. There was little protest when such dubious neutrals as Cuba and Vietnam joined the movement and Cuba began to claim that the USSR ought to be regarded as a 'natural friend' of the non-aligned. Disagreements which came into the open on this score at the last Summit conference of non-aligned nations in Havana in September 1979 were much exaggerated by the western Press.

Blatant attempts made by the Soviet Union to take over the movement and use it for its own aims of aggrandisement of course caused problems, which became particularly acute after Russia's invasion of Afghanistan, a non-aligned country, in 1980. But there has been no sign of the movement breaking up because of that. It has in fact never ceased to grow and win new adherents. Twenty-five nations were represented in Belgrade in September 1961. In September 1979 in Havana there were 95 States and liberation movements speaking on behalf of more than a thousand million people.

In the crystallisation of African attitudes in regard to Palestine the June 1967 war, the 'Six Day War', was undoubtedly a watershed. After this bold attack on Egypt and lightning victory, Israel ceased to be looked on as a 'wolf in sheep's clothing', as Gamal Abdel Nasser saw fit to describe it at the Casablanca conference in 1961. The familiar image of the little David successfully resisting the giant Goliath was also out of place now, seeing the display of military might and efficiency of the Jewish State backed by the world's most powerful nation, America. It was Nasser's Egypt which seemed to be the paper tiger.

The prevailing sentiment in Africa—whatever else it might have been in America and Europe—in regard to Israel's military triumph in the June War was one of anxiety, concern and fear, but mixed with prudent refusal to express any commitment, one way or the other. Only Sekou Touré's Guinea now broke off its relations with Israel, the first African country to do so. The OAU Summit in Kinshasa in September 1967 expressed its concern and offered Egypt its sympathy, but refrained from calling Israel an aggressor and shifted the burden of seeking withdrawal from occupied territories to the United Nations.[5]

At the United Nations, Resolution 242, which was adopted in November 1967, later became a matter of controversy as, according to some, including Israel itself, the English wording of 'territories', rather than 'the territories', or 'all territories', implied that the document only called on the Zionist State to vacate *some* of the Arab land it had conquered. However that may be, it is clear from official reaction in Africa that this was not what the Africans thought. Israel's African friends now indeed became restive as the victorious State made fairly clear it had no intention of giving up 'Arab territories', including East Jerusalem. The Africans were now faced with the fact that one African country, Egypt, had part of its territory occupied by an outside power which showed no intention of giving up the spoils of war, a war of aggression to boot.

Consecutive resolutions passed at OAU assemblies reflected this anxiety as Israel was called upon to withdraw from all the Arab land. Israel's refusal to respond to the initiative of the UN Secretary-General Gunnar Jarring for indirect talks with Egypt and to pledge to withdraw from the occupied territories made in February 1971 also created a deep impression in Africa. The

Africans have come to regard the United Nations as an important guarantor of their own independence and territorial integrity, but here was a country openly defying resolutions and initiatives of that international body.

In a resolution adopted at the OAU Summit in 1971 the Africans not only deplored Israeli defiance but themselves took measures to intervene in the Middle East conflict. Palestine was now no longer a matter solely for the United Nations. OAU was to send a mission to the Middle East, see the two sides and help towards peace.[6] It was significant that the initiative for the mission came from President Kaunda of Zambia, President of the non-alignment movement in the year from September 1970. The movement, at its Summit conference in Lusaka, the capital of Zambia, in that year gave Egypt outspoken support, in considerably stronger terms than the OAU had done so far. President Kaunda's personal motive however was chiefly 'a genuine concern to bring about peace and security in the Middle East, since whatever happens there would affect Africa and the entire world'.[7]

The OAU mission, composed of ten members and a subcommittee of four headed by President Senghor, proved abortive. Israel had no intention of complying with the main request of the OAU, withdrawal from the occupied territories, although this was to be accompanied by guarantees in regard to the existence of Israel as a State.

At the Rabat Summit of the Organisation of African Unity in 1972 a resolution strongly condemning Israel was passed. It was, significantly, moved by the Ivory Coast, a country known for its pro-Israeli sentiments. At the same Summit the Palestinian Liberation Organisation (PLO) was given the status of observer.

A wind of change was now blowing across Black Africa in favour of the Arabs and Afro–Arab solidarity to which several factors contributed, apart from Israel's own policies. There was growing disappointment with continued support, tacit or overt, given by the leading western nations to racist and colonialist regimes in Africa and parallels were increasingly drawn between Zionism and apartheid, Israel and South Africa. Arab leaders themselves actively encouraged African doubts about Israel and indicated the benefits, political as well as economic, that would follow a closer Afro–Arab alliance. King Faisal of Saudi Arabia went on a goodwill visit to Chad, Mauritania, Niger, Senegal and Uganda in November 1972. Before he set out on his journey his Government issued a statement 'that the Arab countries and the entire continent of Africa would work together after the total liberation of Palestine for freeing the occupied African territories one after another, including Rhodesia'.[8]

Sudan now became a model of Afro–Arab co-operation and Khartoum grew into an important centre for Afro–Arab cultural, academic and other activities. BADEA opened its headquarters there in March 1975.

Peace and co-operation in the Sudan were relevant to the decision of Idi Amin, the leader of neighbouring Uganda, to break off relations with Israel in March 1972. This put an end to his own and his country's close involvement with the Jewish State and important Israeli military training and economic ventures. As long as civil war continued in the Sudan relations with Uganda were strained, as thousands of Southerners fled to the latter country. Undoubtedly some help reached the Anyanya fighters through Uganda. Idi Amin, although himself a Muslim, was of southern Sudanese origin and is said to have sympathised with the Anyanya rebellion. Israelis had also assisted the Anyanya freedom fighters, especially those under the direct command of Joseph Lagu, in a bid no doubt to impress African nationalists everywhere as well as to embarrass the Arabs. But when the Africans wished to co-operate with the Arabs, Israeli assistance was not only no longer wanted but best forgotten. The Israelis in the end earned little gratitude for helping the rebellion in southern Sudan, or for that matter assisting Uganda.

Again the problem for Israel was that it was an outsider intervening in what were essentially family affairs. The family was now patching up its quarrels and was getting ready to work in unison as so much remained to be done. What could Israel do to help?

The convergence of Arab and African views in regard to the liberation of their respective territories and the common enemies the two groups of States were facing was now rapidly approaching its apex of consensus. The events themselves helped this development but the contribution of individual statesmen in clarifying the issues and laying down a coherent line to be followed was also very important. President Houari

Boumedienne of Algeria in particular took upon himself a leading role in the task of analysing the situation and setting out a strategy for common struggle.

It was President Boumedienne who presented the Arab cause at the OAU Summit in May 1973 in Addis Ababa with a lucidity and good sense that won him the general support of the Assembly. He pointed out that Israel now occupied one-third of the total area of Egypt, refusing to withdraw in spite of pressure on the part of international organisations and movements. This, he said, was an insult to Africa. Occupation of Arab land was to be compared to the policies of white settler regimes in Rhodesia and South Africa, and 'Africa cannot adopt one attitude towards colonialism in southern Africa and a completely different one towards Zionist colonisation in North Africa'.[9]

In a unanimously adopted resolution the Summit spoke of the inalienable rights of the Palestinians, warning Israel that in continuing to occupy the Arab territories it was committing an act of aggression which threatened the 'security, territorial integrity and unity' of the African continent. This might lead, the resolution concluded, OAU member States to take, individually or collectively, political and economic measures against it, in 'conformity with the principles contained in the OAU and UN Charters'.

But then it was again left to the non-alignment movement to spell out more precisely what ought to be done now. At its Summit in Algiers in September 1973 the non-alignment movement requested all the member countries which had not already done so, to 'boycott Israel diplomatically, economically, militarily and culturally, as well as in the field of sea and air transport'.[10]

In view of this gathering of clouds the ensuing storm should not have surprised anybody. Yet, when President Mobutu Sese Seko, speaking at the General Assembly of the United Nations in New York on 4 October 1973, announced his country's decision to break with Israel, he astounded many. Zaire had been more friendly to Israel than most African countries, and President Mobutu and many of his officers had had training in Israel. But, as he explained, he had now to choose between 'a friend' and 'a brother'. He added that 'Zaire will never back down and will carry out the duties of African co-operation'.[11]

It was now becoming increasingly clear that siding with the

Arabs, and breaking with Israel, meant complying with a moral principle as well as an African and Third World consensus. To do otherwise would mean being out of step with the prevailing opinion which might be inviting trouble and be uncomfortable anyway—quite regardless of any other considerations. Many of the African countries that had not yet broken with Israel now appeared to be looking for a convenient excuse to do so.

This came shortly, on 6 October, when a new war broke out in the Middle East, variously described as the October, Ramadan or Yom Kippur War, unleashed by the Arabs. As distinct from all previous armed confrontations with Israel the Arabs were now holding their own, even inflicting heavy defeats on Israel in the initial stages. Yet when the Israelis subsequently crossed the Canal many Africans professed indignation. It was the first time that Israel had occupied African soil, not just the soil of an African country. Furthermore, the oft-repeated Arab accusation of collusion between imperialism and Zionism now gained new credit as the US, in a desperate bid to save Israel, used the Azores, with the permission of the Portuguese Government, as a staging post for supplies of sophisticated weaponry.[12]

More and more African countries now followed the Zaire lead and from October to 13 November 1973 a total of 21 broke off their diplomatic relations with Israel (although not necessarily trade). By the time an emergency session of the Council of Ministers of OAU took place in Addis Ababa on 19–21 November 1973 to consider the Algerian proposal on 'Consideration of the current Middle East situation with particular reference to its effects in Africa', only four countries—Malawi, Lesotho, Swaziland and Botswana—out of the total of 42 members of the OAU still maintained their ties with the Jewish State.[13]

Now when the bulk of the non-Arab African States had finally broken their diplomatic relations with Israel an important new stage was reached in Afro–Arab relations. It has been argued throughout these pages that Israel and Palestine must not be regarded as the only reason for the political rapprochement between the Arabs and Africans, or even a very important reason, taking into account the fundamental and long-term convergence of interests of the two communities. If there had been no Israel the Africans and Arabs would still undoubtedly have plenty of reason to find themselves on the same path and the future of this co-operation certainly does not depend on what may eventually happen to the Middle East conflict.

The significance of the issue for the Arabs should nonetheless not be minimised. How can one claim to be a friend, indeed a 'brother', of the Arabs if one does not support them in what they themselves see as their most critical problem?

However, why the vast majority of the Africans turned against Israel in the way and the time they did is still to some extent a matter of speculation. Since the issue had been the subject of considerable innuendo and controversy it is worth pausing to look at some of the more relevant statements and observations, especially in view of the contention often made by the critics of Afro–Arab co-operation as well as cynics to the effect that the Africans might have been mainly motivated by expectation of material gain, as Arab oil was now becoming an important 'weapon' in international affairs.

I recall an interview I had with Ahmed Sekou Touré, President of Guinea, in Khartoum in 1978. I put to him that some people thought the Africans had broken with Israel and supported Arab causes principally to receive as a reward Arab aid and concessions. Sekou Touré retorted with some impatience:

'Our support for Arab causes springs from Afro–Arab solidarity which has always been a matter of principle to Guinea. This support does not depend on any financial rewards being paid to us by the Arabs. We have stood by the Arabs because we thought they were right, not because we expected any financial gain. Guinea broke off relations with Israel in 1967, the day when the Zionist State launched its aggression against the Arabs. We did this immediately, without thinking at all about the consequences of our action in regard to financial help we might get from oil-rich Arab States.

'We would have acted in the same way as we did in respect of any country that was victim of external aggression. We would have broken off relations with Israel even if the Arab States themselves had asked us not to.

'I would like to say to those who suggest that we co-operate with the Arabs because of their money: "We are a religious people, believing in God. We have a deep sense of dignity and responsibility. We are no opportunists, and we are no beggars, no matter how poor we may be."'

This was Sekou Touré of Guinea, the first African country to break with Israel, years before any other did so. So how important was the issue of the 'oil weapon' to other African countries as they too, one after another, eventually decided to give up Israel?

Prof. Mazrui, in his work already referred to, made this point: 'Some commentators who should know better (including African journalists) have suggested that Africa broke off relations with Israel for the sake of cheaper oil from the Arabs. Such an analysis distorts the sequence of events. By the time the Organisation of Petroleum Exporting Countries dramatically raised the price of oil, much of Africa had already sided with the Arabs on the Palestine question. The trend against Israel in Black Africa started in 1972, and had converted even Mobutu Sese Seko of Zaire to its side before the outbreak of the October War, so that trend could hardly be attributed to the energy crisis, which did not hit the world until the last few weeks of 1973.'[14]

A noted analyst of African affairs, Zdenek Cervenka, wrote: 'One of the most remarkable aspects of the Afro–Arab alliance was the fact that it was forged as a "political pact" long before a number of European countries became converted by the "oil weapon" from Israeli support to friendship with the Arabs. There is no evidence either that the Arabs ever mentioned the possibility of using the "oil weapon" against African countries or that the African countries threw their support behind the Arabs with financial benefit in mind.'[15]

The Africans have unanimously rejected the view that they had been motivated by material gain when breaking off with Israel as an insult to their dignity. The Arabs for their part had no less consistently rejected the thought, out of respect for the African stand as well as for the practical consideration that to accept such a proposition might open the door wide to blackmail as Africans could start demanding from the Arabs the fulfilment of their part of the bargain.

While this may be the real situation it would be equally wrong and unrealistic to say that economic and financial factors, including the accumulation of surpluses in OPEC countries and balance of payments problems in Africa because of dearer oil, played no part in the emergent alliance. If you marry someone rich for love and not for money this does not mean that you will abstain from discussing money, especially when you happen to be desperately poor. On the contrary, money is likely to be an important topic, even if love remains more important.

Indeed, the topic of economic and financial co-operation entered Arab–African relationship as soon as the new partnership was forged and solidarity confirmed when the Africans gave up their dealings with Israel and opted for friendship with the Arabs. The Africans never hesitated to make plain that they expected their gesture of solidarity to be reciprocated by similar gestures on the part of the Arabs, in the fields of economy, finance and oil trade as well as in regard to political support for the liberation of African territories still under colonial and racist regimes, although in this respect the Arab group of States as a whole had accepted the African line on Rhodesia and South Africa as their own considerably before the Africans had done the same in respect of Palestine.

Proceedings at the emergency meeting of the African Council of Ministers in November 1973 reflected the Arab and African views on these matters as the conference put a seal on the new alliance.

A declaration adopted at the meeting named Africa's enemies as 'colonialism, racial discrimination and apartheid, aggression, foreign occupation and domination, neo-colonialism, imperialism and Zionism'. The Africans would now set about 'to free themselves from colonialism everywhere, to eliminate apartheid and Zionism, to safeguard their own identities and personalities, to recover and enhance their cultural heritage and to assert in every way "authenticity", and finally, to consolidate their national independence by rejecting all forms of foreign domination, interference and pressure'.

The echoes of non-alignment jargon and philosophy are unmistakable in this wording.

The Council then called upon all African countries to sever relations with Israel until she withdraws from the occupied Arab territories, and pledged to 'assist Egypt, the other Arab countries and the Palestinian people to liberate their territories by every means'.[16]

The Council furthermore adopted a resolution appealing to oil-exporting Arab countries and Iran to extend the oil embargo, which the Arabs had just instituted against western countries, to

South Africa, Portugal and Southern Rhodesia. A special committee of seven members was to be set up to liaise with the Arab League in order to supervise the oil embargo and ensure that its operations did not harm African States themselves.[17]

Finally, the Council recommended the strengthening of economic, financial and cultural co-operation between the Arab and African States and the setting up of machinery for such co-operation. The Secretaries-General of the League and OAU were to consult on these matters and there were to be periodic meetings between the two organisations.[18]

A week after the Addis Ababa emergency session a conference of the Arab Kings and Heads of State gathered in Algiers, expressing its delight at the decisions made in Africa. For its part the Conference resolved that all Arab States which had not already done so should 'sever all diplomatic, consular, economic, cultural and other relations with South Africa, Portugal and Rhodesia', and completely banned Arab oil exports to the three offending States. Special measures would, however, be taken to continue regular supplies of Arab oil to sister States in Africa. This Conference too spoke of the need to strengthen economic relations between the two communities and arrange periodic consultations and meetings between them.

President Boumedienne described in his address to the Conference the newly found Afro–Arab solidarity as 'a turning point in African history'. He appealed for co-operation between the political, economic and technical institutions of OAU and the Arab League. 'Such co-operation', he pointed out, 'representing the human and material resources of the Arab and African countries, will constitute a formidable force in international relations capable of playing a decisive role in the service of justice and freedom in the whole world'.[19]

Decision was made to create an Arab development agency for non-Arab Africa, later to be known as the Arab Bank for Economic Development in Africa (BADEA). The decision to establish such a bank marked the first tangible step in the implementation of the Arab–African co-operation programme and the first instance of a machinery being set up for the Arab countries to contribute to the economic development of Africa.[20]

Subsequently, at the meeting of the Arab Oil Ministers on 23 January 1974 in Cairo the Special Arab Aid Fund for Africa

(SAAFA) was established with an initial capital of $200 million to furnish emergency assistance to non-Arab African countries affected by higher prices of oil imports and other contingencies. First administered by the Arab League the Fund was later handled by BADEA with which it was merged in 1977 (see chapter on BADEA). At the meeting of the Arab League Council in Tunis on 25–28 March 1974 an Arab fund for technical assistance to African and Arab countries was set up.

Ideas set forth at the OAU and Arab League assemblies towards the close of 1973 were now being rapidly implemented, and the following milestones marked the road to the first Afro–Arab Summit conference to be held in March 1977 in Cairo.

The initiative for such a conference came from the meeting of the Arab Heads of State and Government held in October 1974 in Rabat, capital of Morocco, where a delegation of nine Arab Foreign Ministers was appointed to visit Africa and explain the Arab point of view on this and other current matters, including the problem of petroleum and its prices.

Then, at a meeting of the OAU Council of Ministers in February 1975 in Addis Ababa, it was decided to enlarge the original committee of seven entrusted with the task of liaising with the Arab League to a total of 12 members, including now also Egypt. The new committee had the following membership: Cameroon, Botswana, Burundi, Ghana, Algeria, Egypt, Sudan, Senegal, Zaire, Tanzania, Sierra Leone and Mali.

For its part the Arab League nominated in April 1975 a similar committee to maintain contact with the OAU, with the following members: Kuwait, Lebanon, UAE, Tunisia, Saudi Arabia, Syria, Iraq, Libya, Somalia, Morocco, Mauritania and the PLO.

The two committees met for the first time in Cairo in July 1975 and prepared a draft co-operation agreement for eventual submission to the planned Afro–Arab Summit. This work was further continued when the Afro–Arab Foreign Ministers met at Dakar, agreeing on a joint Declaration and Plan of Action for Afro–Arab co-operation among the 47 African and 20 Arab States, closely following the text agreed upon at the meeting of the two committees in Cairo in the previous year. But a proposal put forward at the meeting by President Leopold Senghor of

Senegal that there should be a full union between the OAU and the Arab League was not accepted.[21]

On 7–9 March 1977 Arab and African Heads of State and Government, or their deputies, met in Cairo. Fifty-nine countries were represented, 30 by their Kings or Presidents. Malawi was the only African country to stay away.

Progress towards this historic meeting was not smooth; the years from 1973 were filled with events, some having a positive and others a negative impact on the further strengthening of Afro-Arab solidarity.

On the positive side international developments confirmed the wisdom of Africa's option for the Arab friendship rather than continued ties with Israel. The South African Premier John Vorster visited the Jewish State in 1976 among reports of closer economic and military co-operation between Israel and South Africa, widely reported in the African press. The daring raid of Israeli commandos on 28 June 1976 at Entebbe airport in Uganda to liberate Jewish hostages shocked and angered the African world. It demonstrated how vulnerable these newly-independent countries really were in the face of a determined and ruthless agent in full mastery of modern technology. The need for development as well as solidarity with other regions of the Third World, especially Arab, became all the more evident.

But international writers have also mentioned 'the smoother flow of Arab money into the African economies and the intensification of the institutional co-operation between the OAU and the Arab League' as factors on the positive side. Within a year of opening its doors for business in Khartoum—writes Zdenek Cervenka[22]—BADEA 'granted $124·5 million in loans and raised its capital from $231 million in 1973 to $500 million in 1976'. At the meeting in Dakar of the OAU and Arab League Foreign Ministers designed to pave the way for the Afro–Arab Summit, representatives of BADEA as well as the African Development Bank (ADB) took a full and active part in the deliberations.

On the other hand, the problem of petroleum prices and ensuing difficulties for African economies cast shadows on the emergent Afro–Arab partnership.

Oil is the main source of energy for most African countries, in contrast to North America and Western Europe where coal plays an important part. Besides, the development process in Africa itself put new demands for energy, with each percentage point rise in Gross National Product bringing about a 2 per cent rise in energy consumption, compared to less than 1 per cent in the advanced industrial countries. The sharp increase in petroleum prices in 1973/74 dealt a severe blow to the economies of the African countries although Africa's crude oil consumption in 1974 may have been less than 2 per cent of the world's total. The cost of oil for the 30 non-oil developing countries in Africa rose from $500 million in 1973 to $1,300 million in 1974.[23] Furthermore, many other products imported into African countries from the developed world, including fertilisers, rose partly because of the higher cost of fuel.

One of the first themes of conversation between the newly appointed committee of seven of the OAU and Arab Petroleum Exporting Countries (OAPEC) in Cairo in January 1974 was oil, and the Africans were given an assurance of continued and sufficient supplies of the fuel. But a request for special concessional prices of the fuel was turned down on the grounds to be repeated many times subsequently. First, the Arabs have only a limited power over the commercialisation and distribution of oil and products which remain mostly in the hands of international companies. Second, the price of oil is fixed by OPEC as a whole and the Arabs as a group could not offer special prices for a select number of consumers, and third, a system of two sets of prices would soon result in a third level, that of the black market.[24]

Further discussions during 1974 and subsequently between the Africans and Arabs on this topic also produced little agreement. At the same time some African countries expressed dissatisfaction with the level of aid now being made available by the Arabs.

Among the papers submitted to the Afro–Arab Summit was an appeal by the OAU urging greater Arab assistance to African countries seriously affected by oil price rises and world inflation.

There was widespread speculation, particularly in the western press, on the eve of the Summit that the emergent Afro–Arab partnership would prove a non-starter, that the gathering would end in mutual recrimination and controversy. Yet the outcome came as a surprise to most people.

As the distinguished Zambian economist and diplomat, E. C.

Chibwe, has said: 'The success of the conference was beyond the expectations of observers and participants alike. Observers had anticipated confrontation, and participants expected deadlock on most issues. What actually happened was that there was a large measure of agreement on most of the major issues submitted.'[25]

The conference was marked by frankness with such controversial issues as the increases in oil prices, liberation movements in Africa and the Arab World, and Arab financial aid to Africa being freely ventilated and thoroughly discussed. 'The Arab and African leaders concluded their Summit by making economic and policy declarations that, if implemented, could make the Arabs and Africans a joint force to be reckoned with in international forums.'[26]

Undoubtedly the atmosphere at the conference was helped by the positive response of the Arab side to African pleas for more financial aid as Saudi Arabia, Kuwait, the United Arab Emirates and Qatar together pledged an additional $1·45 billion in aid for development in non-Arab Africa. But more important than this was that for the first time now the emergent movement was equipped with a comprehensive set of institutions for mutual co-operation.

The Summit approved four basic documents:
   a. Political declaration;
   b. Declaration on Economic and Financial Co-operation;
   c. Declaration and Programme of Action for Afro–Arab Co-operation;
   d. Agreement on machinery and methods to implement Afro–Arab Co-operation.

The Political Declaration listed 13 points, calling in particular for the support of the struggle on the part of the peoples in Palestine, Zimbabwe, South Africa, French Somaliland and the Comoro Islands. It reaffirmed the commitment of the Arab and African countries to the principles of non-alignment, peaceful co-existence, creation of a just international economic order as well as sovereignty and territorial integrity, non-interference in the domestic affairs of other States and the right to self-determination.

The Declaration on Economic and Financial Co-operation laid down 11 propositions:

1. Encouragement for national and multinational financial institutions with the view of providing technical and financial assistance for four studies of multinational African projects proposed by the Economic Commission for Africa.
2. Enhancing financial resources of the national and multilateral African development agencies.
3. Increase of ADB's capital resources by means of loans raised in Arab financial markets.
4. Increase of BADEA's financial resources.
5. Development of Afro–Arab trade relations.
6. Co-ordination of Arab financial assistance to Africa.
7. Encouragement and safeguarding of Arab investments in Africa.
8. Diversification of Arab financial assistance to Africa.
9. Encouragement of Afro–Arab technical co-operation.
10. Expansion of bilateral aid through Arab national Funds to Africa.
11. Machinery to implement this Declaration, including close co-operation between the Standing Commission on one hand and BADEA, ADB and ECA on the other.

Noting that the volume of Afro–Arab economic and financial co-operation in the past three years had increased sevenfold, mainly on the basis of concessional loans and grants, the Declaration affirmed 'that the backwardness and the economic problems of the African and Arab peoples are originally the results of many centuries of exploitation and imperialism, and also of the state of inequality in the current economic relations and of the nature of the present international economic system engineered basically to serve the objectives of the exploiting industrial States'.

The Declaration and Programme of Action for Afro–Arab Co-operation defined the scope of the joint endeavour in the political and diplomatic, economic—including trade, mining and manu-facturing industry, farming and animal husbandry, energy, transport and communications and finance—social, cultural, educational and scientific and technical fields.

In regard to Machinery and Methods to Implement Afro–Arab Co-operation the following institutional arrangements stood out:

The Standing Commission, consisting of 12 Ministers from the OAU Committee and 12 Ministers from the counterpart Arab League Committee, to meet twice a year with the task of implementing the Afro–Arab co-operation.

Working and Specialised Groups, composed of Arab and African experts and specialists to carry out studies and put forward suggestions for projects designed to promote specific co-operation in the economic, agricultural, financial and other fields.

The Co-ordination Committee consisting of the Chairmen of the two Committees of 12 and Secretaries-General of the OAU and Arab League to co-ordinate the activities pursued under the auspices of the Standing Commission.

An 'ad hoc' Conciliation and Arbitration Committee (yet to be set up) to interpret legal provisions governing Afro–Arab co-operation and settle differences.

It was also decided that the Afro–Arab Summit was to meet every three years.[27]

The Standing Commission, established by the Summit, held its first session from 31 May to 1 June 1977 in Yaoundé in Cameroon. It particularly examined the modalities designed for the implementation of the resolutions on Arab–African co-operation, including the appointment of Working Groups, and invited the Group concerned with economic and financial co-operation to meet in Cairo in order to define and determine these modalities.

In the course of its second session, held in Cairo on 28–29 November 1977 the Standing Commission laid down the functions and responsibilities of the Working Groups and defined the procedures for the implementation of the recommendations adopted at the Cairo Summit.

Thus, four Groups were respectively assigned the following sectors:
1. Agriculture, forestry, fisheries and animal husbandry;
2. Mining, industry and water resources;
3. Transport, communications and telecommunications;
4. Education, social affairs, culture and information.

Meeting on 5–7 June 1978 in Niamey, capital of Niger, for its third ordinary session the Standing Commission, after examining the progress achieved so far voiced 'satisfaction with positive results attained in a comparatively short time'.[28]

But this positive development came to a halt by 1978 and no Afro–Arab institutions in fact held any sessions during 1979 or subsequently. There was no longer any dispute between the Arabs and Africans. The problem was rather between the Arabs themselves. It was nonetheless on the old, sensitive issue of Palestine. The Arab world rejected the Camp David agreements made by one Arab country, Egypt, with the USA and Israel, and the ensuing peace treaty between Egypt and the Jewish State. Egypt was ostracised by the rest of the Arab States, which were not prepared to sit together with a delegation sent by Cairo to any of the Afro–Arab assemblies. But given that Egypt was one of the members of the committee of 12, and now of the Standing Commission, as part of the OAU delegation, no meetings could take place.

For the Africans the matter was both embarrassing and confusing. It has been indicated in the previous pages that Egypt, by virtue of its leadership in the Middle East, Africa and the Third World, as well as by its geographical position at the north-eastern gate of Africa, had played an exceptionally important part in the development of closer relations between the Arabs and the Africans. The fact that Egypt, an African country, was the primary target of Israeli aggression played a major role in the way the Africans finally decided to support the Arab cause to the extent of breaking ties with Israel. But now Egypt was out, treated by the Arabs almost like Israel itself.

The Africans refused to change their view that Egypt, as an African country, should remain a member of the OAU representation in contacts with the Arab League.

This appears to be a technical problem, but not to be minimised in view of the sensitivities which have characterised both the Arabs and the Africans in relations with each other. To an outsider it may appear illogical that the problem should stand in the way of continuing organised co-operation between the two communities as, after all, the question is that of pursuing a partnership between the Arab and the non-Arab African worlds. Egypt is not part of the non-Arab world and it is for the Arabs to decide who will represent *them* in their contacts with Sub-Saharan Africa. Moreover, Egypt's role in the all-important economic co-operation between oil-rich Arab States and non-Arab Africa could only be small.

The setback is all the more regrettable at a time when the growing economic problems in Africa on the one hand and expanding financial surpluses in the oil-rich Arab region on the other make the need for co-operation all the greater.

Recently there have been signs that both sides realise the importance of revitalising the institutions they so hopefully set up at the first Afro–Arab Summit in Cairo in 1977. The recent OAU Summit in Freetown echoed this realisation and more recently, in June 1980, the Secretaries-General of the Arab League and the OAU, Chedli Klibi and Edem Kodjo, met in Tunis, deciding in principle to set the co-operation in motion again. Nonetheless, the flow of Arab funds to Africa has been continuing and there is underlying consensus in both regions that co-operation should be resumed and strengthened. Perhaps the Afro–Arab Summit was too ambitious; it would at all events be very difficult to carry out such a comprehensive programme with the resources of administrative and technical facilities available in the two communities. A more pragmatic and gradual approach might have caused less embarrassment and disappointment.

What then is the Arab view on the future of Afro–Arab co-operation? There is no better man to put this question to than the Secretary-General of the League of Arab States, now, after the big reshuffle in the Arab camp following the Camp David agreements, a Tunisian, Chedli Klibi. The Arab League has also moved its headquarters from Cairo to Tunis.

President Habib Bourguiba must have felt very pleased and vindicated by this choice. There were times, in the sixties, when Tunisia's realistic and pragmatic views were misunderstood by many Arabs as a policy of abdication and weakness. Yet the Tunisians never wavered in their defence of the right of the Palestinian people to self-determination while insisting that only a policy which recognises the world as it is, including the reality of the existing States in the region, can bring positive and beneficial results for the Arabs.

One can only speculate about what might have happened in the Middle East and how different the situation would have been today had the Arabs followed Habib Bourguiba's counsel.

For me to return to Tunis after an absence of 12 years was an experience coloured by emotion. Twelve years may not be much in the life of a nation, but it is a long time in the life of an individual.

It was still the Tunisia that I had known and loved, the country of the friendly and gregarious souks and the fragrance of jasmine, of warm welcome, hospitality and camaraderie; yet it was also a land of purposeful construction and progress, of common sense and eagerness to learn and to co-operate. If all the countries of the developing world were to sit in a classroom Tunisia would get the top marks, I wrote in my book, 12 years ago. Cynics laughed and said I was either naive or simply trying to make propaganda (for cash).

Now I felt vindicated, having a singularly happy feeling, as I watched this new generation of the Tunisian populace thronging the Bourguiba Avenue and its cafés. When I had last strolled in this central artery of Tunis there was still much poverty around, too many beggars and shoeblacks and large numbers of children stretching out their hands for a coin. There were no beggars this time, no trace of degrading poverty (not in the centre of Tunis at any rate), but decently dressed, well-behaved young men and women, alert and sensible, that would have been the pride of any city in the world.

Tunisia must be the only African country without any illiterates. Education for the people has been perhaps the most important single achievement of Bourguibism, but this is also an outward looking education, designed for friendship and co-operation with the outside world rather than being self-centred or bigoted.

Many people had thought foreign tourism, the emergence of which I praised as an important development for a country with few natural resources but much to offer a traveller, was going to corrupt Tunisia and erode its traditions. Tourism has brought money and employment. But contacts with foreigners have not diluted the old values and beliefs. If anything I found this time the Tunisians more Islamic and more Arab although it was a frequent sight to see young Tunisians and young Europeans walking and chatting together, like people that have a great deal to share with each other.

This may seem a digression from the theme of my book, although the book is about people getting on with people, being equal and accepted.

Chedli Klibi did not talk to me as a Tunisian, of course. He was not giving me a Tunisian or a personal point of view, but rather that of the Arab community as he saw it—a point of view on the delicate situation in the Afro–Arab world. Yet it is not difficult to discern in his answers the workings of a Tunisian mind, also that of a highly cultured and erudite man, a craftsman of words, both Arabic and French, a communicator by profession.

A frail-looking, gentle person, M. Klibi weighed his words carefully as he spoke to me.

Why this Afro–Arab co-operation anyway? I have put this question to many people before and I had received characteristically different answers. What does this co-operation mean to the Secretary-General of the Arab League?

'A question', M Klibi commented before giving me an answer, 'of great interest and portent, requiring study in depth.' He then explained his view:

'First of all you must keep in mind that there are a significant number of Arab countries which are at the same time African: Mauritania, Morocco, Algeria, Tunisia, Libya, the Sudan, Somalia and Djibouti—and Egypt itself for that matter—nine countries which are members of the OAU and at the same time of the Arab League.

'Apart from geography, history has brought the two communities closely together. Solid ties have been maintained in social and cultural areas.

'We also believe that the Arab and African countries face a large number of similar problems. To wit, a majority of the Arab countries and all the African ones have been colonised. Both groups of peoples have fought their liberation struggles which bound them together by even closer ties of solidarity.

'At the time of this struggle there were frequent contacts between the respective liberation movements which in turn strengthened the bonds between the two communities. But I also happen to believe that the colonisation left behind on both sides of the Sahara traces that are not entirely negative, consequences that have not been wholly harmful. Among such positive results of the colonial period was that people have been using the same working languages and shared in Western-type administrative practices. This has been done to an extent which even causes problems when the countries concerned want to carry out the process of economic, administrative and cultural decolonisation. But this in its turn shows that we, people on either side of the Sahara, share the same or similar problems.

'We think also that the Africans and Arabs have convergent interests which they can develop in international organisations, the non-alignment movement, the North–South dialogue and in other assemblies into a positive and constructive solidarity, assuming a significant role in the international arena in defence of their views and stands.

'All these and other considerations militate in favour of the two communities becoming increasingly aware of the profound identity of their interests, which should make certain that the Arabs will never be indifferent to the development and future of African countries.

'Moreover the Arabs are increasingly anxious to diversify the placement of their investments in our uncertain world, and to develop their economic and financial co-operation with developing countries. With the industrial part of the world being more and more saturated the Arabs cannot easily gain access to investment opportunities offering high financial returns, particularly in industries with a future growth.

'This is to say that the Arab–African co-operation must be seen in the geographical, historical, sociological, political and economic contexts, making it an objective imperative for the two communities. By joining their forces and their potential the two communities can gain a political credibility and achieve economic development to which they could not aspire if they were left separate.'

I told him that the impression I gained in the Gulf, notably when talking to the Kuwaitis, was that their principal interest in becoming involved in Africa was for altruistic motives, religious and humanitarian, rather than the more mundane considerations of building a joint community of interest with the Africans.

'I believe', he said, 'that as far as our brothers in the Gulf, in Asia in fact, are concerned, there must be a number of considerations that are chiefly important to them. First of all, the Gulf Arabs co-operate with many countries of the world, Asian, African, Latin American and European. For the Gulf Arabs and their leaders this co-operation is based on ethical grounds as much as on strict interests. They believe it is their duty to co-operate, especially with those who are in need. It is, incidentally, the same in the case of wealthy countries in Europe and America which forge their relations with the developing South and for which there is also, over and above the well-understood interest, a moral duty to extend a helping hand to those that need assistance in their struggle with under-development. Similar considerations are valid for our brothers in the Gulf.

'But in regard to Africa there are also other considerations, one of which we have just recalled, namely that many Arab countries are tied to Africa. There is, as far as the Gulf countries are concerned, this indirect link through other brothers, other Arab countries which for their part are in contact with Africa, with countries south of the Sahara, and this is something to which the Gulf countries are certainly not indifferent.

'There is a third dimension, Islam. African countries are either Muslim or else include large Muslim communities which is something that is of great interest to the Gulf countries. But, even when we are dealing with Christian communities there is always a link with Arab countries as these too include Christian populations.

'But there is, finally, the common interest, which all Arabs share, in having African support in the struggle against Zionism. I do not wish to conceal from you the importance of this political support on the part of our African friends. But this cuts both ways. The Africans value the support we, the Arabs, provide for their struggle in Namibia and South Africa, as we have provided it in the past for their liberation wars in Angola and Zimbabwe.

'As far as we are concerned we wish always to have on our side our African friends in the fight against Zionism which is a form of racism. But, being particularly sensitive to racism and colonialism because the Blacks, Arabs and Jews alike have always been the targets of these scourges, they are all the more ready to render us their support.'

I told him I had heard that the Africans had not broken with Israel in order to draw material benefits from the Arabs. Yet the question of petroleum and petro-dollars was on the Afro–Arab agenda as soon as most of Africa severed its ties with the Zionist State in 1973. Besides, certain Africans have said that the Arabs had a duty to help Africa . . .

'I don't think our African friends', M Klibi explained, 'broke with Israel in order to acquire oil or petro-dollars. For them this was a question of principle, of morality. It is also in this sense that we understand their support for us to be. This gives them credit as their support to us is not tied to any material gain whatever. But, if the Arabs render Africa their material assistance they are thereby accomplishing a duty stemming from the principle of mutual solidarity, not honouring their part of a bargain.

'Yet, having said that, I must emphasise that in my view this mutual support has a very important bearing on our relations. That is why it is also highly important to us that relations between Africa and Israel should remain severed as long as the Palestinian people have not regained their legitimate rights.'

But the problem of Israel and Palestine, however important, cannot be the crux of the matter between two communities embarking on a long-term co-operation covering every conceivable field of activity. After all, the Middle East conflict will one day be solved. Will Afro–Arab co-operation then lose much of its significance?

'Certainly not', M. Klibi replied. 'Among the reasons I gave for Arab–African co-operation I did not mention in the first place the political aspect of the matter, as the community of interests binding the two parties rests on other foundations than the mere supply of African votes at the UNO and other international fora. The subject of Palestine is enormously important to us, but once this political problem is solved common destiny with the Africans remains.'

But the problem now was that some Africans apparently failed to appreciate the strength of the Arab feeling in regard to Palestine as they insisted that Egypt, which the rest of the Arabs had rejected and condemned, should continue to take part in Afro–Arab deliberations. This failure to understand the Arab point of view might have dangerous consequences for Africa in the Gulf. As M. Klibi explained:

'Clearly, our African friends have been having scruples when it comes to victimising Egypt, which, after all, is a great African country. Yet, the Arabs have not been demanding that the Africans should expel Egypt from the OAU as they might well have asked if it was strictly a question of their interests. So there is no question of interfering in the internal affairs of OAU. The Arabs have merely been insisting that Egypt should be excluded from joint Arab–African institutions, as the Arab States, having condemned Egypt's political decisions as being contrary to Arab interests, categorically refuse to sit with Egypt in such organisations.

'Recently I paid a visit to Arab Gulf countries and I wish to say to our African friends that the leaders there were very unhappy about the stand adopted by the African countries as these insist on imposing the presence of Egypt in joint Arab–African bodies.

'The Arab view on this is: we are concerned in this Arab–African co-operation with economic and financial relations between the Arab countries on one side and African countries on the other, under the auspices both of the OAU and the Arab League. But Egypt is no longer an active member of the League. It is therefore necessary that the Africans should take account of these Arab feelings and of the fact that we, the Arabs, cannot accept to be sitting in joint Arab–African institutions in which an Egyptian delegation is present.

'This is all the more necessary as Egypt's role in Arab–African co-operation would not have been essential anyway. On one hand Egypt could not benefit from the financial co-operation which only involves countries south of the Sahara on the African side. On the other hand, Egypt cannot really claim to be a donor, seeing her economic difficulties and limited resources.

'In view of all this I believe it would be also in the interest of the Africans to find a solution to this problem on an amicable basis.

'We attach a great deal of importance to Arab–African co-operation, which we regard as far too significant to remain the victim of what are in any event temporary problems, as Egypt will sooner or later return to the fold.

'But it is now a question of life or death for the Arabs. It is not only the freedom of the Palestinian people that is at stake, but its very survival. We expect from all our friends, and more particularly from our African friends who are among the closest to us, that they should show their solidarity with our struggle by removing Egypt from all the joint Arab–African institutions.'

Now, how seriously has this problem affected Afro–Arab

relations and the activities that were envisaged by the first Afro–Arab Summit?

'It is necessary to take account of the rather limited nature of the damage which is being done. In a general way, Arab–African co-operation is continuing and showing results. In the economic, financial and technical fields the co-operation has been developing in a manner satisfactory to both parties.

'What, on the other hand, are not making very good progress are the joint institutions of political character. The Standing Commission, composed of 12 Arab and 12 African Ministers, one of them Egyptian, has not been meeting since 1979, although the working groups consisting of Arab and African specialists continue to carry out their missions of studying the projects designed to fulfil Arab–African co-operation in the most varied domains of economic and social development.'

But now, M. Klibi revealed, an agreement had been reached with Edem Kodjo, the Secretary-General of the OAU, to reactivate the Arab–African political dialogue—on the level of the Co-ordination Committee, one of the institutions created at the Cairo Summit, for co-ordinating joint activities, the committee consisting of the two Secretaries-General and the Chairmen of the two delegations making up the Standing Commission. There is no Egyptian on this Committee. The first meeting of the Co-ordinating Committee was to be held in December 1980.

There was no hope that a Summit Conference of the Arab and African Heads of Government could take place now. But as M. Klibi explained: 'The Co-ordinating Committee could guarantee, in case that it should continue to be impossible to reactivate the Standing Commission, a broad continuation of Arab–African co-operation as envisaged by the Cairo Summit.

'What interests us particularly is that the present political problems arising from the presence of Egypt in certain Arab–African institutions should not affect the economic co-operation between the two communities, and we have agreed in the course of a meeting with M. Kodjo to take steps in order that this co-operation should be given a new impulse. We also agreed that the private sectors should be associated with the co-operation. What is particularly important is that financial transfers should be effected in a regular manner and for the benefit of the projects in non-Arab Africa which are important for economic development.'

Had the machinery established in March 1977 not been too ambitious anyway? M. Klibi commented:

'The fact that we shall now be working on the level of the Co-ordination Committee will also compel us to look on things more realistically, more pragmatically, leaving aside all that might unnecessarily burden our meetings without leading to any positive results.'

Would now the Arabs be willing to increase substantially their aid to Africa, seeing the much greater need for this in the continent? M Klibi was non-committal, but, while emphasising that the Arabs had so far largely honoured all their commitments and that it was also important to appreciate the quality of the Arab aid rendered, as this was free of any strings whatever, he said that 'our Arab brothers are open to any positive suggestions for increased assistance', and he added that it was in the Arabs' own interests 'to diversify the scope of their investments and deepen the co-operation between the two brotherly communities'.

But how important was the Arab–African movement in his present scale of priorities? Surely, the Arab League right now had many other worries. M. Klibi:

'Our first priority, of course, remains the liberation of the Palestine people. After that we regard it as very important that the Arab world as a whole should have a balanced economic development and that the widening gap between the wealthy and the poor Arab countries should be narrowed, all with the ultimate hope that our region may as far as possible catch up with the development in the industrial countries.

'Having said that, I should also stress the importance of Arab–African co-operation and indeed the solidarity with all other developing countries. In the same way as we endeavour to co-operate with the industrial world, particularly Europe, we must think of those who need our co-operation for their development.'

Turning again to Arab–African co-operation, M. Klibi summed up the Arab interests as he saw them:

'We help Africa because the African for us is a neighbour and we are geographically and culturally tied to Africa. From the economic point of view too our major interests are converging. In the political domain I see the benefit arising from a great Arab–African grouping active on the international stage. Then, of course, there is the support that Africa can give the cause of Palestine. But when one talks of this particular subject, is it not the conscience of the Africans themselves that will determine their attitude rather than any amount of co-operation with us, economic or other?'

NOTES

1. See 'The Afro–Arab Alliance: Dream or Reality', by Adeoye Akinsanya, African Affairs, p. 513.
2. Ibid.
3. Data on Israeli aid to Africa have been taken from 'Africa and the Arab States, Documentation on the Development of Political and Economic Relations since 1973', Institute of African Studies, Hamburg, 1980, pp. 5 and 53.
4. See Africa's International Relations, by Ali A. Mazrui, Heinemann, London, 137.
5. See The Unfinished Quest for Unity, by Zdenek Cervenka, Julian Friedmann, London, 1977, p. 158.
6. Ibid, pp. 159–160. (For details on how individual members of the mission saw its aim.)
7. Ibid, p. 160.
8. Ibid, p. 220.
9. Ibid, p. 164.
10. Africa Contemporary Record (ACR), Rex Collings, London, 1974, p. C 59.
11. See Africa's International Relations, op. cit. p. 144.
12. See ACR, op. cit. 1974, p. A 6.
13. The Unfinished Quest, op. cit. p. 164.
14. Africa's International Relations, op. cit. p. 144.
15. The Unfinished Quest, op. cit. p. 162. See also ACR, op. cit. 1974, p. A 14.
16. Ibid. p. 165. See also ACR, op. cit. 1974, p. A 7.
17. The Unfinished Quest, op. cit. p. 165.
18. ACR, op. cit. p. A 12.
19. The Unfinished Quest, op. cit. p. 166.
20. Arab–African Co-operation, BADEA, Khartoum, December 1978.
21. See, ACR, 1977, p. A 97.
22. See, The Unfinished Quest, op. cit. p. 171.
23. Ibid, p. 167.
24. Ibid, p. 168.
25. Afro–Arab Relations in the New World Order, by E. C. Chibwe, Julian Friedmann, London, 1977, p. 11.
26. Ibid, p. 11.
27. For details on the documents adopted at the First Afro–Arab Summit Conference see Afro–Arab Co-operation: Landmarks of Progress, BADEA 1977, F.S. 1/77 pp. 5–9; ACR, op. cit. 1977 (in the section The Afro–Arab Summit), and Afro–Arab Relations, by E. C. Chibwe, op. cit. pp. 137–146.
28. See, Arab–African Co-operation, BADEA, op. cit.

CONCLUSION

As 1980 draws to its close one can say with some confidence that
Afro–Arab co-operation, as a specific relationship between two
communities of the Third World, is here to stay. Both the Arab
and African States and their respective organisations have
confirmed this. There is a wide consensus that the two groups of
countries have much more to gain than to lose by working
together, in the political as well as in the economic field.

Arab aid commitment in favour of non-Arab Africa has been
substantial by any standards, and the specialised institution
created to help development in the region, BADEA, has worked
successfully since it started operations in 1975. This, one ought
to point out, is the first agency of its kind set up by one
developing region to help another. Beyond being a source of
development capital provided on concessional terms BADEA has
been acting as a catalyst for other Arab aid flows to Africa and is
becoming an increasingly significant voice in the world counsels
concerned with development in the region of its activity.

Growing co-operation among development agencies, often
under the aegis of BADEA, needs stressing, especially in regard to
joint deliberations and operations undertaken by the Arab Funds.
Indeed, BADEA likes to be seen as only one of the Arab
institutions, part of a common Arab effort for help to non-Arab
Africa, although having a special position by virtue of its
geographical scope and political commitment.

Arab agencies operating in non-Arab Africa may be motivated
by varying considerations, political, humanitarian, religious and
others, and may apply different criteria in deciding what aid they
will extend, but collectively they represent a common Arab
endeavour and are co-operating closely among themselves.

Again, taken together, the Arab countries and their organisations have become an important factor in the world development scene, adopting and advocating points of view which
favour the interests and claims of the developing world,
notably in respect to the need for a New International Economic

Order. In this the views and interests of the Arabs and Africans have been converging.

There can on the other hand be no doubt that the high hopes generated by the first Afro–Arab Summit Conference in 1977 had not been fulfilled by 1980. The progress of the institutions then created received a serious setback from the problem of the attitude to be taken to Egypt, a country of major significance, both as Arab and as African. The Arabs and Africans must now decide how far they will allow this problem to remain an obstacle to the growth of their partnership, which, as they both say, should not be governed by momentary or tactical considerations but by vital long-term interests.

However, we have seen signs of movement and there is every likelihood that the deadlock will soon be broken. At all events, African commitment to Arab causes, notably in respect of Palestine, stands and there is no wavering on the Arab side as far as their support for the cause of a free Africa is concerned. Most Arabs and Africans agree that their political solidarity in the face of unresolved problems of the right of Palestinians to self-determination and end to oppression and racial discrimination in southern Africa is as necessary as ever.

Yet, for the Africans, political preoccupations have given way to worries about the catastrophic economic situation developing in large parts of the continent. Particularly disturbing has been the lack of progress in food and agricultural production which has made Africa critically dependent on outside supplies of food at a time when many countries of the continent are suffering from staggering balance of payments problems.

The causes of this situation have been many and complex. Above all African countries have seen the prices of their exported commodities largely stagnating because of slack demand for them in the industrial countries, at a time when the cost of imports has been rising very fast. This includes the cost of industrial products as well as food and petroleum.

Large adjustments, including better utilisation of domestic power resources and energy conservation measures are needed everywhere in oil-importing countries. But such adjustments are far easier to make for an industrial country than for one that is poor and in the process of development.

No one can reproach the oil-rich Arabs or for that matter

other petroleum-exporting countries for raising the prices of their commodity in response to the interplay of supply and demand for oil. Yet at a time of desperate economic plight in so many African countries on the one hand and considerably larger revenues accruing to oil-exporting Arab countries on the other (although these revenues may in 1980 only equal those of 1974 in real terms) one can see the urgent need for stronger economic co-operation between the two communities, Arab and African.

This co-operation has been largely confined to the transfer of official capital funds from Arab countries to developing Africa. But there is also need for co-operation involving private capital investment and trade, and discussions on these issues are currently in progress.

Arab–African co-operation for development would be incomplete without a third partner, the industrial world, whose technology and expertise are indispensable if progress is to be made. Such trilateral co-operation is also vitally important to the western countries and it is therefore in their interest to see that the emerging partnership is based on terms acceptable to all concerned. At present, both the Arabs and the Africans believe that the co-operation, as currently practised, is open to serious criticism, fundamentally because of the unequal position in which the Arabs as suppliers of finance, and the Africans as owners of the natural resource to be developed, have been placed in relation to the industrial world. It is particularly important to the Africans that such trilateral co-operation should not contribute to an ever greater dependence on imports of goods and technology from the industrial world but that it should be accompanied by such transfer of technology and other measures as would lead to an eventual economic emancipation of the developing countries.

At a 'trialogue' held in October 1980 in Paris between the Secretary-General of the OAU, M. Edem Kodjo, French and EEC officials, and Dr Ayari, President of BADEA, the latter thus summed up the conditions on which trilateral co-operation would be acceptable to the Arabs:

'There must be a commitment by all the partners to balanced economic development in the country hosting a joint project, and technology must be transferred on fair terms.

'The partner supplying the technology must not be allowed to play an active, decision-making role while the other two remain passive. And even if the Arabs do contribute funds while the industrial countries provide technology, this ought not to be seen as an excuse for the developed world to shift all responsibility for financial assistance to the Third World on to Arab shoulders.

'Political and cultural diversity must be respected and co-operation must be outward-looking—not designed to foster restrictive practices of benefit only to certain countries or regions. It must also be considered an integral part of world efforts to bring about the New International Economic Order.'

This Arab view is shared and echoed by the Africans, and a common stand on this vital point of how co-operation with the industrial world should develop provides yet another reason why Arab and African countries find a working partnership between them so desirable and necessary.

STATISTICAL
APPENDIX

I

Arab Concessional Aid to Non-Arab African Countries, Commitments[1] $ millions 1973–1979

BENEFICIARIES	1973	1974	1975	1976	1977	1978	1979	1973–79
Sahel Zone	24·962	132·284	148·791	178·952	164·623	120·286	135·096	904·994
Other LDCs	1·004	97·649	166·594	136·573	92·417	114·608	151·742	760·587
Other MSACs	—	28·331	65·190	165·230	144·276	66·093	100·997	570·117
Others	5·335	64·990	62·705	58·652	60·815	126·654	138·082	517·234
Unspecified	3·490	26·676	13·404	17·328	95·524	112·223	2·000	270·645
TOTALS	34·791	349·931	456·684	556·735	557·655	519·864	527·917	3,023·577

[1] Arab Governments and their bilateral and multilateral agencies and IMF oil facility.

Source: BADEA

II
BADEA Loans 1975–1980

Country	Project	Amounts of Loans $m	Repayment (years)	Interest %	Grace (years)
Benin	Cement Factory	8	25	6	5
Cameroon	Port of Douala	10	25	4	5
Congo	Railway	10	25	4	5
Ghana	Cocoa	5	25	4	5
Madagascar	Highway	5	25	3	5
Niger	Highway	7	25	2	5
Senegal	Livestock	1·6	25	2	5
Tanzania	Maize	5	20	2	5
Zaire	Water Supply	10	25	4	5
Togo, Ghana, Ivory Coast	Cement Factory	10	15	6	5
TOTAL 1975		71·6			
Burundi	Sewerage	4	25	2	5
Gambia	Rural Development	3·3	25	2	5
Kenya	Rural Development	5	25	4	5
Mali	Sélingué Dam	15	25	2	5
Mauritius	Electric Power	10	15	4	5
Rwanda	Rural Development	5	25	2	5
Sierra Leone	Electric Power	5	15	4	5
Upper Volta	Rural Development	4·5	25	2	5
Zambia	Highway	10	25	4	5
PANAFTEL	Seminar	0·1	—	—	—
TOTAL 1976		61·9			

Country	Project	Amounts of Loans $m	Repayment (years)	Interest %	Grace (years)
Cameroon	Pulp Mill	10	11	7	3
Ghana	Kpong Dam	10	17	6	5
Guinea	Cement Factory	4·84	17	5	5
Liberia	Industrial Free Zone	3·2	14	5	4
Madagascar	Hydro-electric Plant	10	20	4	5
Mali	Rural Development	5	25	2	5
Rwanda	Electric Power	6	20	4	5
Senegal	Fishing Port	7·2	20	5	5
Tanzania	Brick and Tiles	10	15	7	3
TOTAL 1977		66·24			
Benin	Ext. of Cotonou Port	4·6	13	6	3
Burundi	Highway	6	20	2	5
Chad	Agricultural Development	7·8	20	3	5
Guinea-Bissau	Feasibility Study	0·1	—	—	—
Lesotho	Airport	6	18	4	3
Liberia	Electric Power	3·92	13	7	3
Uganda	Textiles	4·7	15	4	3
Uganda	Feasibility Study	0·15	—	—	—
Zaire	Oil Palm Rehabilitation	4·4	15	7	5
PANAFTEL	Feasibility Study	1	—	—	—
BDEAC	Line of Credit	5	12	4·5	3
Sahel countries	Emergency Aid Programme	15	25	1	10
Niger	Power	7	15	7	3
Botswana	Livestock	2·2	10	2	3
TOTAL 1978		67·87			

II—*continued*

Country	Project	Amounts of Loans $m	Repayment (years)	Interest %	Grace (years)
Angola	Rehabilitation of Lobito Route (Benguela Railways)	10	15	4	5
Cape Verde	Fishing	2·4	15	4	3
Comoro Is.	Telecommunications Network Development	1·57	20	2	5
Gambia	Yundum Airport Extension Project	5·2	15	5	2
Guinea	Road Rehabilitation	6·0	20	4	4
Kenya	Industrial Development Bank	5·0	12	7	3
Lesotho	Road Construction	3·9	20	4	5
Mali	Sevare-Gao Road	10·0	20	4	5
TOTAL 1979		44·07			
Botswana	Airport	7·25	15	5	3
Burundi	Sugar Complex	10	17	5	4
Cameroon	Route	9	15	6	3
Comoro Is.	Mutsamudu Port	8	20	5	5
Mozambique	Wood Factory	10	13	6	3
Senegal	Chemical Industries	10	15	8	5
Seychelles	Electricity	1·2	12	5	2
Sierra Leone	Integrated Agricultural Development	8·5	20	5	5
Tanzania	Road	8	20	5	4
TOTAL 1980		71·95			

GRAND TOTAL $383·63m

Source: BADEA Annual Report 1980

III
Kuwait Fund for Arab Economic Development
Loans signed for the benefit of non-Arab Africa, 1975–1979 (June)

Country	Project	Amount (KDm.)	Repayment (years)	Interest %	Grace (years)
1975					
Rwanda	Tea Plantation	1·00	27	3	6·6
Uganda	Livestock	5·75	25	2·5	4·5
Tanzania	Textile Plant	4·50	22	4	4·6
1976					
Guinea	Communications	2·7	17	4	3
Comoros	Roads	1·8	40	1	10
Burundi	Coffee Plantation	0·36	26·2	3	6·2
Mali	Sélingué Dam	5·00	26	2·5	6
Senegal	Livestock	1·2	25	3	5
1977					
Cameroon	Songloulou Hydroelectric	4·5	25	4	5
Madagascar	Highway	2·1	16·1	4	3·6
Ghana	Kpong Hydroelectric	8·97	20	4	5
Congo	Railways	4·00	16·7	4	3·7
Gambia	Soma- Yoroberikunde Rd.	4·5	25	2	5
Burundi	Bujumbura- Mutambara Rd.	1·75	24·9	3	4·9
1978					
Benin	Roads	2·25	20	2	4·6
Guinea-Bissau	Bissalanca Airport	2·00	20	2	4·6
Congo	Railways	1·0	15	4	1·7
Lesotho	Maseru Airport	1·2	24	2	4·2
Liberia	Roads	2·2	18	4	3·3
Madagascar	Andekaleka Hydro.	2·9	25	4	4·6

Country	Project	Amount (KDm.)	Repayment (years)	Interest %	Grace (years)
1979 (to June)					
Central African Rep.	Bangui–Bossembele Highway	1·0	24	3	4·5
1979					
Comoros	Pomoni–Moya Road	1·5	39	1	9
Senegal	Debi–Lampsar Irrigation	1·6	24	3	3·9

Total loans for non-Arab Africa, not including technical assistance, 1975–1979 (June) KD 63·78 million (1 KD equalled $3·64 at the end of 1979)

Source: Kuwait Fund for Arab Economic Development.

IV
Abu Dhabi Fund for Arab Economic Development
Project loans signed, 1976–1979, for the benefit of non-Arab Africa

Country	Project	Amount UAE Dirhams m.	Repayment (years)	Interest %	Grace (years)
1976					
Burundi	Fisheries	4	21·6	2·5	6·6
Mali	Sélingué Dam	16	20	3	5
1977					
Gambia	Yundum Airport	5·2	15	3	3
Tanzania	Sugar Factory	2·4	15	4	5
Guinea	Clinker Grinding Plant	16	14	4·5	4
1978					
Lesotho	Lesotho Airport Study	3	15	4	5
Senegal	Dam Construction Study	4	20	4	5
Uganda	Rehabilitation of Textile Industry	25	14	5	4
1979					
Comoros	Airport Development	4	n.a.	n.a.	n.a.
Madagascar	Andekaleka Hydroelectric	16	15	4	5
Seychelles	Praslin Island Electricity	3·20	12	5	2
Seychelles	Ice Plant and Store	0·80	12	5	2

Total 111·2 million UAE Dirhams

1 UAE Dirham was worth $0·27 at the end of 1979.

Sources: Abu Dhabi Fund, for 1978 and 1979, the Co-ordination Secretariat at the Arab Fund for Economic and Social Development (AFESD) in Kuwait.

V
Saudi Fund for Development
Loans and grants signed 1975–1980 for the benefit of non-Arab African countries

Country	Project	Amount (SR m)	Repayment (years)	Interest %	Grace (years)
1975					
Uganda	Agr. and Livestock Dev.	105	20	2	5
1976					
Mali	Various	21	20	2	5
Congo	Railways	88·3	20	4	5
Niger	Housing and Grain Storage	20·3	20	2	5
Rwanda	Kigali-Gutuna Rd.	17·65	20	2	5
1977					
Guinea	Study Guekedou-Nezerekore Rd.	6·00	20	2	5
Mali	Sélingué Dam	52·95	20	2	5
Ghana	Kpong Hydroelectric	114·7	20	2	5
Gambia	Yundum Airport	23·3	20	2	5
Cameroon	Songloulou Hydroelectric	105·9	20	2	5
1978					
Senegal	Dakar-Thies Rd.	125·64	20	3	5
Mali	Livestock	46·845	20	2	5
Gabon	Railways	70·6	20	4	5
Guinea-Bissau	Industrial Complex	15·9	20	2	5
Liberia	Tubman Bridge-Bomi Hills Rd.	31·8	20	2	5
Liberia	Bushrod Power Station	38·8	20	2	5
Kenya	Nairobi Water Supply	87·25	20	3	5
Madagascar	Andekaleka Hydro.	42·4	20	3	5
Senegal	Anamby Pilot Proj.	13·2	20	3	5

V—continued

Country	Project	Amount (SR m)	Repay-ment (years)	Interest %	Grace (years)
1979					
Togo	Economic and Social Development	16·6 (Grant)	—	—	—
Comoro	Roads	48·00	20	2	5
Cameroon	Highway Project	12·30	20	2	5
1980					
Gambia	Bangol Yandom Highway	20·16	20	2	5
Gambia	Yundum Airport Runway	6·72	20	2	5
Gabon	Study Institute Marsuki	9·00	20	2	5
Zaire	Railway	116·00	20	3	7

Total Non-Arab Africa, 1975–1980, SR 1,256·315 million, or about $418·6 million

Source: Saudi Fund for Development.

VI
Islamic Development Bank
Project loans, equity participation, technical assistance and trade financing for the benefit of Muslim non-Arab Africa 1976–1979. Aid approved.

Country	Project	Amount ($ m)	Repayment (years)	Month of approval
Project loans				
Cameroon	Songloulou Hydro.	7	27	October 1976
Chad	Mamdi Polder Irrigation	7	30	May 1978
Mali	Sevare-Gao Road	8·00	30	1979
Niger	Birmi N'Konni Irrigation	5·6	30	May 1977
Senegal	Cap-Skirring-Ziguinchor Road	6·25	25	December 1977
Uganda	Kampala Water Supply	5·61	15	April 1978
Equity				
Cameroon	Cellucam Paper Pulp Mill	8·33	—	September 1977
Guinea	Clinker Grinding Plant	4·68	—	August 1977
Niger	Sonichar Thermal Power Station	8·88	—	April 1978
Technical assistance				
Guinea	Feasibility Study for Conakry Oil Refinery	0·05	—	June 1977
Guinea	Feasibility Study for Aluminium Plant	0·40	—	August 1977
Guinea	Survey of Lole Forest	0·16	—	August 1977
Niger	Design of Niamey—Falingie Road	1·00	—	1979
Uganda	Feasibility Study for Third Cement Works	0·60	—	March 1978
Uganda	Feasibility Study for Glass Factory	0·15	—	March 1978
Uganda	Feasibility Study for Road Project	0·40	—	1979

Country	Project	Amount ($ m)	Repayment (years)	Month of approval
Upper Volta	Feasibility Study and Design of Petroleum Tank	0·097	—	1979

Foreign trade financing

Import of

Country	Project	Amount ($ m)	Repayment (years)	Month of approval
Guinea	Petroleum Product	10·80	—	June 1978
Guinea	Cement	6·00	—	May 1979
Guinea-Bissau	Petroleum Product	10·00	—	June 1979
Mali	Cement	2·62	—	January 1979
Mali	Metal Construction Materials	2·62	—	January 1979
Mali	Urea Fertiliser	2·73	—	January 1979
Niger	Cement	4·35	—	January 1979
Niger	Petroleum Product	20·00	—	July 1979
Senegal	Crude Petroleum	15·00	—	July 1978
Uganda	Bicycles	1·76	—	June 1978

Total project loans, equity participation, technical assistance and trade financing for the benefit of Muslim non-Arab Africa, 1976–1979: $139·187 million.

Source: Islamic Development Bank.

237

VII a
OPEC Fund for International Development
Project and Programme Lending Operations, 1976–1979, Commitments for the benefit of non-Arab Africa.

Country	Project or programme	Amount ($ m.)	Repayment (years)	Service charge or interest %	Grace (years)
Benin	Highway	1·6	20	0·75	5
	Line of Credit for Development Bank	4·5	20	0·75	5
Botswana	Road	1·00	20	0·75	5
Cameroon	Line of Credit for Development Bank	4·50	20	0·75	5
Chad	Mamdi Polder Irrigation	2·45	20	0·75	5
Comoro	Road Expansion	1·00	20	0·75	5
Ghana	Kpong Hydroelectric	3·70	20	0·75	4
Kenya	Tea Factories	5·30	20	0·75	4
	Nairobi Water Supply	3·00	20	0·75	5
Lesotho	Maseru Airport	3·00	20	0·75	5
Liberia	Tubman Bridge—Bomi Hills Road	3·00	20	4·00	4
Madagascar	Andekaleka Hydro.	6·50	20	0·75	5
Malawi	Kasungu-Jenda Road	1·80	20	0·75	3
Mali	Sevare-Gao Road	7·00	20	0·75	5
Rwanda	Makungwa Hydro.	2·35	20	0·75	4
Tanzania	Pulp and Paper	5·00	20	0·75	5
Upper Volta	Sakoince-Hounde Road	4·50	20	0·75	5
Zaire	Line of Credit for Development Bank	5·00	20	0·75	5
	Railways	7·00	20	0·75	4
Zambia	Third Railway Project	4·50	20	4·00	5

Total of loans   78·30

VII b

OPEC Fund for International Development

Balance of Payments Support Loans, 1976–1979, Commitments for the benefit of non-Arab Africa.

Country	Amount ($ m)	Country	Amount ($ m)
Benin	2·00	Kenya	5·00
Botswana	2·00	Lesotho	1·90
Burundi	4·50	Madagascar	3·10
	1·70	Mali	3·55
Cameroon	4·95		3·50
Cape Verde	1·55	Mozambique	6·55
	1·00		5·00
	1·00	Niger	2·90
Central African Republic	1·75		3·85
Chad	2·40	Rwanda	1·70
Comoro	0·50		4·70
	0·50	São Tomé and Principe	0·35
Congo	4·00	Senegal	3·40
Equatorial Guinea	0·50		4·00
	1·00	Seychelles	0·30
Ethiopia	4·80		0·30
Gambia	1·65		0·20
	2·00	Sierra Leone	2·05
	1·00	Tanzania	5·45
Ghana	7·80	Togo	3·50
Guinea	2·35	Uganda	4·55
	4·50	Upper Volta	2·25
	2·00		3.00
Guinea-Bissau	1·65		1.50
	1·00		
	1·00		

See note overleaf

239

Note to table overleaf

Total BOP Support Loans $131·50

No interest is charged on loans to the low-income countries, only 0·5 per cent annual service charge on amounts disbursed and outstanding. There is a grace period of three years and a repayment period of seven years after that. But repayment period is subject to reduction of five years if no agreement is reached on the financing of a development project or programme from counterpart funds in local currency.

Grand Total of OPEC Fund Loans to Non-Arab Africa by end of 1979
$209·80 million.

Source: OPEC Fund.

VII c

OPEC Fund for International Development

Project and Programme Lending and Balance of Payments Support Operations in 1980 (by 21 July), Commitments for the benefit of non-Arab Africa.

Country	Project or Programme	Amount ($ m)	Balance of payments support Country	Amount ($ m)
Angola	Railway	3·0	Mauritius	2·0
Burundi	Rural development	2·0	Tanzania	5·0
			Comoros	1·0
Ghana	Line of credit	1·5	Upper Volta	6·0
Uganda	Rehabilitation programme	5·0	Guinea-Bissau	2·0
			Cape Verde	1·5
Kenya	Restructuring programme	4·0	Seychelles	0·5
			Niger	4·0
Tanzania	Power transmission	5·0	Gambia	1·5
			Madagascar	5·0
Ghana	Energy	6·0	Mali	6·0
	TOTAL	$26·5 m	Benin	4·5
			Lesotho	1·5
			Mozambique	3·5
			Senegal	4·5
			TOTAL	$48·5 m

Grand total of project and programme and b.o.p. support loans committed in 1980, to 21 July, $75 million

Grand total of project and programme and b.o.p. support loans committed from 1976 to 21 July 1980 $284·8 million

ABBREVIATIONS

ADB African Development Bank.

ADF African Development Fund.

ADFAED Abu Dhabi Fund for Arab Economic Development.

AFESD Arab Fund for Economic and Social Development.

AFTAAC Arab Fund for Technical Assistance to African and Arab Countries.

BADEA Banque arabe pour le développement en Afrique (Arab Bank for Economic Development in Africa).

BDEAC Banque de développement des Etats de l'Afrique centrale (Development Bank of Central African States)

BOAD Banque ouest africaine de développement (West African Development Bank).

CCCE Caisse centrale pour la coopération économique (French Central Fund for Economic Development).

CIDA Canadian International Development Agency.

DAC Development Assistance Committee of the OECD.

ECA Economic Commission for Africa of the UNO.

ECOWAS Economic Community of West African States.

EDF European Development Fund

EIB European Investment Bank.

FAC Fonds pour l'assistance et coopération (French Fund for Assistance and Development).

FAO Food and Agriculature Organisation of the UNO.

GNP Gross National Product.

IBRD International Bank for Reconstruction and Development.

IDA International Development Association

IDB Islamic Development Bank.

IDB (Kenya) Industrial Development Bank (Kenya).

IFAD International Fund for Agricultural Development.

IFED Iraqi Fund for External Development.

IMF International Monetary Fund.

KFAED Kuwait Fund for Arab Economic Development.

KFW Kreditanstalt für Wiederaufbau (German Credit Institution for Reconstruction).

LAFB Libyan Arab Foreign Bank.

LDCS Least Developed Countries.

MSACS Most Seriously Affected Countries.

OAPEC Organisation of Arab Petroleum Exporting Countries.

ABBREVIATIONS

OAU Organisation of African Unity.

ODA Official Development Assistance.

OECD Organisation for Economic Cooperation and Development.

OF OPEC Fund.

OMVS Organisation pour la mise en valeur du fleuve Sénégal (Senegal River Basin Development Organisation).

PANAFTEL Pan-African Telecommunication network.

PLO Palestine Liberation Organisation.

SAAFA Special Arab Aid Fund for Africa.

SFD Saudi Fund for Development.

SIDA Swedish International Development Agency.

UNCTAD United Nations Conference on Trade and Development.

UNDP United Nations Development Programme.

UNESCO United Nations Educational, Scientific and Cultural Organisation.

INDEX